DREISER
and His Fiction

DREISER

A Twentieth-Century

Lawrence E. Hussman, Jr.

 UNIVERSITY OF PENNSYLVANIA PRESS
Philadelphia · 1983

and His Fiction
Quest

For Stephen and Sarah

This work was published with the support of the Haney Foundation.

Copyright © 1983 by the University of Pennsylvania Press
All rights reserved

Library of Congress Cataloging in Publication Data

Hussman, Lawrence E., 1932–
    Dreiser and his fiction.

        Includes bibliographical references and index.
        1. Dreiser, Theodore, 1871–1945—Criticism
and interpretation.   I. Title.
PS3507.R55Z639   1983   813'.52   82-40493
ISBN 0-8122-7875-5

Printed in the United States of America

Designed by Adrianne Onderdonk Dudden

Contents

PREFACE

1   Before *Sister Carrie:* An Introduction   3
2   *Sister Carrie*   18
3   *Jennie Gerhardt*   50
4   *The Financier* and *The Titan*   70
5. *The "Genius"*   91
6   "The Marriage Group"   113
7   *An American Tragedy* and the Thirties   126
8   *The Bulwark*   153
9   *The Stoic*   180
    Conclusion   194

NOTES   197
INDEX   209

Preface

DURING the last years of his life, Theodore Dreiser began to speak and write about the meaning of existence in a way that contrasted markedly with the beliefs he had long professed. Although he had traditionally been regarded as a dour scientific determinist and a Social Darwinian, his final statements and his posthumously published novels—*The Bulwark* (1946) and *The Stoic* (1947)—posited a benevolent Creative Force and endorsed an ethic of love and service. There were several sympathetic and understanding critical reactions to this shift of ground, notably from Robert Spiller and F. O. Matthiessen. Others, however, were less perceptive and friendly, misreading the last novels as further evidence of determinism or professing puzzlement over them or even denouncing them as the products of failing faculties and insincerity. The difficulty in dealing with this final phase encouraged a neglect of Dreiser's work during the fifties that was compounded by the sway of the New Criticism, which was ill-equipped to deal with his sprawling novels. By the mid-sixties, however, a modest revival of his fiction had begun. Books and articles about Dreiser appeared steadily during the late sixties and the seventies. Some of this more recent work, for example Ellen Moers's *Two Dreisers*, has identified literary and scientific sources for the novelist's ideas. Some works, like Donald Pizer's *The Novels of Theodore Dreiser*, have focused on the composition process through manuscript study. Other analyses, of which Richard Lehan's *Theodore Dreiser: His World and His Novels* is the most influential, have stressed the philosophical and political ideas as keys to an appreciation of Dreiser's writing. Although most contemporary criticism has exhibited increased understanding of Dreiser's late change of heart, we have no extended study focusing on the intellectual and emotional tensions of the earlier novels which the spiritual affirmation of *The Bulwark* and *The Stoic* was meant to resolve. I have tried to fill this gap by identifying in the novelist's early experiences the seeds of certain intrinsically religious and moral ideas and by tracing their development through his life and career. My approach has made possible a reassessment of Dreiser's work that, I believe, directs new light on his earlier fiction and makes his final phase more comprehensible. My aim has been to contribute to a fuller understanding of the man and his art.

I have placed the major emphasis on the novels because I am convinced that they are and will continue to be regarded as Dreiser's most solid contribution to American literature. I have also discussed those short stories which can most clearly contribute to our understanding of the novels. I have made references to the plays, the poetry, the political and philosophical essays, and *The Notes on Life* only when such references would clarify points to be made about the fiction. My analysis of *Sister Carrie* makes use of the recent University of Pennsylvania edition with its discoveries based on contemporary textual studies and its hypotheses about the composition of the novel. This edition of *Sister Carrie* is an essential record of Dreiser's grappling at the outset of his career with the concepts and the feelings that were to remain at the center of his subsequent fiction. I have pegged each discussion of a particular novel or story to a summary of its plotted action, since few people other than specialists have read much Dreiser beyond *Sister Carrie* and fewer still will have had the opportunity to read that work in the Pennsylvania edition. To make certain crucial points, I have used some previously unexplored sections of extant manuscripts. I have allowed the novelist to speak for himself as much as possible, through liberal use of his autobiographical books and his letters. My study approaches his life and his novels in chronological sequence. This arrangement is necessitated by the nature of my task, which is to document what I believe to have been Dreiser's spiritual and intellectual growth, mirrored in fiction, building from *Sister Carrie* and culminating in *The Bulwark* and the last section of *The Stoic*.

I wish to record my heartfelt thanks to those persons who provided valuable aid in the accomplishment of my work. In particular, Mrs. Neda Westlake, curator of the Theodore Dreiser Collection in the Charles Patterson Van Pelt Library at the University of Pennsylvania, proved cooperative beyond the call of duty in guiding me through the maze of materials that Dreiser left behind. Marguerite Tjader Harris, Dreiser's long-time confidante and literary secretary, provided personal remembrances, especially of her work on the manuscript of *The Bulwark*. I am indebted to the many scholars and critics whose discoveries eased my task and whose insights helped to pattern my own perception of Dreiser's fiction, particularly Donald Pizer, Richard Lehan, Robert H. Elias, Phillip Gerber, Jack Salzman, and F. O. Matthiessen. My debt extends to the many students in my American literature classes whose fresh responses to Dreiser's writing have colored my own. I thank Professor Richard Dowell and John Desmond for their careful reading of my manuscript. Felicia Lewis and Professor Peter Bracher provided research and technical assistance. Eileen Sestito, Carol Taulbee, Shirley Nicholson, and Leanne Smith aided in the preparation stages. I wish also to express my gratitude to two of my graduate professors at the University of Michigan, Robert Haugh and the late Joe Lee Davis. Their guidance and encouragement first directed me toward Dreiser as a rewarding subject for critical study.

Permission to consult Dreiser holdings and to quote from unpublished material was generously provided by the University of Pennsylvania Library. The Wright State University Library also supplied assistance through its interlibrary loan facilities. Portions of my manuscript, used here by permission, have appeared in *American Literary Realism* and *The Dreiser Newsletter*.

My work has benefited immeasurably from three research grants from the Liberal Arts College of Wright State University and a sabbatical leave granted by Wright State University.

DREISER
and His Fiction

1 / Before *Sister Carrie*

An Introduction

ALFRED Kazin has observed that "naturalism has always been divided between those who know its drab environment from personal experience, to whom writing is always a form of autobiographical discourse, and those who employ it as a literary idea."[1] Dreiser was most assuredly one of the former. Born in 1871, he was the twelfth child in a family whose head was a mostly unemployed millworker. His father's financial misfortunes led his mother and her brood from one small Indiana town to another and briefly to Chicago in search of inexpensive housing. The children were often assigned such ignominious chores as stealing coal from the railroad yards so that the family might survive another winter. This difficult situation was made worse by the father's narrow religious outlook. A strict and intolerant German Catholic, the elder Dreiser pummeled his offspring with moral preachments and exiled several of his daughters from the family circle because of their moral lapses. Most of the children rebelled against the confining strictures of their father's beliefs, and Theodore especially resented what he called the "religious mooning" which he believed rendered his father "entirely unsuited for the humming world of commerce" and therefore contributed to the family's precarious circumstances (*Dawn*, p. 4). Theodore never overcame his acute fear of poverty, even when he was relatively well off, and his father's brand of Catholicism embittered him toward nearly all organized religions for most of his life.

Although Dreiser later came to forgive his father and even to appreciate his positive traits, the rancor he felt for the parochial schools was, first to last, unmitigated. An extremely conservative Catholic school was the source of his early elementary education, a less intellectually defensible, Teutonic version of James Joyce's Irish Catholic training. The language of the classroom was German, and the organizing principle was apparently Prussian regimentation. Allowing for the exaggeration that doubtlessly colors Dreiser's remembrances of his youth, the attempt seems to have been made in the school to inculcate a highly legalistic Catholicism with blind acceptance of pious legend as well as dogma. Dreiser recalls that the priests and nuns engaged in the "fierce beating of recalcitrant pupils" (A Hoosier Holiday, p. 462). The school offered no instruction in fields of genuine interest to Dreiser, such as botany, chemistry, and physics. Moreover, he asserts that he was advised in the confessional that reading scientific books was sinful. Equally important in Dreiser's rejection of his inherited Catholicism was the sentimental world view he learned in the school. According to his frequent recollections, he was taught by the priests and nuns that the world was organized and functioned on the basis of the Beatitudes and the Sermon on the Mount. This conception of life was soon found wanting when measured against the real world, or even against the classroom, wherein Protestants were regularly reviled. It was with a sense of deliverance that he entered the public school midway through his education.

Dreiser's formal break with Catholicism, and indeed with all organized religion, occurred when his mother was denied burial in consecrated ground because of her neglect of confession and communion. The incident embittered Dreiser and blunted his religious perceptions for many years. The institutional Church always incited his utmost contempt. When he was well past sixty, for example, he wrote to the French novelist Henri Barbusse that his battle cry was for the destruction of the Catholic church which seeks universal "domination for itself" by "darkening the minds of all the citizens of all the lands that it invades."[2]

If Dreiser's youthful experience with poverty, the religion of his father, and the shallowness of the parochial school left him apprehensive and rancorous, not all of the early influences on him were negative. In contrast to his attitude toward his father, he had a strong devotion to his brothers and sisters and an especially intense love for his mother, whom he perceived to be a beautiful woman blessed with simple warmth of heart. Tributes to her "tenderness and consideration" abound in Dreiser's autobiographies. He wrote a number of poems about her patient giving. She is the model for the selfless Jennie Gerhardt. Recent scholarship has called into question the reality of Sarah Schänäb Dreiser's untarnished virtue. Moreover, Dreiser's niece Vera, a psychologist, has said that the special relationship between the young Theodore and his mother was owing to the woman's lavish expenditure of attention on her favorite son at considerable emotional expense to her other children.[3] A number of recent critics have accepted Dreiser's status as a "mama's boy," perhaps pathologically devoted to his mother's memory to the point of seeking and never finding her in his countless sexual conquests. But my purpose here is not to decide whether the relationship between the son and his mother was pathological but rather to underscore the importance of the novelist's perception of his mother in the formation of the religious and moral ideas that are present in his earliest work and which slowly matured and emerged fully developed in his last two novels.

Although Dreiser often speaks of his mother's "pagan" love of life and although some of the most distinguished Dreiser scholars have uncritically appropriated the word "pagan" to describe her, he clearly extols her Christian charity above all else. His remembrances portray her as a woman of ingenuous selflessness, engaged in ceaseless missions of mercy to family members, neighbors, acquaintances, strangers. Although Dreiser believed until late in his life that such a spirit was an anomalous ideal that nearly all of humanity could admire but never hope to approximate, from the beginning his mother's example, her love of life and giving nature, tempered his dark pessimism. She had become a convert at the time of her marriage, but she seems not to have taken her Catholic duties seriously. Her simple faith and benevolent feelings were the products of a Mennonite background, and they sharply contrasted with the austere brand of Catholicism practiced by her husband. The contrast did not go unnoticed by Dreiser. The extent to which his mother's example influenced him is displayed in the numerous exhortations to charity that appear in his books and in the compassion he exhibits for his fictional characters. Dreiser could find sympathy in his heart for the rich as well as the poor, for the financier as well as the bowery derelict. This compassion cannot be accounted for by any part of the naturalistic philosophy that informs his first six novels. If one truly believes that the survival of the fittest is the ordained fate of humans as well as of the lower animals, there is no necessity to view with compassion or even concern the plight of the poor or the ultimate frustration of the powerful. If one truly believes man to be merely a complex animal, there is no need to protest the predicament of a Clyde Griffiths or a Hurstwood any more than the role of the beasts that become man's food. But in spite of his reputation as an objective determinist, Dreiser always led with his heart. If he did not believe that he could locate, until late in his life, the source of the dignity he implicitly ascribed to man through his compassion, the possibility for that belief was always there.

Another inheritance from his mother (and from his father as well) was a mind open to the possibility of supernatural intrusion into human events. Even in his earlier books, Dreiser often speculated about the possibilities of supernatural causation for things that seemed inexplicable, and he collected, over his lifetime, newspaper and magazine articles about rains of frogs, levitation, all manner of strange happenings. This unwillingness to discount the miraculous was shared by most of the members of Dreiser's family. His mother claimed to have seen a vision of the Blessed Virgin. One of his brothers talked of receiving a supernatural communication telling him of his mother's death. Dreiser's discussions of these incidents in his autobiographies never betray any doubt about their authenticity. Moreover, he often attested to similar experiences, including his meeting a certain Jew at every turning point in his life. He believed in the predictions of gypsy fortune tellers, in mental telepathy and premonition. His critics have viewed this strain in Dreiser's thought as indicative of either a mystical nature or merely a superstitious streak. What we choose to call it is of less importance than our recognition that Dreiser was always curious about things for which there seemed to be no material explanation, and this provided the impetus for his lifelong research into science and pseudo-science. Even those who deplore what they regard as Dreiser's superstitions should note the relationship of his speculations about the occult to the religious ideas of his last novels. Huston Smith, a noted authority on religion, has asserted that the connection between magic, mysticism, miracles, and religion is understandable despite the complaints of rationalists because "religion's final business is the infinite, the beyond, the beckoning," and it will therefore always "lie tangential to what is mundane, ordinary, and prosaic and move away from these even when it can only grope in the direction of their alternative."[4]

From the beginning, Dreiser was filled with awe and wonder for existence and the unknowable, an attitude that allowed him to relish the ritual of the Catholic church, especially the sense of mystery in the Mass. He was too much the questioner and the seeker, too much given to dreamy speculation to tolerate the confines of a narrow philosophy for long. The reader should take this into consideration when he encounters the bravado with which Dreiser sometimes pushes his determinism. Ultimately, he relegated even the findings of the naturalistic philosophers to the realm of theory.

Another early influence which kept Dreiser receptive to religions without the dogma of Catholicism was exerted by several liberal preachers of the Social Gospel whom he heard lecture in the auditoriums of Chicago in the days before *Sister Carrie*. The two speakers who most appealed to him were the Reverend Jenkin Lloyd Jones and Rabbi Emil Gustav Hirsch. Jones was a Unitarian minister of striking appearance, a prominent pacifist who was instrumental in the founding of the "Unity Clubs," small mutual-improvement societies. He published Sunday school lessons which backed the evolutionary hypothesis. He also argued for a universal religion based on the ethics of Christianity and the great modern poets. Hirsch was a brilliant, extremely liberal scholar who was noted for his advocacy of unpopular humanitarian causes. He had come to Chicago's Sinai Congregation in 1880 and was awarded the chair in rabbinical literature and philosophy at the University of Chicago in 1892. Both Jones and Hirsch were important leaders of the World Parliament of Religions associated with the World's Columbian Exposition in Chicago in 1893. Dreiser attended the Exposition as a reporter. The future novelist marvelled at the liberal interpretation of life that these men exhibited because it contrasted so markedly with his father's circumscribed perceptions. He pays lengthy tribute in *Dawn* to these preachers "unshackled of dogma," and the memory of their lectures doubtlessly made him psychologically receptive to the two religions that most influenced his last novels, Quakerism with its simple faith in the Inner Light and Hinduism with its reverence for cosmic mystery.

Dreiser also recounts his early reading experiences in *Dawn*. They reveal that long before he encountered the naturalistic philosophers, he reveled in romance. At the parochial school, the one class that he looked forward to was in Bible history with its richly dramatic stories. But it was only when a teacher at the public high school informed him of his privilege of drawing books from the local public library that he began to read somewhat systematically. He recalled, years later, the delight with which he discovered Hawthorne, Irving, Goldsmith, Longfellow, Bryant, Whittier, Cooper, Ouida, Laura Jean Libby, and the recollection led him to a self-estimate that has been too often overlooked by the many critics who have insisted on seeing him as a grim and narrow determinist:

For all my modest repute as a realist, I seem, to my self-analyzing eyes, somewhat more of a romanticist than a realist. The wonder of something that I cannot analyze! The mystic something of beauty that perennially transfigures the world! The freshness of dawns and evenings! The endless changes of state and condition in individuals! How these things grip and mystify! Life itself is so unstable, water-slippery, shifty, cruel, insatiate, and yet so generous, merciful, forgiving. How like all or nothing it seems, according to one's compound and experiences! Yet never would I say of any picture of it, realistic or otherwise, that so much as fragmentarily suggests its variety or force, that it is dull. The individual himself—the writer, I mean—might well be a fool, and therefore all that he attempts to convey would taste of his foolishness or lack of wisdom or drama, but life, true life, by whomsoever set forth or discussed, cannot want utterly of romance or drama, and realism in its most artistic and forceful form is the very substance of both. It is only the ignorant or insensitive who fail to perceive it. [Pp. 198–99.]

In his classic study *Rousseau and Romanticism*, Irving Babbitt considered romanticism and naturalism as opposite sides of the same coin, both extremes of the "despotism of mood." Babbitt was arguing for a return to the golden mean of the classical tradition, but whatever the merits of that case, one should not underestimate the value of some of his insights when applied to a writer like Dreiser. They provide a meaningful context in which to put his predilection for oscillating between opposites and his frequent justification of extremes by an appeal to nature's need to express "equation." His richly romantic side, strengthened by his early reading, broadened his earlier "naturalistic" novels and played a crucial role in the development of the religious ideas in *The Bulwark* and *The Stoic*.

In addition to his love of romantic literature, the young Dreiser developed an intense feeling for the pastoral beauty of rural Indiana. The rolling countryside, the lakes and rivers quickened in most of the members of the Dreiser family, Theodore included, a rich, romantic response. His brother Paul Dresser was an eminently successful songwriter whose love of landscape often found expression in his lyrics, and Dreiser took pride in reminding his friends that he had written some of the words to his brother's "On the Banks of the Wabash." But Dreiser's observations of the natural world were not always tinctured with sentimentality. His often expressed admiration for the hawk, a bird that seemed designed to illustrate nature's cruelty, balanced his romantic feeling for the dove. Nature plays an important role in most of his fiction, but it is in *The Bulwark* that it is most substantial, since it becomes the aperture through which Solon Barnes approaches the Creative Force.

Dreiser responded emotionally to man-made as well as natural wonders. During one of his mother's periodic forays in search of a lower cost of living, she took her children to Chicago. Dreiser's senses were overawed, his mind fixed on the high drama that radiated from this great American metropolis in the making. Chicago was then in its most dynamic state of development. Five hundred thousand souls already lived in the city which drew pilgrims from all parts of the nation and the world in search of the new secular salvation, success. By the time Sarah Dreiser removed her family and settled in Warsaw, another rural Indiana community, Theodore had resolved to return to Chicago to make his fortune. The sight of a train moving toward the city through the fields near his home induced in him an extravagance of longing. When he went to Chicago in 1892 he was enraptured. His level of expectation matched that of his fictional creation Carrie Meeber on her journey to the same city. Dreiser was overwhelmed by the skyscrapers, the whirl of activity, the possibilities for financial, professional, social, and sexual conquests.

But he soon observed that the city could be terribly cruel as well as fascinating, that it could devastate the ill-equipped as well as delight the financially secure. One of Dreiser's first jobs was as a reporter, assigned to the police beat, for the Chicago *Globe* in 1892. He became a daily witness to scenes of human degradation. The cruelty of the city was a vital primer in the doctrine which he was later to know by name as the survival of the fittest. The many examples of urban man's inhumanity made a joke of the world view taught him in the parochial schools. One might half believe in the widespread application of justice and mercy in rural Indiana, but not in Chicago in the 1890s. One trip through the slums would be enough to destroy the last vestiges of such illusions. Yet his first taste of life in the metropolis satisfied him immensely as spectacle and he never lost his romantic fascination with it. He resolved to be a fit survivor by making his way in a large city as a newspaperman. During the next few years he wrote for a number of dailies, working his way toward New York, the ultimate metropolis. On the way, he read several books which were to profoundly influence his own writing.

While working for the Pittsburgh *Dispatch* in 1894, Dreiser discovered the philosophical tracts of T. H. Huxley, John Tyndall, and Herbert Spencer. Already brooding over the apparent purposelessness of his own life and the failure of his previous education to provide him with a convincing world view, Dreiser was psychologically ready for the decisive impression that these philosophers made on him. He testified to the experience in an often quoted passage from *A Book About Myself*:

> At this time I had the fortune to discover Huxley and Tyndall and Herbert Spencer, whose introductory volume to his *Synthetic Philosophy (First Principles)* quite blew me, intellectually, to bits. Hitherto, until I had read Huxley, I had some lingering filaments of Catholicism trailing about me, faith in the existence of Christ, the soundness of his moral and sociological deductions, the brotherhood of man. But on reading *Science and Hebrew Tradition* and *Science and Christian Tradition*, and finding both the Old and New Testaments to be not compendiums of revealed truth but mere records of religious experience, and very erroneous ones at that, and then taking up *First Principles* and discovering that all I had deemed substantial—man's place in nature, his importance in the universe, this too, too solid earth, man's very identity save as an infinitesimal speck of energy or a "suspended equation" drawn or blown here and there by larger forces in which he moved quite unconsciously as an atom— all questioned and dissolved into other and less understandable things, I was completely thrown down in my conceptions or non-conceptions of life. [Pp. 457–58.]

Thus Dreiser records the central event in his conversion to philosophic naturalism and the touchstone used by several generations of critics to situate his books in literary history. Through his exposure to Huxley, Tyndall, and Spencer, Dreiser formulated his declared beliefs that life is without purpose or plan, that man has no soul, that free will and original sin are myths, that human morality and motivation are based on physiological and sociological fate and that the only discernible laws are the laws of change and chance.

But to pigeonhole Dreiser's art within the naturalistic movement is to stop far short of an understanding of that art at its deepest. The way he uses the naturalistic hypothesis to explore fundamental questions about man and his institutions constitutes Dreiser's unique contribution to our literature and to our understanding of ourselves. Having accepted the belief that was to become the common inheritance of the major writers of the twentieth century, the belief that "God is dead," Dreiser was among the first to explore the question of what to make of this seemingly diminished thing called existence. One might speculate on its meaninglessness for a time, but the question of how to organize oneself for living persisted. His fiction represents an implicit attempt to answer that question. Through it he explores various paths that might lead the modern pilgrim around the Slough of Despond to personal fulfillment. Furthermore, although Dreiser's negative experiences led him to embrace the precepts of naturalism intellectually, he was never able to accept them emotionally. We need only recall that he was given to speculating that man was no more important to the universe than an expiring beetle, yet he wrote four volumes of autobiography and an autobiographical novel. The exploration of alternative ways to live life coupled with the emotional need to believe in a transcendent reality led tortuously from *Sister Carrie* to *The Bulwark.* And the passage was made possible by Dreiser's fascinated observation of an ancient problem in its modern context, man's disillusioned longing for ultimate fulfillment and the moral questions which that longing raised.

In 1898, the year before he began *Sister Carrie*, Dreiser was working as a consulting editor for *Success* magazine, a monthly which highlighted the accomplishments of the nation's prosperous and famous by describing how they became so. He interviewed a number of rich and celebrated men for *Success*, and though most of them piously professed that spiritual peace was far more important than material well being, a remark made by Thomas Edison during Dreiser's interview of him made a far more profound impression. Edison told Dreiser that his only pleasure came from the process of working on inventions and that he lost all interest when the work was completed. This remark crystallized for Dreiser his own vague feelings of disillusionment with things he had longed for and achieved. It became, along with other of Edison's ideas expressed in the interview, a source for character and theme in *Sister Carrie* and a subject for lifelong brooding. Dreiser had always been a dreamer of large dreams and intensely ambitious for financial security, material comforts, social acceptance, and the glamour of a writer's career. His sexual appetite was enormous. When he had secured some of his wants in Chicago, however, he remained curiously restless. By the time he came to interview Edison, this aspect of human nature which makes the attainment of an object of desire disappointing had stirred Dreiser's imagination. Since he believed from his reading that existence is meaningless and since he was naturally of a melancholy turn, he was concerned less with the pleasure in the pursuit of an object than with the disillusionment that attended its acquisition. And he found his insight prefigured in the era in which he lived. With the dawning of the age of conspicuous consumption in America had come the realization that material things do not bring fulfillment. The frenzied pursuit of an illusory happiness had already struck the young writer as the most fascinating and poetic phase of American city life around the turn of the century.

Ultimate fulfillment has always been seen as beyond man's grasp in his earthly state. A religious person might take the fact in stride, perform his duties and bide his time in anticipation of the perfect bliss promised in another world. But a mechanist could find this aspect of the human predicament another persuasive demonstration of life's essential senselessness. Dreiser began brooding about disillusionment at a time when his thinking was at least tacitly mechanistic. Furthermore, if man had overpowering yearnings that could be neither resisted nor satisfied, not only must life be purposeless but also free will must indeed be a myth. Some such interpretation surely played a part in Dreiser's reading of Huxley, Tyndall, and Spencer. Because they are in the grip of inscrutable desire, Carrie Meeber, Clyde Griffiths, and even Frank Cowperwood appear to be mere pawns of blind force. Each of Dreiser's books is remarkable for its author's profound preoccupation with frustrated desire. One of his most perceptive early critics, Randolph Bourne, remarked in a review of The "Genius" that "the insistent theme of Mr. Dreiser's works is desire, perennial, unquenchable."[5]

Dreiser employs a variety of terms to describe and translate desire. At times he refers to mystic longing, unreasoning passion, or chemic compulsion, but always the reference is to the fact that his characters' desires are unquenchable. They are so because the objects of these desires are not sufficient to explain the intensity of the longing. This phenomenon was hardly a discovery of Dreiser's. Plato describes the inability of the objects of our desires to satisfy us through the analogy of a perforated vessel into which water is poured. Lucretius calls desire the "thirst for life" and observes that "so long as we have not what we crave, it seems to surpass all else; afterward, when it is ours, we crave something else, and the same thirst of life besets us as ever, open-mouthed."[6] What makes Dreiser's treatment of desire new in his time and still fresh is its twentieth-century context. The naturalistic philosophers had cast doubt on the theological foundations of the western world, and the crumbling of the religious edifice would be so swift that by the twenties most of the books written by intellectuals would begin with the assumption that God was no longer an issue. Dreiser was among the first of American artists to try to make sense of a world in which science and religion seemed hopelessly split, a chasm which was to prove to be the foremost cultural fact of the first half of the twentieth century. Without a religious explanation of man's yearning for ultimate fulfillment, later writers would try to fill the void by establishing their own ersatz religions. Thus, Wallace Stevens wrote in "The Man with the Blue Guitar": "Art, surpassing music must replace empty Heaven and its hymns." James Joyce and Virginia Woolf agreed that art was the only surviving modern ideal. For D. H. Lawrence, the new faith was to be found in blood consciousness, for Ernest Hemingway, in modern stoicism, for John Steinbeck, in biological evolution. Dreiser's fiction transcribes through his characters his own relentless and vain search for a worthy reality. Carrie's aching need for material, social, and artistic success is answered with gowns, carriages, position, and career, but the end of the novel finds her still hopeful of release from "longings" and "heartaches." Frank Cowperwood, the robber baron hero of the *Trilogy of Desire*, acquires a succession of mansions, priceless paintings, and enchanting mistresses, but fulfillment eludes him. Eugene Witla, the artist hero of *The "Genius,"* is sustained neither by his art nor by the many liaisons that mark his frenzied pursuit of the "impossible she." Clyde Griffiths's doomed dream of money, importance, and sexual power leads inexorably to the electric chair.

Dreiser's autobiographies offer ample evidence that he was, himself, afflicted to an unusual degree with romantic desire that could never be satisfied. The absence of fulfillment intensified his brooding melancholy. For example, he writes of his youth:

I tell you, in those days, wonderful, amazing moods were generated in the blood of me. I felt and saw things which have never come true—glories, moods, gayeties, perfections. There was a lilt in my heart and my soul. I wanted, oh! I wanted all that Nature can breed in her wealth of stars and universes – and I found – what have I found – ? [A Hoosier Holiday, p. 325.]

The insatiable desire to experience all things simultaneously which stirs his characters stirred their creator as well. He often protested gloomily against what George Santayana called "the deepest curse of existence," the need of "rejecting and destroying some things that are beautiful," for in that direction Dreiser saw accommodation, compromise, decay, and death.[7] His brooding over the extent to which mankind's reach extends beyond its grasp penetrates his very style, through which he conveys a sense of gnawing unrest.

Although Dreiser empathized with most people who seemed fated to strive for the objects of their personal desires, he admired those few who were able to transcend desire by dedicating themselves to a higher good, as he believed his mother had. He often regretted that most were essentially self-serving and that compassion and charity were not more widespread. As a consequence, his novels before The Bulwark seem curiously contradictory, for they are simultaneously deterministic and humanistic. Dreiser critics have frequently identified this seeming contradiction without tracing it to its source and relating it to the novelist's ongoing quest for moral as well as spiritual moorings in a postreligious world. The apparently incompatible impulses to take what one desires for personal happiness and to give of oneself for others were the alternatives that presented themselves as a result of the new freedom that attended Dreiser's loss of religious faith with its moral imperatives. In A Book About Myself, he wrote two long, contiguous confessional paragraphs in which he admitted to a ravenous appetite for the world's goods as well as a profound compassion for those whose possessions were minimal (pp. 106–7). Although he sometimes seemed simply to accept these two sides of himself, he continually explored them through fictional characters and situations as alternate paths to a possible secular salvation. Could a man or woman find true happiness by storing up treasures or by succoring those who had none? It must be remembered that although Dreiser thought of himself as a determinist, he did not consistently deny free will. In A Hoosier Holiday, for example, he cited historical precedence in the overthrow of monarchy as evidence of the people's will. And even the characters in a determinist novel must attempt to manage their lives by making moral choices, whether or not those choices are merely illusory against the backdrop of meaninglessness. Thus, the morally uncommitted heroine of *Sister Carrie* is motivated by her "guiding principle" of self-interest in her languid quest for position and possessions, but by the end of the novel she has begun to indulge her compassionate side. Jennie Gerhardt gives totally in an utterly selfless manner. Cowperwood shamelessly indulges his will to power. Clyde Griffiths follows his tawdry dreams to their tragic terminus and begins to see in prison that responsibilities to others might be a more crucial call than desire. Thus, Dreiser's novels scrutinize characters struggling to invest their lives with meaning by pursuing self-interested goals or by curbing their personal desires to devote themselves to others. Seen in this light, they have an existential dimension that has not been previously explored.

The relationships between men and women provided Dreiser with the most illuminating case studies for his examination of the conflict between the self and the other. He was himself a notorious womanizer whose affairs of the heart and exploits in the bedroom numbered in the hundreds and spanned his entire lifetime. In the give and take of these affairs he found a useful paradigm for abstract moral considerations. He returned to such relationships again and again in his fiction. The institution of marriage was an even richer source of moral speculation for Dreiser. He met his first wife in 1893. Assigned by the St. Louis *Republic* to escort a group of school teachers on a trip to the Chicago World's Fair, he picked Sara Osborne White (also known as "Jug") from among the twenty-five teachers as the most worthy of his attentions. Soon he was lost in romance, writing highly charged, emotional letters to her and constructing a miniature shrine in his room to display her picture. Despite the warnings of friends that Sara was too old for him (at nearly twenty-five she was two years his senior) and that as a conservative churchgoer she might be too narrow for him, Dreiser decided that he must marry her. Although he went East to further his career as a reporter, he resolved to return for Sara when he had sufficient money to support her. Their five-year courtship resulted in marriage late in 1898, even though his sojourn in the East had provided him with a succession of other women and the excitement of New York. Dreiser would later recall that the marriage was prompted by his obedience to "the pale flame of duty." He soon began to find his wife too conventional and possessive and himself too driven not to crave the "artistic" freedom to pursue younger women.

His disillusionment grew incrementally, but Dreiser and Sara were not permanently separated until 1912. She refused him a divorce, preventing his remarriage until her death in 1942.

Dreiser often used marriage as a literary subject. His novels from *Sister Carrie* up to *The Bulwark* portray the institution with a mostly jaundiced eye. But it is in *The "Genius"* and in his "marriage group," a series of short stories including among others "Married," "The Second Choice," and "Free," that he records his most subtle analysis of the concept of lifelong commitment to one sexual partner. In these works, marriage becomes a vehicle for discussing the struggle within the individual between the desire for the world's most alluring and abundant commodity—what Dreiser called "the show of soul in some passing eye"—and the wish to know that soul intimately and fully, possible only through an emotional expenditure and commitment which disallows our knowing as intimately and fully the souls that animate the many other equally tantalizing "passing eyes." Dreiser tried to resolve the dilemma through a series of intense, mostly short-lived relationships with a legendary number of women.

By 1899, he had contributed about forty articles and poems to magazines (most to *Metropolitan* and *Cosmopolitan*), had his first short story published by *Ainslee's*, and had seen his name appear in *Who's Who in America*. He began writing his first extended work in the autumn of that year, spurred by his newspaper colleague Arthur Henry's suggestion that they both attempt a novel. Dreiser confessed that he addressed himself to the task with no idea of how to proceed. He was probably indulging in his characteristic exaggeration when he said that he wrote the title on a blank sheet of paper with no conception of the story that was to follow. After writing about one third of the book, he was forced to abandon it for several months because he could not untangle the plot complications that had developed to that point. Although he ultimately managed to realize the narrative line of the novel in impressive fashion, his admitted amateurism was responsible for several flaws in the logical underpinning of *Sister Carrie*. But he was able to successfully transform into his first major work the experiences and conflicts that were to remain among the most important sources of all of his fiction. These included the grinding poverty of his youth, which stirred his sympathy for the poor as well as his resolve not to be among them; the contrasting examples of his father's narrow outlook and his mother's rich sympathy; his struggle for survival and

Dreiser is clearly recalling here the emotions that his own first view of Chicago stirred in him. He recorded those feelings in *Dawn*, and his remembrance was of a youthful idealism even more intense than Carrie's—a remembrance that inspired this urban rhapsody:

> The city of which I am now about to write never was on land or sea; or if it appears to have the outlines of reality, they are but shadow to the glory that was in my own mind. Compassed by a shell or skull, there was a mirror inside me which colored all it reflected. There was some mulch of chemistry that transmuted walls of yellow brick and streets of cedar block and horses and men into amethyst and gold and silver and pegasi and archangels of flaming light. There was a lute or harp which sang as the wind sings. The city of which I sing was not of land or sea or any time or place. Look for it in vain! I can scarcely find it in my own soul now. [P. 156.]

Clearly, in this passage from *Dawn* Dreiser is investing city streets and tall buildings with emotions akin to religious awe. A seventeenth-century Englishman could not have found any district of John Bunyan's "Celestial City" more inspiring than Dreiser found The Loop. With the gates to the ethereal capital locked to the modern mechanist while the desire for ultimate fulfillment remained unassuaged, Dreiser was forced to channel his need in the direction of Vanity Fair. C. S. Lewis has described the "Sweet Desire" for ultimate fulfillment in the preface to *Pilgrim's Regress*, his modern sequel to Bunyan's visionary classic. Surfeit ever beckons the twentieth-century pilgrim from beyond a further hill and "pierces us like a rapier at the smell of a bonfire, the sound of wild ducks flying overhead, the title of *The Well at the World's End*, the opening lines of 'Kubla Khan,' the morning cobwebs in late summer, or the noise of falling waves."[1] But the level of expectation Dreiser brought to Chicago invited the disillusionment that darkens his nostalgia in the lines from *Dawn*. And since he began *Sister Carrie* with the benefit of knowledge his leading players do not possess, he foreshadows Carrie's disenchantment with her attainments in an early passage which compares the city to a seducer whose resistless charms include "the gleam of a thousand lights" and "a blare of sound, a roar of life, a vast array of human hives" (p. 4). The metaphor is particularly apt because like those of the human seducer, the promises with which the city tempts Carrie are false. But she is highly susceptible to seduction because youth is the golden time in

Dreiser's world when illusion reigns unchastened and all things are bathed in light.

Carrie arrives in Chicago "dreaming wild dreams of some vague, far-off supremacy" (p. 4). Despite the promising welcome which the traveling salesman Drouet extends to her on the train into town, she is soon brought up short by the bleak world of her sister's home and a grim job in a shoe factory. But a girl of Carrie's romantic nature could not be expected to endure for long either a household in which the simplest pleasure is regarded as an extravagance or one dominated by the necessity of prosaic labor. After she loses her only source of money, her factory job, she is presented with the opportunity to be kept by Drouet. Carrie drifts into the relationship, since it offers the possibility of actualizing her nagging yearning for clothes and jewelry. Chicago's department stores woo her with their persuasive pleading in the "language of the stones" (p. 98). Drouet's wardrobe first attracts Carrie to him, just as Hurstwood's imported suits spur her later dissatisfaction with Drouet. Dreiser uses clothes in the way that William Dean Howells uses houses in his fiction, as symbols of varying levels of aspiration, taste, and success. In transcribing the allure of goods for Carrie, Dreiser was again making fictional use of his own youthful desire at the onset of the age of conspicuous consumption. He described those ambitions in *Dawn*:

I was beginning to be caught by the American spirit of material advancement. Here was no land or day to be satisfied with well enough. Anyone could legitimately aspire to be anything in America, and nearly all aspired. Not to want to be rich or to be willing and able to work for riches was to write yourself down as nobody. Material possessions were already the goal as well as the sum of most American life, and so one could not help feeling the state of isolation and indifference which accompanied a lack of means. [P. 293.]

Equipped only with her "average little conscience" (p. 89), Carrie does not trouble much over the moral implications of her liaison with Drouet, who is himself described as a "merry, unthinking moth of the lamp" (p. 63). In a passage often quoted by critics, Dreiser points out that even if Carrie were to agonize over the situation, she could not possibly know with certainty the right path because our perception of morals is infantile despite the strides in understanding made by Herbert Spencer and other naturalists (presumably their contention that morality is relative to time and place and always evolving). Then Dreiser adds that if we wish to understand ethical questions, we must place them in the context of desire. The first principles of morality lie in such questions as "why the heart thrills" or "wherefore some plaintive note goes wandering about the world undying," and in the reason for "the rose's subtle alchemy, evolving its ruddy lamp in light and rain" (p. 88). In such passages Dreiser attempts to articulate an existential answer to the plaguing question of whether to take or to forego. If unquenchable desire is man's strongest characteristic, who dares quarrel with his pursuit of its objects?

When Drouet introduces Carrie to George Hurstwood, the modish manager of a Chicago bar, mutual dissatisfaction with their lives spurs another relationship unsanctioned by conventional morality. Carrie is attracted by Hurstwood's superior social position compared to Drouet's, to his fine clothes and elegant manner. She has been nursing a growing ambition to become an actress, and Hurstwood has hinted that he can do more than simply encourage her. She has also grown restive because of Drouet's neglect. Hurstwood sees in Carrie a delicious avenue of escape from his shrewish wife and social-climbing children.

This is the point in the novel at which Dreiser was forced to abandon the writing for several months. He could not think of a way for Hurstwood to get sufficient money to begin a new life with Carrie. Dreiser had the real-life example of his own sister's suitor who had stolen money to finance his flight with his lover, but the novelist needed to find a convincing set of fictional circumstances. He finally decided on a turn of fate that was to become one of the most famous incidents in the novel. The opportunity for the theft of ten thousand dollars presents itself when Hurstwood, slightly inebriated, discovers the bar safe open while he is alone after closing time. The chance thus afforded triggers a moral debate within the manager. In a long passage, Dreiser describes the conflict between "duty and desire," which rages when an average conscience is faced with a situation such as the one presented by the open safe. Even the "dullest specimen of humanity, when drawn by desire toward evil, is recalled by a sense of right, which is proportionate in power and strength to his evil tendency" (p. 269). (Note that theft is described here as an "evil," whether or not the "heart thrills" to the possibilities it engenders.) Blind chance intervenes. When the safe clicks shut while Hurstwood is handling the cash receipts, he decides to steal the money rather than return it to his employer.

Dreiser's difficulty with this section is understandable because the situation in which Hurstwood is placed is the first in the novel that calls for one of the characters to make an unmistakable moral choice that has to be subsumed within the amoral, naturalistic form. Carrie's drift into her relationships with Drouet and Hurstwood is handled in such a way that conscious decisions do not seem to be involved. Dreiser points out that Drouet's string of mistresses are meant no harm by the drummer because he is not a "cold-blooded, dark, scheming villain," but rather an average fellow whose "inborn desire urged him to that [seduction] as a chief delight" (p. 63). In fact, nearly all of the players in the novel are passive, more acted upon than acting. The reason is that such characterizations best fit the naturalistic design. To deal with Hurstwood at the safe door, however, Dreiser was forced to fall back on prenaturalistic language, finally absolving him because conscience is ineffectual when strong desire is duty's adversary. The strength of Hurstwood's desire for Carrie is overwhelming—his passion is "no longer colored with reason." He decides to make his "try for Paradise" by spiriting her off to Montreal and New York with the help of a ruse and the weakness of her will to resist (pp. 209–10).

Many critics have remarked on the device Dreiser uses to structure the novel after Carrie and Hurstwood reach New York, namely, the antiphonal relationship based on the rise of the former and the fall of the latter. Carrie rises rapidly to fame and some fortune while Hurstwood slowly declines into despair and ends in suicide. His resolve to return the stolen money and his inability to find what he considers to be suitable employment through which to gain the means of restitution lead steadily to his demise. Although he has Carrie, the prize he believed would make up for all other lacks, he is far from fulfilled. Dreiser's portrait of Hurstwood's deterioration has been justly praised by critics for its psychological realism. Significantly, the manager's grip on life loosens as soon as he begins to suffer a diminishing of future-oriented desire. As his sad odyssey unfolds in New York, he begins to brood more and more over "the good old days," luxuriating in pleasures past that he had turned his back on. For Dreiser, the man who lives in the past has already begun to die. When the future is no longer colored by "Sweet Desire," the game of life is all but over. When Hurstwood loses his investment in a New York bar, he loses his pride as well. Soon, he is walking the streets looking for employment of any kind. We are reminded that Carrie had made the same quest for work earlier in Chicago. But there is a vital difference in Hurstwood's quest. He lacks the resiliency of youth, the dream of a succession of ever more golden tomorrows which had sustained Carrie. She indulges temporarily in retrospect during the worst of her experiences with factory drudgery, remembering her native town and "the better side of her home life" (p. 40). But she soon recovers and resumes looking ahead. Hurstwood, however, gives up the search for work and stays at home instead, reading newspaper accounts of the doings of the Vanderbilts and the theatrical people. The newspaper becomes his passport to a fantasy world providing reverie and release from his problems. After his abortive try at gambling, his condition worsens to the point that he actually begins to hear "the old voices and the clink of glasses" back at the Chicago bar (p. 432). By the time he has lost his job as a scab motorman during a Brooklyn street-railway strike, he is living primarily in a half-world of memory. With a touch of Dreiserian irony, he longs to return to what he now remembers as his happy domestic arrangement with Mrs. Hurstwood: "As the present became darker, the past grew brighter, and all that concerned it stood in relief" (p. 459). Finally, the weight of the present is too great to be lifted even by a reconstructed past and, turning on the gas jets in a Bowery flophouse, he achieves his release.

Earlier, Dreiser had diagnosed Hurstwood's terminal condition as an imbalance of "katastates" and "anastates" in the blood caused by "comparison between his old state and his new" which "produced a constant state of gloom, or at least depression" (p. 339). The first indication of the onset of the bar manager's chemical imbalance occurs during the train trip to Montreal with Carrie. Instead of his looking forward single-mindedly to life with his prized possession, "nostalgy" begins to "affect his vitals." When the realization of what he has done begins to sink in, he longs for Chicago, "his old ways and pleasant places," and he wants to "go back and remain there, let the cost be what it would" (p. 288). Ellen Moers has identified the source of the brain metabolism theory exhibited in *Sister Carrie* as Elmer Gates, a "scientific psychologist" of the day. Dreiser appears to have read in manuscript form Gates's *The Relations and Development of the Mind and Brain*, which was published in 1903.[2] With the help of Gates's materialist explanations of human psychology in terms of anastates and katastates, Dreiser fixes the cause of Hurstwood's death as a strain of naturalistic blood poisoning. The unmistakable symptom of the disease is the waning of desire.

While Hurstwood is drifting inexorably toward his suicide which ends the novel, his only solace is nostalgia. Conversely, Carrie is simultaneously moving toward the apogee of her good fortune, untroubled by any thought of yesterday. When Hurstwood's money runs out, she rekindles her dream of becoming an actress and, thanks to a tip from a friendly showgirl, she lands a bit part in a Broadway play. Helped by a series of lucky breaks and a previously unrealized talent, her career is launched. By the end of the novel she has attained nearly all of the things she had dreamed about at the beginning. She has money, carriages, gowns, social acceptance, applause, a great city at her feet. But she has begun to see that these achievements cannot bring her the fulfillment she has wished for from the beginning.

One of the more perplexing aspects of the novel is Dreiser's handling of Carrie's disillusionment with all of the things she had valued so highly when she coveted them from afar. He tries to explain the causes of this disillusionment with the help of the third man in her life, Bob Ames, an intriguing character who appears in two extended scenes late in the novel. Ames appears to function as the author's spokesman in offering Carrie some perspective on her pursuits and in pointing the way to what he thinks may be her higher calling. But some of his own ideas turn out to be less than lucid and consistent. The resulting confusion might well lead a close reader to doubt that Dreiser himself fully understood all of the ramifications of his story, or at least to doubt his ability to make his understanding manifest. Despite the undeniable power and impressive architectonics of *Sister Carrie*, critical questions concerning the novel's definitive message can be raised through a detailed examination of Ames's role and an analysis of related authorial intrusions into the narrative. Such a detailed examination and analysis is offered here not to denigrate Dreiser's achievement in *Sister Carrie*, but to show that the flaws in the novel resulted inevitably from the complexity of the ideas he was trying to dramatize and the formative state of his intellectual development.

Just before her stage career is launched in New York, Carrie meets the Vances, a rich couple who sponsor her socially at the moment when her longing is sharpest for material success. Her friendship with the couple allows Carrie for the first time to step within the magic circle of New York's luxurious restaurants and glittering theaters. At a pre-theater dinner party at Sherry's restaurant, the Vances introduce Carrie to Ames, an engineer and inventor who works for an Indianapolis electrical company. As his characters sit down to dine, Dreiser interrupts the narrative to counsel the reader that Sherry's represents the epitome of American upper-class decadence, being an institution given over to "that exhibition of showy, wasteful and unwholesome gastronomy as practised by wealthy Americans which is the wonder and astonishment of true culture and dignity the world over" (p. 332). Ames's function in this scene is to corroborate and amplify Dreiser's judgment and to begin to show Carrie that her dreams of luxury and pleasure are misguided. Although Carrie is enthralled by the glamour of the restaurant, Ames tells her that he would not care to be rich enough to spend his money in such a vulgar manner. This remark overawes Carrie, for whom such pleasures represent the essence of the good life. With slim evidence for the analogy, she begins to think of her new acquaintance in connection with "the sorrows and the sacrifices" she had seen portrayed on the stage. The alert reader should be less impressed when he notes that Carrie's new idol is "well-dressed" and that his repugnance for Sherry's does not noticeably spoil his meal.

During the dinner conversation, Ames disparages a book which Carrie had enjoyed (*Dora Thorne*) and an author whom Mrs. Vance admires (E. P. Roe) by simply declaring that neither amounts to much. These judgments further establish Ames's credentials in Carrie's mind. Her longing to pursue a stage career is quickened when Ames praises those who take the acting profession seriously. He is firmly established as a "scholar" in Carrie's view by this pronouncement. Indeed, Dreiser seems as impressed by Ames as his heroine is, since he interrupts the narrative again to assure the reader that Carrie's instant esteem for this "genius" shows her "saving grace," the ability to "understand that people could be wiser." For further proof of Ames's mental magnetism, Dreiser has Carrie gaze several times at the inventor's forehead, and at his hair, which is bathed in a red glow. After parting with this fascinating man, Carrie returns to her apartment to muse in her rocking chair, an activity that marks every turning point in her life. In this first scene between the budding actress and the inventor, Ames is established as chief spokesman for Dreiser and as an incisive critic of the American success formula. (His name itself suggests a play on "aims.")

Throughout the novel, Dreiser reveals his transcendence of Carrie's worldly values. He characterizes her expectations as the "illusion of hope" and frequently reminds the reader of the futility of her dreams of fulfillment through material things. Carrie displays various qualities in a rudimentary form—intelligence, feeling, compassion—which the omniscient narrator of the novel presumably possesses in considerable abundance. When he introduces Ames, Dreiser makes use of him as an intermediary to carry his enhancing message to Carrie. And Dreiser invites the reader to believe that Ames's wisdom significantly affects Carrie, writing that now, "through a fog of longing and conflicting desires, she was beginning to see" (pp. 333–37). Between their first meeting and their next, the "call of the ideal" that Ames has awakened occasionally troubles Carrie's thoughts.

When they meet anew at the Vance's dinner party in the next-to-last chapter of the novel, Ames, who has set up a laboratory in New York, again arrests Carrie's attention. This time he surprises her with his unexpected indifference to the theatrical notoriety she has achieved since they last talked. Instead of offering her praise for her accomplishments, he implies that she has wasted her time on insufficiently serious plays. Dreiser credits Ames with a mind that is "speculative and idealistic—far above anything which she had as yet conceived." But close attention to his advice to Carrie in the scene reveals that he is anything but consistent and clear. This inconsistency and obscurity could be ascribed in part to his sexual attraction to Carrie, which may somehow cloud his thinking. More fundamentally, however, the problem lies in the fact that he is attempting to address incompatible impulses at war not only within Carrie but within Dreiser as well.

Examples of Ames's inconsistency abound. First, the inventor informs Carrie about Hardy and Balzac, whom she had read at his suggestion. When Carrie reacts with sadness to the failure of Lucien de Rubempré in *The Great Man from the Provinces*, Ames defines true success for her. He interprets the failure of Balzac's hero as merely the result of his being deprived of wealth, position, and romantic love which would have been truly tragic only if de Rubempré had realized that the pursuit of these things had deflected him from the authentic human goal of knowledge. He tells her that when a person "doesn't make knowledge his object, he's very likely to fail." But just how Carrie's theatrical talent is related to the acquisition of knowledge is not explained. Furthermore, Ames criticizes Balzac for making too much of wealth and material possessions, even though five lines earlier he had urged her to read all of the French writer's works for the "good" they would do her. Again, the inventor finds Carrie's melancholia unbefitting a person so young, thus linking happiness to youth but failing to explain the necessity of youth for the accumulation of knowledge or the renunciation of worldly values.

Next, Ames cautions against dreaming of far-off things. Life is "full of desirable situations, but unfortunately we can only occupy one at a time," he tells her. Most people do not realize this and never taste contentment, because they "neglect" their particular desirable situation to "long for others." Yet, the inventor's own message is calculated at nearly every other point in the scene to stir Carrie's dissatisfaction with herself and her situation. Indeed, Ames's prescription for her salvation becomes more confusing as it unfolds. When he tries to locate the source of her acting talent, he finds it in her "large, sympathetic eyes and pathetic mouth" which express the world's longing. But he warns that her power will disappear if she becomes "self-interested, selfish and luxurious." He warns her further that her gift can be squandered if she lives only to satisfy herself: "The sympathetic look will leave your eyes, your mouth will change, your power to act will disappear. You may think they won't, but they will. Nature takes care of that." In short, on the one hand Ames locates Carrie's talent in her longing facial expression and, in fact, insists that she retain above all her "own aspirations." On the other hand he tells her to dampen her personal dreams or run the risk of losing her talent. Moreover, Ames seems to exhort Carrie to some altruistic action: "If you want to do most, do good. Serve the many. Be kind and humanitarian. Then you can't help but be great." In addition to being so general that it nearly evaporates, the call to humanitarianism is incongruously linked to personal greatness. Ames likens Carrie's talent to the gifts of "great musicians, great painters, great writers and actors." Even though he had argued a little earlier in the scene that her acting ability reflected "no credit" on her because of the importance of the thing portrayed rather than the portrayer, surely the comparison with great artists is a provocative compliment to a young woman with Carrie's dreams of personal glory. Again, when she expresses some humility in relation to her stage success, Ames assures her that it is deserved because no one "gets up" without having something the world needs in a "high place." But Carrie considers "the solution being offered her," namely, "goodness—labor for others," performed as a willing "medium" of some mysterious force, to be "absolutely true." She admires Ames's freedom from pretensions in clothing (although his dress suit and gleaming white shirt front had earlier in the scene arrested her attention) and the absence of any craving for applause (although he has become a famous celebrity as a result of his inventions). Equally disconcerting is Ames's final estimate of Carrie. He finds "something exceedingly human and unaffected about this woman—a something which craved neither money nor praise" (although the novel is about her endless dreaming of both). Conveniently, Carrie will not be forced to give up her career, since the only concrete advice Ames proffers is to seek out more serious dramatic roles. Little wonder that by the end of the evening with Ames, all her nature is "stirred to unrest" and she is once again "the old, mournful Carrie—the desireful Carrie,—unsatisfied" (pp. 478–87). The inventor's counsel does little to assuage the infinite, indeterminate longing that characterizes Carrie from the opening pages of the novel.

Dreiser's own misgivings about Ames's role in *Sister Carrie* may have been responsible for his decision to change this scene, which was both considerably shortened and revised between the completion of the holograph and the Doubleday, Page and Company first edition.[3] But the changes only made Ames's message more cryptic and no less confusing. In the first edition, for example, the inventor's reference to the world's many desirable situations which cannot be occupied simultaneously is preceded by an opportunity for him to chasten Carrie's vagrant longing for something better. When a piece of sentimental music is played by a group at the Vances' dinner party, instead of cautioning his pupil that such a "pathetic strain" might well promote her nebulous dreaming of superior states, Ames in fact joins her in an extravagant emotional response. Both the inventor and the actress are transfixed by the music, "touched by the same feeling, only hers reached her through the heart." (Presumably, Ames had been reached through the mind.) Carrie's response is totally in character: "'I don't know what it is about music,' she started to say, moved to explain the inexplicable longings which surged within her; 'but it always makes me feel as if I wanted something—I—'" The man who helped author the lyrics to "On the Banks of the Wabash" could not be expected to whisper to his spokesman in the novel that sentimental music was bound to induce in Carrie the very indeterminate yearning he had been warning against. Furthermore, other segments of this altered scene show Ames to be an oracle at the same cross purposes as his creator. In response to Carrie's appeals for guidance, he adds to the confusion with a vague exhortation to "change," though he specifies no course of action beyond moving from light to serious drama. Despite his references to her innate sympathy, he suggests nothing she might do for those who need not only sympathy but also help, except to urge her to reproduce the world's longing on the stage. While his conception of the solemn duty of the stage personality to the world to express its longing makes Carrie feel "slightly guilty of neglect," the inventor's praise of her talent "unlocked the door to a new desire." Stimulated as it is by flattery (Ames praises her gifts in the altered scene as well), this new desire is not likely to reduce Carrie's self-absorption. Understandably, Ames's influence produces no immediate change. For a time, at least, she will continue to live for herself: "Still she did nothing, grieving. It was a long way to this better thing, or seemed to be, and comfort was about her. Hence the inactivity and the longing."[4] Surely her hesitancy to embrace "this better thing" stems from Ames's inability to define it.

The two scenes involving Ames demonstrate in graphic detail the difficulty Dreiser faced in constructing a fictional spokesman for his ideas. Strikingly, very little has been written by critics over the years about Ames. He is most often ignored in discussions of *Sister Carrie*, even though it can be justly said that his characterization is the key to understanding the novel and Dreiser at the time that he wrote it. Most critiques of the book either ignore Ames altogether or afford him only a passing reference. There cannot be said to be a standard interpretation of the inventor's role in the novel. Opinions about him range from that of Ellen Moers, who finds him "impossibly perfect,"[5] to those of several critics who try to explain away his inconsistent message as a part of Dreiser's purposeful use of him as an unsound guide for Carrie, more sophisticated but only slightly less deficient than Drouet and Hurstwood. The truth seems to lie somewhere between these points of view. Certainly Ames is anything but "perfect." Dreiser hints in the concluding lines of the inventor's last scene that his philosophy represents for Carrie a way station at which she will tarry only temporarily: "Carrie! Oh Carrie! ever whole in that thou art ever hopeful, know that the light is but now in these his eyes. Tomorrow it shall be melted and dissolved. Tomorrow it shall be on and further on, still leading, still alluring, until thought is not with you and heart-aches are no more." (p. 487). On the other hand, there is little reason to doubt that Dreiser's idea was to portray Ames as a trustworthy phi-losopher. His own descriptions of the inventor's insight are uniformly laudatory, sprinkled with references to his genius, his scholarly acu-men, his bright mind.

If, in truth, Dreiser had his own misgivings about Ames, they may have been owing to the fact that he developed his character not only from his own ideas but also from the imperfectly related ideas of others, including most notably Thomas Edison. Apparently, there were at least three sources for the ideas expressed by Ames in the novel. Dreiser's mother was probably the inspiration for the fictional inventor's stress on giving. From his brother Paul may have come Ames's passionate response to sentimental music, although Dreiser himself often responded in like measure. His reaction to his own read-ing doubtlessly formed the basis for Ames's literary pronouncements. Most of the inventor's ideas, however, appear to be based on state-ments made by Thomas Edison during an interview he gave Dreiser for *Success* magazine shortly before *Sister Carrie* was begun. Of all the remarks offered by the genius of Menlo Park during the interview, the one that seems to have struck Dreiser most forcefully was his assertion that his only happiness came from the process of working on an in-vention and that once the project was completed, he hated the prod-uct: "'When it is all done and is a success, I can't bear the sight of it.'"[6] This observation may have crystallized for Dreiser his own youthful experience and verified his reading of Balzac. Like Carrie and many of Balzac's characters, Dreiser had been unfulfilled when the apparent objects of his desires had been attained. But Edison had also stressed the satisfaction to be found in the work itself. The task of propound-ing this wisdom in *Sister Carrie* falls to Ames.

During the second scene between Carrie and her counselor, several of Edison's specific prescriptions for true success are transferred to Ames, including the injunction to take pure knowledge as her goal. Edison had impressed Dreiser with his exhaustive reading of general as well as technical literature. In the interview, he had told Dreiser that as a boy without a common school education, he had attempted to read through the entire Detroit Free Library. Edison had also told Dreiser that the first requisite of success in any field was the willingness "to apply your physical and mental energies to one problem incessantly without growing weary." Dreiser had found Edison willing to spend twenty hours daily in the cultivation of his talent and ready to chide others whose day was not only short, but also fragmented. Their trouble was that any writing or thinking they did was done "about a great many things and I do it about one." Ames urges Carrie to concentrate on her acting talent and his reasoning relates to the Edison interview as well. His advice is based on his keen sense of the mutability of existence. Soon, he tells the actress, she might "die and dissolve" and be lost to the world, and so it is extremely important that she "do something" with her talent immediately. In the *Success* interview, Dreiser records an anecdote concerning Edison's absorption in his work told by a friend. Edison had explained his running to breakfast on a certain occasion: "'I have got so much to do, and life is so short, that I have got to hustle.'" Ames's stress on Carrie's duty to express the world's longing may also have its source in Dreiser's conversation with Edison. The inventor told his interviewer that he always took pains to insure that the things he made benefited society.[7]

There are a number of additional details linking Ames to Edison. The fictional inventor's fame results from his development of a new kind of light. In his piece on Edison, Dreiser stresses the real-life inventor's background of economic deprivation. Ames alludes to his own deprived youth. Dreiser wonders in the interview because Edison cared not in the least for money. The same indifference in Ames fascinates Carrie. When Dreiser had asked Edison if want urged a man to greater success, the inventor had responded affirmatively. Ames tells Carrie that her unhappiness results from her being too comfortably situated. In the Edison essay, Dreiser makes an extended point about the inventor's abstinence from drink, a virtue attributed to Ames as well. Even Carrie's fascination with Ames's forehead has its analogue in the interview. Dreiser found Edison's "broad forehead" his most arresting feature. Finally, Ames's function is to philosophize on the nature of success, the very thing Edison was asked to do for Dreiser's article.[8]

The evidence is convincing that Dreiser based Ames's ideas primarily on Edison's philosophy as it emerged in the *Success* interview. But there are inherent problems with the way he implemented the decision as well as with the decision itself. First, he muddied the waters by unsuccessfully mixing Edison's thoughts with competitive or marginally related ideas and feelings of his own and others. As we have seen, for example, Ames's soft spot for sentimental music validates and stimulates Carrie's dreaming of far-off things, as opposed to concentrating on the present, and the fictional inventor's insistence on linking Carrie's sympathy to artistic greatness further stirs her "unrest." Second, Edison's unelaborated ideas as expressed in the interview do not in themselves add up to a coherent philosophy—or at least to one that can be applied to Carrie's situation. How, for instance, does the single-minded dedication to one "problem" mesh with the nervous need to move on to some equally compelling project?

What may be most telling in all of this is Dreiser's primary reliance on someone else's ideas to construe the meaning of Carrie's experience. Although he is not hesitant to interrupt the narrative earlier on to comment about various ramifications of his story or to correct some societal views or values, a summarizing voice beyond that of Ames/Edison is conspicuously missing at the end of the novel. He may have rewritten the second scene between Ames and Carrie out of a sense of his not having successfully integrated the ideas the inventor expresses. Ames's reduced speaking part in the Doubleday, Page first edition may represent, therefore, an eleventh-hour decision on Dreiser's part to shroud his character in as much mystery as possible. Whether a serious rethinking by Dreiser of Ames's ideas would have resolved the problem is questionable, however. The tasks which Dreiser had assigned Ames were simply too formidable, amounting to no less than a gloss of the modern experience and a recommendation for personal fulfillment in a naturalistically conceived world.

Nonetheless, the mini-scene that marks Carrie's final appearance in the novel shows her apparently changed. Her compassion stirred by her reading of *Père Goriot* at Ames's suggestion, she chides her friend Lola for thinking only of sleigh riding on a bitter winter evening when the poor must be suffering most acutely. Dreiser tells the reader that Carrie has "caught nearly the full sympathetic significance" of Balzac and has discovered "how silly and worthless had been her earlier reading, as a whole" (p. 495). Presumably, this expansion of sympathy and sensibility has been wrought by her conversations with Ames. But the final, fleeting glimpse of Carrie ends with her concern over the need to hire a coach for the evening. She has put aside her worry about the suffering being endured by others outside her window at the Waldorf. No action is taken appropriate to her feeling for the less fortunate. Nor does Dreiser indicate that she owes any debt to them beyond romantic identification.

Again, it may have been Dreiser's sense that he had not satisfactorily dramatized Carrie's ultimate state of mind that led him to decide to rewrite the final scene and add a coda before submitting the novel for publication.[9] But the coda suggests as much as the original version Dreiser's difficulty in naming an appropriate channel for Carrie's desire. It demonstrates, moreover, that Ames's attempts at changing her have merely brought to the surface of Carrie's mind one side of an inner dialectic between getting and giving.

In the first-edition coda, Carrie is unfulfilled despite her own dramatic charisma, gowns, carriages, influential friends, substantial income, applause, and publicity. She rocks and thinks about the direction of her life. Although she perceives vaguely that worldly success cannot fulfill her, she has still not discovered nor has she been provided with a clear course of action. An isolated line informs the reader that as she walks on Broadway, her purse will be "open to those whose need is the greatest." This single line was apparently the cause of what was surely one of the most misleading judgments ever made about the novel. Leslie Fiedler, probably using Carrie's open purse as his evidence, has written that by the end of the Doubleday, Page first edition Dreiser contrives to convert Carrie into "a kind of unchurched nun, celibate, lonely, and dedicated to charity."[10] But there is no indication that she will revert to celibacy (Ames assumes she is married and respects the institution)[11] or that she is particularly lonely and certainly none that she is dedicated to anything beyond her vague longing. Dreiser gives no indication that Carrie plans to abstain from refilling her purse once it has been emptied through almsgiving. Nor does it seem likely that she will distribute her belongings among the destitute, become an urban missionary like those described elsewhere in the novel, or accomplish anything notably spiritual. Since her charitable impulse manifests itself on Broadway and not in the Bowery, we must conclude that Carrie's "open purse" results more from sentiment than from genuine sympathy. Moreover, only three sentences after we are told of her benevolent instincts, we learn that she will always remain unaware of Hurstwood's death as well as of

Drouet's whereabouts and that, thus, "all that was of interest" regarding them had passed. To so blithely ignore Hurstwood's plight after he has supported her for three years and when she knows of his dire predicament is surely not the response to be expected from a nun, churched or unchurched. At this point, Dreiser's defense of Carrie's attitude toward Drouet and especially toward Hurstwood is not particularly convincing: "Their influence upon her life is explicable alone by the nature of her longings. Time was when both represented for her all that was most potent in earthly success. They were the personal representatives of a state most blessed to attain—the titled ambassadors of comfort and peace—aglow with their credentials. It is but natural that when the world which they represented no longer allured her its ambassadors should be discredited." Surely one is justified in judging from such an explanation that Carrie is guilty of having used the two men as much as she has been used by them.

In the final moments of the first-edition coda, Carrie lapses into a torpor of undifferentiated emotion, dreaming of a happiness she "may never feel," longing simultaneously for that "peace and beauty which glimmered afar off" and "that radiance of delight which tints the distant hilltops of the world."[12] These would surely seem to represent diametrically opposed dreams. Certainly, the one thing that Carrie might have been expected to learn from her experience is that she cannot possibly find peace so long as she must pursue her personal delight. By the end of the coda, Carrie has still neither charted nor set her course. She remains a drifting dreamer crippled by incompatible impulses and, significantly, she had exhibited the same impulses very early in the novel, long before she had met Ames. When she is still living with Drouet, two extended, contiguous paragraphs ascribe to Carrie these irreconcilable pulls. One paragraph describes her acquisitive side. She craves pleasure and position so intensely that always "the kaleidoscope of human affairs threw a new lustre upon something, and therewith it became for her the desired—the all." But the next paragraph indicates that spiritually she was "rich in feeling," often experiencing "an uncritical upwelling of grief for the weak and the helpless" and actual pain at the sight of the poor (p. 145). These pulls toward acquisitiveness and humanitarianism seem to account for most of the trouble that the close reader experiences throughout the novel. In the first chapter, for example, Dreiser describes Carrie's motivation in significantly equivocal terms, informing the reader that her self-interest is "high, but not strong." The very next sentence refers to that same self-interest as her "guiding characteristic" (p. 4). After Drouet rescues her from her menial labor at the shoe factory, Carrie's sympathies are "ever with that underworld of toil from which she had so recently sprung and which she best understood" (p. 146). But when she had been among the toilers, she had rejected them as "common" and vulgar, undeserving of her friendship despite their kindnesses to her (pp. 41, 53). Contrary to her supposedly rich sympathy for the poor, she considers her struggling sister and brother-in-law only when they can be used. On the other hand, she is troubled by her treatment of Drouet and her perceived injustices to him. Her first impulse is to use Hurstwood, imagining that "his attraction to her could only mean that entrance for her in a higher world which she craved" (p. 138). In New York, she holds back money from him, resents spending her own on him until he is destitute, yet she seems genuinely moved at times by his plight when he is near the end of his rope. What is fairly consistent in this behavior is her tendency to be more sympathetic in inverse ratio to the proximity of the object of her sympathy.

During several of his occasional explanatory interruptions of the narrative, Dreiser addresses the conflicting pulls within Carrie. These explanations connect with the conflict between duty and desire within Hurstwood at the safe door. At one early point, Dreiser expresses the dichotomy in terms of instinct and reason: "In Carrie, as in how many of our worldlings do they not, instinct and reason, desire and understanding warred for the mastery. In Carrie, as in how many of our worldlings are they not, instinct and desire were yet in part the victors. She followed whither her craving led. She was as yet more drawn than she drew" (pp. 73–74). Again, in an extended, restored section of the novel comprising five paragraphs just after Carrie's introduction to Hurstwood has spurred her longing for things that are beyond Drouet's capacity to give her, Dreiser intrudes to explain the difference between desire and selfishness (pp. 97–98). Although he is not a writer whose work generally repays exceedingly close analysis, his differentiation between desire and selfishness invites extended scrutiny because it demonstrates the difficulty he was having with the abstract ideas that the narrative line of *Sister Carrie* is meant to illustrate. The five paragraphs begin as follows:

In considering Carrie's mental state, the culmination of reasoning which held her at anchorage is so strange a harbor, we must fail of a just appreciation if we do not give due weight to those subtle influences, not human, which environ and appeal to the young imagination when it drifts. Trite though it may seem, it is well to remember that in life, after all, we are most wholly controlled by desire. The things that appeal to desire are not always visible objects. Let us not confuse this with selfishness. It is more virtuous than that. Desire is the variable wind which blows now zephyrlike, now shrill, filling our sails for some far-off port, flapping them idly upon the high seas in sunny weather, scudding us now here, now there, before its terrific breath, speeding us anon to accomplishment; as often rending our sails and leaving us battered and dismantled, a picturesque wreck in some forgotten harbor. Selfishness is the twin-screw motive power of the human steamer. It drives unchangingly, unpoetically on. Its one danger is that of miscalculation. Personalities such as Carrie's would come under the former category. The art by which her rather confused consciousness of right and duty might be overcome is not easily perceived.

Dreiser's explanation of Carrie's motivation here stimulates more questions than it supplies answers that would help the reader figure out her character. Has she reached her current "mental state" through consecutive reasoning, as he implies at the beginning of the first sentence, or by a species of imaginative drift, as he seems to be saying at the end of the same sentence? What is the relationship between desire, which controls our lives, and reasoning and imagination? Such things as fame and status can be understood as objects of desire that are not material and, therefore, not visible, yet they are tangible. Desire is not synonymous with selfishness in Dreiser's view. He sees desire as more attractive than selfishness. But is Carrie's neglect of her sister and brother-in-law after she leaves their home or her dismissal of Hurstwood in the first-edition coda merely a function of "more virtuous" desire or a manifestation of selfishness? If it is simply a function of desire, how does it differ from the motivation attributed to Mrs. Hurstwood? She is described as "a cold, self-centered woman with many a thought of her own which never found expression, not even so much as in the glint of an eye" (p. 112). Does Ames's recommended humanitarianism represent a virtue still higher than desire, or is it part of desire itself?

The extended metaphor which likens man to a ship, desire to the wind, and selfishness to a twin-screw (and by metonymic extension to a steam engine), muddies rather than clarifies the reader's perception of Carrie's motivation, thereby undercutting the very sanction for an authorial intrusion. Desire can provide both the direction and motivation to accomplishment, Dreiser says, but too strong a desire can destroy the human being. That is clear enough. But what is unclear is the role selfishness plays in direction and motivation. How selfishness can be unchanging while desire changes and how selfishness sometimes leads to miscalculation are two questions Dreiser leaves unanswered for the reader. The reason these questions remain unanswered is that he fails to complete the metaphor of the ship; he leaves the reader without an explanation in terms of the ship metaphor, or in any terms for that matter, of what he means by selfishness leading to miscalculation. The reader is left to ponder a distinction without a discernible difference between desire and selfishness, especially since either can presumably lead us to our goals or to our destruction.

His next paragraph is a straightforward description of the way environment stimulates the onset of desire. "Fine clothes, rich foods, superior residence, a conspicuously apparent assumption of position in others" stimulate Carrie's longing, for example. But the third paragraph of the restored section presents the reader with more problems:

It must next be considered that if desire be rife in the mind and no channel of satisfaction is provided; if there be ambition, however weak, and it is not schooled in lovely principle and precept—if no way be shown, be sure it will learn a way of the world. Need it be said that the lesson of the latter is not always uplifting. We know that the common run of mortals *struggle* to be happy. Is not that comment sufficient?

The antecedent of the second pronoun "it" in the first sentence of the paragraph is confusing. Does Dreiser mean "it" to refer back to desire or to ambition or to both? The parallel clauses suggest that he may be equating desire and ambition. Therefore, "it" may be referring to both ambition and desire. The reader cannot be sure. This uncertainty leads to the second problem of the paragraph: the relationship between desire and man's control of it. In the first paragraph of the restored section, Dreiser suggests that man is passive before the winds of desire, yet in this paragraph he seems to suggest that man may control desire through principles and precepts or he may actively control the direction of his ambition.

In the fourth paragraph, Dreiser introduces a new subject, virtue, without an effective transition from his previous subjects, desire and ambition.

> Lastly, let all men remember that in the main, the world's virtue has never been tested. Wherefore was he good—the heavens rained goodness on the soil that nourished him. Where severe tests have been made, there have been some lamentable failures. Too often we move along ignoring the fact of our own advantages in every criticism we make concerning others. We do this because we are ignorant of the subtleties of life. Be sure that the vileness which you attribute to some object is a mirage. It is a sky illumination of your own lack of understanding—the confusion of your own soul.

What does Dreiser mean by virtue in this passage? He has previously linked desire with virtue, but we cannot be sure that he is doing so again. He asserts that "the world's virtue has never been tested," yet he alludes to "severe tests" that have been failed without providing illuminating examples that would resolve this apparent contradiction. Furthermore, Dreiser makes the assumption that the reader will attribute vileness to some object which he does not name, when in fact, the reader may do nothing of the kind. By attributing this attitude to the reader, he indulges the very vice he rails against. What is clear from the paragraph is that Dreiser warns against judging others on the basis of one's own experiences and prejudices.

The final paragraph of the restored section comes down to the specifics of the narrative—Drouet and his relationship to Carrie's desire: "In the light of these truths, it is well to admit the possibility of persuasion and control other than by men. Did Drouet persuade her entirely? Ah, the magnitude attributed to simple Drouet! The leading strings were with neither of them." The salesman's function is thus described as that of a catalyst for her desire. We are asked not to attribute all of the responsibility for Carrie's actions to Drouet since he is not assigned any deliberate manipulation of her. The problem here is that Drouet's role does not correspond to any item in the initial metaphor comparing man to a ship, desire to the wind, and selfishness to a twin-screw. In this metaphor, there is no place for a catalyst.

The writing in this long, restored section leaves much to be desired in terms of both content and rhetoric. Dreiser was often sloppy in his diction and grammar. He was always after bigger game than pronoun antecedents. But the passages quoted above also show clearly that he was not in total control of the abstract ideas with which he intended to explain Carrie's motivations. However, these paragraphs are certainly noteworthy. They illustrate Dreiser's attempt to grapple with extremely subtle ideas and their expression. There is a kind of power in his search for the right rhetorical tools. Moreover, this restored section shows in a most interesting fashion the way in which his mind worked over the concept of desire and its moral concomitants during the composition of the novel. An indication is provided here as well of *Sister Carrie*'s audience as he conceived of it. He seems to be attempting to address an educated, yet sheltered readership. He is trying to express abstract ideas that he presumably assumes they will understand. Yet ironically, he himself does not fully understand them, or at least he has great difficulty expressing his understanding as the very distinction between selfishness and desire demonstrates. Surely, selfishness is rather a subclass of desire, since we speak of both selfish and unselfish desires.

Donald Pizer sees Carrie finally as a vehicle for Dreiser's depiction of "the very confusion at the center of life itself" which Pizer defines as "the amoral need most individuals have to fulfill themselves in a world controlled by moral assumptions, and the pathetically superficial but moving instances of man's pursuit of beauty."[13] Pizer may well be right, if he infers this conclusion from the novel in its entirety; the restored paragraphs analyzed above as well as other passages may suggest, however, that there is a second confusion to be dealt with here. This second confusion is Dreiser's inability to explain in his authorial intrusions how this "amoral need" functions as Carrie's motivation and how her actions are "more virtuous" than selfish.

But to return to Ames and his influence on Carrie, when he supposes she has a nature that is susceptible to spiritual enrichment, he is, of course, not altogether deceived. She is unable to accept her success without at least thinking about the less fortunate. Dreiser vaguely connects this compassionate impulse with her sensitivity to beauty at several points in the novel. But her commitment to self-interest is nearly total, for she lacks a suitable channel for her "other-oriented" side. Ames urges a lessening of self-absorption, but he fails to suggest an outlet for her "better" self beyond more serious performances on the stage. Such performances would merely duplicate in the audience her own vicarious identification with those who suffer, neither fulfilling the sympathizer nor helping the recipient of the sympathy. Certainly, the novel does not lack examples of genuine compassion such as "the captain" who cajoles passersby for money to buy sleeping quarters for New York derelicts, the Sisters of Mercy who run soup kitchens, and Fleischmann, the caterer who donates bread to the needy.

Understandably, Dreiser was not certain about the most promising path to secular salvation, and therefore he could not see either Ames or his pupil on it. Both characters finally coalesce in a point of view coequal to Dreiser's when he began the novel. In the autobiographical portrait of his youth cited above from *A Book About Myself* in the Introduction (see p. 14), Dreiser almost exactly reproduced the two paragraphs in the novel that describe the conflicting sides of Carrie's temperament. Describing himself as a "poetic melancholiac, crossed with a vivid materialistic lust of life," he found his burning "desire for material and social supremacy" balanced by an "intense sympathy for the woes of others," his eyes brimming with tears and his throat "parched and painful" over scenes of poverty (pp. 106–7). The very commodities that Carrie values until the end Dreiser pursued himself long after he completed the novel (even though he recognized, like Ames, that those commodities did not satisfy). On the other hand, his inherited status as an outsider developed in him a strong sympathy for the poor. Through the interaction of Ames and Carrie, Dreiser explores the alternatives of supremacy through self-seeking and peace through self-sacrifice. In this context, phrases such as "The Lure of the Spirit, the Flesh in Pursuit," included among the chapter titles that accompany the Doubleday first edition, make perfect sense. [14] Dreiser would continue the exploration of the opposing pulls of these two forces throughout his life and his fiction.

Critics have tried in various ways to deal with the relationship between Dreiser's own psychology and the narrative of *Sister Carrie*. For example, Phillip Gerber has asserted that the players in the novel "derive largely from Dreiser himself, each depicting a separate facet of the writer's own nature." [15] But as we have seen, rather than depicting a single facet of Dreiser, Carrie is split by warring sides. Even Ames's advice reflects Dreiser's difficulty in either separating or integrating the two sides of his own nature into distinct fictional characters whose interaction could effect a cohesive intellectual statement. Contrastingly, Fitzgerald handled a nearly identical problem much more coherently in *The Great Gatsby* through the interaction of Jay Gatsby and Nick Carraway. But we should not underestimate the formidable task that Dreiser set for himself a quarter century before Fitzgerald, no less than the exploration of the way to secular salvation in a modern world without moral signposts.

Richard Lehan observes that Carrie at the close of the novel "would like to relieve general suffering at exactly the same moment that Hurstwood, to whom she is now almost indifferent, commits suicide," and that Carrie "feels that time will bring complete fulfillment while in reality it will bring only death." He sees these facts as part of a pattern of irony which fits within the general deterministic framework of the novel. [16] Such a judgment stems from Lehan's wish to separate Dreiser the man from Dreiser the artist and his contention, stated elsewhere in his book, that somehow Dreiser's ideas were "inchoate" in his life though not so in his fiction. [17] But there are, in fact, inchoate passages in *Sister Carrie* as I have pointed out. I introduce the views of Gerber and Lehan here not to disparage their work. They are among the very best of the scholars who have chosen Dreiser as a subject. My purpose is to indicate what I think is a serious problem with most *Sister Carrie* criticism—the inclination to impute to Dreiser more detached control over the material of his first novel than is justified. Too few succeeding critics have heeded F. O. Matthiessen's depiction of Dreiser at the time of *Sister Carrie* as an authentic primitive, "only half-educated" and "scarcely a conscious artist at all." [18] On the other hand, Dreiser does not need defenses such as Lehan's, quoted above. He is an undeniably powerful, albeit flawed artist, even in his first work of fiction.

Misleading responses to *Sister Carrie* have not been confined to the overly complimentary. Critics unfriendly to Dreiser have not always seen the value of what he was trying to do. In a landmark essay on the novel, Kenneth Lynn maintained that in Carrie, Dreiser had described "quite accurately an attitude of mind which he did not consciously understand, but which psychoanalysis explains is notably characteristic of gold diggers, namely, that they are 'invariably severely neurotic . . . capable of achieving their conscious aim temporarily, only to find themselves depressed, dissatisfied, bored.'" [19] But Dreiser would have been shocked and offended by such a reading since he was seeking to describe human desire and discontent in much larger terms. He was attempting to put into cosmic perspective the fact that man's reach exceeds his grasp and trying to understand and explain what the psychoanalyst (or the novelist given to "dramatic development" as opposed to an "intruding narrator") might be content simply to describe. The attempt was an audacious undertaking for a writer in his first major work, especially for an "authentic primitive" and the results were not unmixed. The most conspicuous failure is in the rocking-chair coda that was printed in the Doubleday, Page first edition and most embarrassingly evident in its concluding lines.

Louis Auchincloss has rendered the most negative judgment about the coda, pronouncing its last paragraph "sheer drivel."[20] He was referring specifically to the lines:

Oh, Carrie, Carrie! Oh, blind strivings of the human heart. Onward, onward it saith, and where beauty leads there it follows. Whether it be the tinkle of a lone sheep-bell o'er some quiet landscape or the glimmer of beauty in sylvan places, or the show of soul in some passing eye, the heart knows and makes answer, following. It is when the feet weary and hope seems vain that the heartaches and the longings arise. Know then that for you is neither surfeit nor content. In your rocking chair by your window dreaming, shall you long alone. In your rocking chair by your window shall you dream such happiness as you may never feel. [Pp. 659.]

An ardent defender of Dreiser might be hard put to argue the point with Auchincloss, and not merely because the prose is swollen and ineffective or because its pastoral setting makes for an inappropriate conclusion to an urban novel. The problem results more fundamentally from Dreiser's failure to clarify earlier the ideas he has broached through Ames and Carrie, a failure which the final paragraph of the coda only underscores. Critics characteristically excuse this kind of failure by asserting that, as a naturalist, Dreiser is not bound to interpret states of mind but merely to describe them in the context of a mechanistic world view. But as we have seen, such allowance has inherent dangers because it fails to recognize how personal was Dreiser's interest in Carrie's ambivalence. His failure to provide a cogent analysis of her dilemma was caused, I believe, by the fact that he was still unconvinced of the vanity of human wishes despite the preponderance of his own evidence. Witness his continued quest in later life for many of the very same commodities from which Carrie derives no satisfaction and his inability to translate his sympathy for the masses into concerted and sustained social action until the 1930s. The omniscient, naturalistic point of view which he donned for the occasion of this first novel was not a perfect fit. Hence the ill-suited final paragraph of the coda and his several other equally ineffective attempts to provide a philosophical context for Carrie's experience.

But in spite of all the protests one might legitimately make about Dreiser's handling of certain ideas in the novel, especially in the various unclear authorial intrusions, *Sister Carrie* is one of the very finest achievements in fiction by an American. It displays a remarkable cohesion of subject, symbol, style, and structure. The pervasive themes are desire and disillusionment in the context of the modern metropolis. Chicago and New York are used as symbols and the metaphors that cluster about them are highly appropriate to the theme. They effectively express the guileful invitation of modern life. The city is likened to a great magnet and its pilgrims to iron filings, or again it is a seducer luring its victims "with all the soulfulness of expression possible in the most cultured human" (p. 4). Characters are helpless "moths of the lamp." Hannah and Hogg's bar, which Hurstwood manages, is "an insect-infested rose of pleasure" (p. 47). Carrie is "charmed" by a fragment of music and responds "much as certain strings of a harp vibrate when a corresponding key of a piano is struck" (p. 102). Style serves subject, for Dreiser's halting dialogue and labored intrusions, so often cited as incriminating evidence by his detractors, convey a gnawing sense of restless groping which, whether designed or accidental, is in fact appropriate. The novel's structure is perfectly suited to the theme as well. Carrie's rise and Hurstwood's fall not only provide a satisfying symmetry, but also signify desire and disillusionment.

Perhaps the most underestimated virtue of *Sister Carrie* is its story line. With the small-town girl who survives the city maelstrom to make it on Broadway, the dapper salesman who specializes in keeping women, the affluent, married man who is brought low through his illicit love for a younger woman, the revenge of the scorned wife, the street-railway strike, the "captain" who begs for alms from theater crowds to buy flophouse rooms for derelicts, and other characters and situations in the novel, Dreiser created a heady dramatic brew which has pleased generations of readers. The story is doubtlessly one that C. P. Snow had in mind when he asserted that American literature reached its peak at the very latest with Dreiser because he is not, like so many highly rated novelists who succeeded him, a "purely verbal performer." Snow saw Dreiser as a writer like Tolstoy in that their actual prose "is not the first thing of interest," and therefore, they are not the sort of writers that "modern academic apparatus is used to coping with."²¹ Ironically, Dreiser unconsciously justified himself before future manipulators of "modern academic apparatus" when he warned several times in *Sister Carrie* of the danger of putting too much stock in words per se. As Drouet and Carrie are engaging in banter on the train when they first meet, Dreiser intrudes to explain that "words are but vague shadows of the volumes we mean" and they are but "little audible links" that chain together "great inaudible feelings and purposes" (p. 9). Later, when a glance from Hurstwood communicates his love for Carrie more effectively than Drouet's spoken words had, Dreiser offers this interpolation:

People in general attach too much importance to words. They are under the illusion that talking effects great results. As a matter of fact, words are as a rule the shallowest portion of all the argument. They but dimly represent the great surging feelings and desires which lie behind. When the distraction of the tongue is removed, the heart listens. [P. 118.]

In the interjected comments in *Sister Carrie* that discount the adequacy of language as such in expressing real messages, Dreiser provides a clue to the neglect of his work for such a long time by the New Criticism, whose practitioners characteristically focus on "the shallowest portion of all the argument." Moreover, he provides a clue as well to the uncommon power his novels generate. If a claim can be made for Dreiser's greatness, it must be made on the basis of his emotional power rather than his intellectual incisiveness. As we have seen, certain crucial sections of *Sister Carrie* do not bear concerted thinking on, and yet, ultimately, this matters far less than Dreiser's evocative treatment of "the great surging feelings and desires which lie behind" the words men and women speak. The reader perceives in the ambitions of his characters an underlying need to embrace the universe, to realize ideal beauty, to achieve ultimate fulfillment. He shows us that even simple people can be bewilderingly complex in their need to satisfy their own incompatible longings. His much maligned style, his labored intrusions and sometimes inchoate dialogue convey a sense of our own yearning for transcendence which only unweakened religious faith had the power to address. We easily identify with his characters because their search for substance in the modern world is our own. Although Dreiser never analyzed the twentieth century's loss of moorings in a perfectly consistent way, he always had a sure grasp of the way it feels to live in the modern world, especially in modern

America. There has never been a more accurate chronicler of the American dream. If few would hold that his philosophy exhibits flawless logic, the importance of his subjects is not to be doubted. Nor is the latent religious feeling in his evocation of urgent desire or in Carrie's response to music, which could "arouse thoughts which started the tears" (p. 105), or in the analysis of the city's "hypnotic influence" produced by "super-intelligible forces," which leads Dreiser to conclude that "the origin of human action has neither yet been measured nor calculated" (p. 78). *Sister Carrie* powerfully suggests Dreiser's intense feeling about these subjects.

Literary power is most assuredly in the eye of the beholder, however, and the first and most influential beholder to demur in Dreiser's case was someone at Doubleday, Page and Company. According to the legend launched and perpetuated by Dreiser, after the New York publishing house accepted the novel on the recommendation of Frank Norris, and in fact printed it, Mrs. Frank Doubleday read it and was so shocked by its content that she succeeded in having it withdrawn from circulation. When Dreiser insisted that Doubleday live up to its agreement, the firm responded through its legal advisor that its obligation was to publish but not necessarily to sell the book and that the printed copies could be thrown into a cellar, which, in fact, was done. Although the supposed suppression of *Sister Carrie* became the most famous piece of literary scandal surrounding Dreiser's career and although it provided a weapon with which generations of liberals might flay generations of bluenoses, modern scholars have cast doubt on the authenticity of nearly every detail. What is clear is that Doubleday was not enthusiastic about publishing the novel in spite of Norris's recommendation and that the novel was not advertised. Despite Dreiser's insistent claims to the contrary, the reviews were not all uncomplimentary. The sale of the book was very poor, however, and its author became more and more depressed about the possibility that his new career might have to be aborted. Although he had managed in 1901 to get a small advance from the relatively obscure firm of J. F. Taylor for a novel to be called *The Transgressor*, his worsening psychological health impeded his writing. He did manage to finish two short character sketches, "A True Patriarch," which is based on his wife's father, and "A Doer of the Word," which describes a man who lived in the picturesque fishing village of Noank, Connecticut. Dreiser had met the Connecticut man there during a visit. "A Doer of the Word" was later included in *Twelve Men*, and its subject was a person quite different from any of the major characters in *Sister Carrie*, one whose dedication to giving anticipated that of the heroine of his next novel. His fictional name is Charley Potter. He is a fisherman who earns the respect if not the understanding of his fellow townsmen because he actually lives according to the dictates of the New Testament. Although he belongs to no church, he is seen as living proof of the possibility of a truly religious life. Charley's friends admire him, yet they regard him as somewhat foolish because he does not think first of himself but instead gives all that he has to the poor. One of his cronies describes him as "naturally big hearted." Charley explains his beliefs to the fascinated narrator of the story in a conversation included in the sketch:

"Nothing to do except to be good to others." "True religion and undefiled before our God and Father is this," he quoted, "to visit the widow and the orphan in their affliction and to keep unspotted from the world. Charity is kind," you know. "Charity vaunteth not itself, is not puffed up, seeketh not its own."

"Well," I said, rather aimlessly, I will admit, for this high faith staggered me. (How high! How high!) "And then what?"

"Well, then the world would come about. It would be so much better. All the misery is in the lack of sympathy one with another. When we get that straightened out we can work in peace. There are lots of things to do, you know."

Yes, I thought, looking down on the mills and the driving force of self-interest—on greed, lust, love of pleasure, all their fantastic and yet moving dreams. [*Twelve Men*, p. 72.]

The alternatives of giving and getting were obviously still much on his mind in the recounting of his experience with the saintly citizen of Noank. Dreiser had always been moved by the message of the Scriptures, although he did not accept them as either divinely inspired or in the least realistic. So long as men's material pursuits have their mysterious magnetism, he believed, we can expect only exceptional men like Charley Potter to heed the scriptural call to charity. Like the heroine of Dreiser's next novel, Charley is viewed as an inspiring anomaly. Despite Dreiser's reputation for portraying average people, it was the uncommon who most compelled his interest. In this story, the ideal of absolute self-denial, exemplified by a simple fisherman, could be examined against its opposite, "the driving force of self-interest." But Dreiser was years away from resolving the conflict between these two pulls within himself.

In the months after the publication of *Sister Carrie*, his brooding over the fate of the novel, his worsening financial situation, and the growing unhappiness in his marriage led him inexorably to a mental breakdown. There are two accounts of this period of emotional collapse, and they provide further evidence of the extent of Dreiser's absorption in the personal conflicts he had turned to fictional use in *Sister Carrie*. The first is a medical diary he kept at his physician's suggestion from October 1902 to February 1903. In it, Dreiser complains of a variety of nervous sensations including a "vague throbbing as if the mental fibre itself were worn," a continual "played out" feeling, and a sense of being as "incapable of consecutive thought as a child." Interestingly, Dreiser was attending Sunday Mass on a fairly regular basis during this siege, long after his self-proclaimed break with the Church.[22] As the diary progresses through the winter months, the entries become fuller and the writing more literary, as if intended for an audience, an index of his impending recovery. He recalled this period again in 1905 in the early chapters of a long, unpublished account of his experience as a railroad hand.[23] He begins the account with an admission that during the previous three years he had been a victim of neuresthenia and that at least two distinguished medical practitioners had attempted to provide him with insight into his problem. One who "held a chair of nervous disease in a great university" told him that his oscillation between exaltation and despair was pathological and another "learned specialist" talked of "psychic stretch" and told him that his symptoms were caused by his being "cross fired by antipathetic waves of some kind." Dreiser writes that, during his illness, when he viewed the world it "seemed a great dark sombre sphere in which all life was being maintained by a sad and unutterably revolting struggle" and that when he looked into the eyes of men he saw "only anger, unrest, selfishness, greed." He asks why the "creative force" wills this "constant turmoil and worry in which so few could get food and clothing, let alone the flashing tinsels of joy that were forever being waved, Tantalus wise, before the hungry eye." Significantly, he wrote that one of his symptoms was the physical sense of being two distinct persons, one of whom was acquisitive, the other detached, yet compassionate. The first was a "tall, thin, greedy individual who had struggled and thought always for himself and how he would prosper," while the second was "a silent, philosophical soul" who "seemed to brood apart over my fate." Dreiser came to believe that this second person whom he described as a "sane, conservative oversoul" and a "superior consciousness" saved his sanity, though he was led to the very brink of suicide before he recovered. Dreiser seems never to have fully realized the psychological implications of this contest between the two persons within him. Yet they are clearly consistent with his divided self as revealed in *Sister Carrie*. Even the images he chose to describe his sensations during his bout with "neuresthenia" were appropriate and familiar. The "superior consciousness" considered the "greedy individual" as one might look at flies caught in flypaper or moths circling a lamp, burning their wings.

Dreiser wandered through New York, Virginia, Delaware, and Philadelphia in this condition. His wife stayed on her father's Missouri farm during part of this time. Finally, he returned to New York and several tiny rooms in Brooklyn to confront his fate. Slowly, he recovered his psychological equilibrium. With the help of his brother Paul, who found him and packed him off to a sanitarium, his physical vitality was restored to the point that he was able to take a job in the railroad yards. When he had recovered sufficiently to face the city again, he managed to get an assistant editorship at *Munsey's*, from which he moved over the next six years to a series of magazine positions culminating in the editorship of *The Delineator* for Butterick Publications at a salary of ten thousand dollars per year. For the first time he was making big money and enjoying the power that went with his position. He might never have returned to fiction, in fact, had it not been for fate and his ever active libido. He made the mistake of sleeping with Thelma Cudlipp, the daughter of a woman at Butterick's. The mother complained about his indiscretions not only to her superiors but also to his wife. Mrs. Cudlipp managed to force his resignation. Rather than seek other employment with a magazine, he decided to return to fiction. He had not only the encouragement of friends but also the incitement of the small success that had been made by *Sister Carrie* in the interim. In 1901, while Dreiser was struggling with mental illness, the British publisher William Heinemann brought out the novel in England, and though the reviews were mixed as they had been in America, the fact that some British reviewers could find strength in Dreiser was deemed a higher compliment than the same opinion rendered by American reviewers. As a result, American firms became interested in republishing the novel. In 1907, after having saved sufficient money to buy the plates of the novel from the J. F. Taylor Company, which had purchased them from Doubleday, Page, Dreiser entered into an agreement with B. W. Dodge and Company for republication. This time the reviews were more plentiful and somewhat more favorable. They gave Dreiser the impetus to begin what was to become the most prolific decade of his career.

He had begun planning his second novel in 1900 amidst the flap with Doubleday, Page and between 1901 and 1904 had managed to draft some forty chapters before putting them aside until 1910, the year after the Thelma Cudlipp affair. The early version of the novel was to be called *The Transgressor*, a title that placed the main emphasis on the heroine's flaunting of conventional morality. By 1910 when he set about revising and completing the novel, he changed the title to *Jennie Gerhardt*, emphasizing his heroine's individuality rather than her subgroup. Between the first draft and the version that was published in 1911, Dreiser had developed Jennie into the kind of woman Carrie has barely the possibility of becoming—a noble heart programmed for duty and sacrifice.

3 / Jennie Gerhardt

IKE *Sister Carrie, Jennie Gerhardt* is concerned with a pretty young woman of the 1880s. Like Carrie's, Jennie's liaisons defy the established conventions of the day. Both Carrie and Jennie progress in knowledge and sophistication under the tutelage of the men in their lives. Both women ultimately fail to achieve fulfillment; each is finally puzzled by her experiences. But in spite of these and other parallels which have led many critics to consider them of a piece, the two women are motivated by diametrically opposed instincts. Whereas Carrie is guided almost exclusively by her self-interest, Jennie is a model of selfless dedication to others. She is Dreiser's personification of giving as a way of life.

In *Jennie Gerhardt*, Dreiser turned again to his own family for source material. Jennie's totally selfless nature owes most to his romantic remembrance of his mother, while the plot of the novel is based roughly on circumstances in the life of his sister Mame. Like Carrie, Jennie is an outsider. She is first encountered as she helps her mother scrub floors in a posh Columbus, Ohio, hotel where the two have been assigned odd jobs. Jennie has known only bleak poverty, but she has a keen sense of life's potential for beauty. When she observes the spectacle of wealth in the hotel and the imposing houses nearby, she is filled with "half-defined emotions." The relaxing sound of a piano being played before the dinner hour in a parlor at the hotel fills her with hope that she might some day experience firsthand the comfortable world that the music signifies (p. 8). Again, while helping her brothers and sisters steal coal from the railroad yards to provide winter warmth for the family, Jennie reacts with silent wonder at the sight of a passing passenger train, its drawing-room cars and plate-glass windows revealing travelers in comfortable chairs (pp. 28–29). But Dreiser does not dwell on Jennie's material desire as he does on Carrie's. Indeed, Jennie's relatively lukewarm longing is included in her makeup simply to underscore the poverty of her background. Moreover, those "far dreams" she is permitted are always subordinated to her wish to help her struggling family. For her to even tentatively dream Carrie's dream of personal possessions and power would be out of character because early on Dreiser establishes that, since Jennie's childhood, "goodness and mercy had molded her every impulse." It never occurs to her to be "meanly envious," although she is frequently ashamed of being poor (p. 16). Dreiser is quick to point out that like Charley Potter in "A Doer of the Word," Jennie is the exception in human nature. "Caged in the world of the material," a person of Jennie's self-effacing spirit is "almost invariably an anomaly" (p. 15).

While collecting laundry at the hotel, Jennie meets a United States senator, George Brander, who appeals to her less because of the luxury and comfort that surrounds him than because he is "gentle, distinguished, and considerate." She is interested in his influence and wealth because of their potential to help others, including her parents and brothers and sisters, since the "privilege of being generous particularly appealed to her" (p. 23). Once she gets to know the senator, who finds her "artistically, temperamentally . . . far and beyond the keenest suspicion of the herd," her own opportunity to be generous is presented (p. 76). She finds herself late one evening in his hotel room awaiting his return from the jail where he has arranged the release of her brother, who had been arrested for stealing coal. Responding to Brander's own supplications, Jennie yields to him sexually. Although her action is partly ascribed to her naiveté, she wishes mostly to repay the senator for his growing generosity to her family.

Dreiser does not deal harshly with Senator Brander for having compromised Jennie. Brander, a more admirable character than either Drouet or Hurstwood, is a fifty-two-year-old bachelor possessing political integrity and a philosophic mind, often "speculating upon the futility of his political energy in the light of the impermanence of life and fame" (p. 21). His love for Jennie precipitates a moral crisis that parallels Hurstwood's at the safe door. Brander wavers "between the strict fulfillment of justice and duty and the great possibilities for personal happiness which another line of conduct seems to assure" (p.

75–76). The old struggle is replayed, and again desire is the victor. But to use the word *seduction* to describe Brander's action would be inappropriate in view of Dreiser's sympathetic handling of the situation. Although the senator appreciates Jennie's "developing form," he also respects her for her all-encompassing goodness. Indeed, his interest in Jennie and his desire to help her family are portrayed as the products of "a spirit of mingled charity and self-gratification" (p. 42). Ultimately, he is overwhelmed by the purity of her soul, her physical beauty, and the "wonder and tenderness of youth" that like a "few sprigs of green" have enlivened his barren materialism (p. 81). Moments before he takes her physically, he tells her that she is an "angel" and a "sister of mercy."

If the reader is led to sympathize with Jennie and Brander under the circumstances, her father cannot. F. O. Matthiessen has called old Gerhardt one of Dreiser's minor masterpieces. The accolade is just, since old Gerhardt is at the center of the most memorable and moving scenes in the novel. Patterned in part after Dreiser's father, he is a German true-believer who is honest, as a matter of unreasoned principle, and militantly moralistic. Dreiser makes him a Lutheran instead of a Catholic, probably in order to blunt his own bitterness and objectify the characterization as much as possible. (Jennie's angelic mother is a former Mennonite turned Lutheran.) Old Gerhardt's beliefs have fostered and fed on the blind bigotry Dreiser associated with "religionists." He is "prone to scan with a narrow eye the pleasures and foibles of youthful desire" (p. 56). When a neighbor tells him that Brander is courting Jennie, he is capable only of shock and confusion, his concern as much for "what the neighbors will think" as for moral considerations. His only recourse when he learns of Jennie's pregnancy is to exile her. But the seeds of his redemption are to be found in the love for his family which his actions obscure. The reader feels with him his depression because he cannot provide his wife and children an enjoyable Christmas. His painful struggle to understand his children's transgressions, rendered with consummate skill, start him on an agonizingly slow intellectual and emotional maturing process which remains incomplete at his death. Eventually, Jennie's father begins to appreciate her innate goodness. Indeed, he comes finally to see that Jennie is the noblest heart among all of his children. He thereby displays a capacity for change and growth that is invariably greatest among Dreiser's religiously committed characters, including the minister McMillan in *An American Tragedy* and Solon Barnes in *The Bulwark.*

But not all of his religious characters are capable of increased awareness and compassion. Certainly no such redemption is possible for the Gerhardts' Lutheran minister. Through Pastor Wundt, Dreiser unmercifully flays the permanently unbending moralist. Described by Dreiser as a "sincere and ardent Christian," he is the consummate bigot, dogmatically condemning to perdition all who are guilty of dancing, card playing, theater going, drinking, smoking, wrong conduct in marriage, and lack of innocence before marriage (p. 55). Given Dreiser's view of "sincere and ardent" Christianity as exemplified by Pastor Wundt, it is little wonder that Helen Dreiser was led to remark about her husband that: "No one with organized religious training or prejudice could ever be of any constructive value to him."[1]

After Jennie is exiled by her father, Senator Brander dies, leaving her pregnant. Forced to look for work, she finds it as a maid for a well-to-do family in Cleveland. Here she meets the second man in her life, Lester Kane, the thirty-six-year-old son of a prominent Cincinnati family. The introductory description of him perfectly encapsulates the qualities of the twentieth-century man and of Dreiser himself, a portrait that paradoxically mixes determinism and free will. Kane is the product of "an age in which the impact of materialized forces is well-nigh irresistible," one in which "the spiritual nature is overwhelmed by the shock." The "kaleidoscopic glitter" and the "vastness of the panorama of life" have left him uncertain of everything. An apostate Catholic, he has become a pragmatic democrat and liberal who has brought the whole of reality "under the knife of his mental surgery" and has left it "but half dissected." The result is a skepticism which carries with it the necessity of existential choice: "Life was not proved to him. Not a single idea of his, unless it were the need of being honest, was finally settled." Hence he enjoys "almost uncounted freedom of thought and action" (pp. 132–33). When he meets Jennie, he is magnetically and chemically drawn by her beauty, but above all by her purity of spirit and her attitude toward sex which is "bound up with love, tenderness, service" (p. 144). Since the only moral imperative for Kane is honesty, he is able with an untroubled conscience to take, through his powers of persuasion, that prize that Jennie alone among his female acquaintances can give—total devotion. In an attempt "to seize the happiness of life without paying the cost," he overcomes her objections and sets up with her a common-law relationship which is sustained for several years (p. 136). This arrangement contains the seeds of tragedy, however, for it meets with the active disapproval of Lester's socially sensitive family.

Moreover, even after he possesses the angelic Jennie, Lester remains restless, fearing that his relationship with her will cost him his material comfort. Before Lester's father dies, he puts Lester's inheritance in his brother Robert's trust against the day when Lester should decide to see reason, abandon Jennie, and take over the family business. Lester's uncertainty about his best course of action is extensively examined, and Dreiser attributes his indecision to his appreciation of Jennie's ideal character and to a deficiency that the hero of his next novel, Frank Cowperwood, would not suffer—"he lacked the ruthless, narrow-minded insistence on his individual superiority which is a necessary element in almost every great business success" (p. 303). But when the chance to better his position at what he deems a fair price presents itself, Lester succumbs. Spurred by his desire to return to society and affluence, he leaves Jennie for the socialite Letty Pace, whom he had known in his youth. But Lester does not submit to temptation without a struggle involving existential choices. Now, he is conscience-stricken in the knowledge that he owes his duty to his self-sacrificing mistress. Despite the exhilarating freedom Kane enjoys as a result of his "mental surgery," he cannot discard Jennie with a clear conscience. He is ashamed that his love is outweighed by his desire for material advantage: "His was not the sorrow of lacerated affection, of discarded and despised love, but of that painful sense of unfairness which comes to one who knows that he is making a sacrifice of the virtues—kindness, loyalty, affection—to policy" (p. 369). The extent of Lester's guilty sense of spiritual error sets him quite apart from the characters in *Sister Carrie* and introduces an ethical dimension missing from the earlier novel. But he capitulates to his desire for comfort and security, conscience notwithstanding. Dreiser's marriage was in the final stages of its ultimate breakup when he was completing *Jennie Gerhardt*. He must have had his situation and his own twinges of conscience in mind when he wrote of the parting of Lester and Jennie: "The relationship of man and woman which we study so passionately in the hope of finding heaven knows what key to the mystery of existence holds no more difficult or trying situation than this of mutual compatibility broken or disrupted by untoward conditions which in themselves have so little to do with the real force and beauty of the relationship itself" (p. 367–68).

Jennie's loss of Lester is compounded by the death of her daughter, Vesta. Confronted with the "immense darkness of her existence" without Vesta, she is spiritually lacerated. Yet she accepts rather than despairs. She displays what F. O. Matthiessen calls her "growing stature in human dignity" by adopting two homeless orphans.[2] (One is named Rose Perpetua, since she is to be a stay against the overwhelming confusion and change that assault her adoptive mother.) But Jennie is soon tested again. She is summoned by the grievously ill Lester, who undergoes a secular, deathbed conversion. He tells her that he has come to see how wrong it was for him to leave her, because he has not found greater happiness by turning his back on "their real spiritual compatibility" (p. 422). But Dreiser has not managed to make their compatibility totally believable in the novel. Lester's dying change of heart does not exactly ring true. Although he had been kind to Jennie's family and had helped her grow in learning and experience, their relationship rests primarily on her willingness to give and his to receive. Dreiser had earlier described Kane as an admirable man in every way "save his gift of love," and his need for Jennie is at several points described as basically selfish (p. 363). Therefore, his protestations that he had always loved Jennie, coming as they do on the heels of his opting for creature comforts, are not entirely convincing, however much Dreiser wants to convince us.

Lester's death casts Jennie once again into bewilderment. The final scene of the narrative pierces with irony. Jennie has come to the railway station in order to be at hand when Lester's body is shipped to his home, although she cannot board the train with the socially respectable mourners. As the truck containing Lester's coffin approaches the baggage car, a workman calls: "'Hey, Jack! Give us a hand here. There's a stiff outside!'" The incident underscores a theme that pervades all of Dreiser's fiction—material attainments come to nothing. Lester had seen through the selfish pursuit of earthly pleasures long before he met Jennie. Yet he had chosen material comfort over commitment. It had all been meaningless. Dreiser implies that the majority are concerned only with their own selfish, material diversions, as evidenced by other features of the final scene, which takes place on Thanksgiving Eve. Passersby are "gay with the anticipation of coming pleasures," and the names of many cities are cried over and over again through the station loud speaker—the world's chatter and bustle signifying nothing (pp. 430–31).

But if Lester's life has been made meaningless by a deficiency of love, what of Jennie's? The last paragraph of the narrative pictures for her a long "vista of lonely years" given over to the raising of the orphan children followed by "days and days in endless reiteration." Assuming during this denouement the mantle of the amoral naturalist, Dreiser consigns Jennie's life as well as Lester's to meaninglessness and papers over another instance of incomplete control over the intellectual content of his fiction. We can most readily approach the conflict just below the surface of *Jennie Gerhardt* by looking at various critics' contradictory reactions to the novel's ending. Donald Pizer, for example, sees Jennie at the conclusion as a victim of "a tragedy of deprivation" whose "constantly narrowing focus for her love" reduces her to "the artifice of adopting orphans" who will soon leave her. Pizer's point of view downgrades Jennie's will or ability to widen the focus of her love. Richard Lehan sees Jennie's life leading to a "lonely and empty end." Phillip Gerber, on the other hand, finds the ending "replete with implications of happiness—or at least peace, contentment—which render it a far more optimistic work than *Sister Carrie*." Gerber implies that Jennie can continue to seek out love objects. John McAleer asserts that "outside the American dream [Jennie] finds the happiness Carrie vainly sought within it."[3] In spite of the gloomy conclusion of the narrative, there is other evidence that validates these more optimistic readings. Dreiser in fact sends mixed signals which account for the conflicting interpretations. On the one hand, there are numerous instances that urge the reader to see the actions of the characters in mechanistic terms. For example, Lester makes a speech late in the novel justifying to Jennie his choice of Letty Pace over her, and his naturalistic explanation has been taken by many critics as a fair copy of Dreiser's beliefs. He tells Jennie that the individual "doesn't count much" in such situations because "all of us are more or less pawns" moved around "like chessmen by circumstances over which we have no control" (p. 401). Passages such as this provide evidence for Lehan's interpretation of Jennie's self-sacrifice as an unwilled manifestation of temperament, a product of the "bodily nature" of "an impersonal machine."[4] On the other hand there are many passages that make apparent Dreiser's preference for Jennie's way of life over others, certainly enough to justify the statement made in a 1911 *Harper and Brothers* advertisement for the novel that called it "a book which does not preach a moral but makes one felt." At least one key passage makes a moral felt by imputing preeminence to "goodness of heart." Lester takes Jennie to Egypt, and the experience puts her life in a new perspective. While she is musing over the ruins of Luxor and Karnak, she comes to an understanding strengthened by Lester's tutelage and seemingly concurred in by Dreiser:

For the first time in her life Jennie gained a clear idea of how vast the world is. Now from this point of view—of decayed Greece, of fallen Rome, of forgotten Egypt, she saw how pointless are our minor difficulties, our minor beliefs. Her father's Lutheranism—it did not seem so significant any more; and the social economy of Columbus, Ohio—rather pointless, perhaps. Her mother had worried so of what people—her neighbors—thought, but here were dead worlds of people, some bad, some good. Lester explained that their differences in standards of morals were due sometimes to climate, sometimes to religious beliefs, and sometimes to the rise of peculiar personalities like Mohammed. Lester liked to point out how small conventions bulked in this, the larger world, and vaguely she began to see. Admitting that she had been bad—locally it was important, perhaps, but in the sum of civilization, in the sum of big forces, what did it amount to? They would be dead after a little while, she and Lester and all these people. Did anything matter except goodness—goodness of heart? What else was there that was real. [Pp. 305–6.]

One might be tempted to ascribe Jennie's confirmed belief in the efficacy of "goodness of heart," which surely here means dedication to giving such as her own, to the fact that she is only beginning to see "vaguely." But the primacy of "goodness" is precisely the lesson that the infinitely more sophisticated Lester learns just before his death, and Jennie's father is brought to the painful admission that his daughter's self-sacrifice outweighs conventional judgments of her. Indeed, early in the novel Dreiser celebrates the "song of goodness" Jennie's character evokes, a song that "all the earth may some day hope to hear" (p. 15). The fact is that Dreiser's vision of the consequence of his heroine's life is no less elusive in *Jennie Gerhardt* than it is in *Sister Carrie*. Significantly, Dreiser wrote an epilogue which appeared in the first edition of *Jennie Gerhardt* but was dropped from subsequent printings on advice. Just as the rocking-chair coda in the Doubleday, Page first edition of *Sister Carrie* had been an attempt to put that story in perspective, the epilogue expunged from *Jennie Gerhardt* was meant to translate his heroine's experience. Called "In Passing," it summarizes Dreiser's own competitive thoughts about his subject. First, the reader is cautioned that he should not try to judge the success or failure of the heroine, because we know so little about the meaning of those words in the context of "the chemic drift and flow of things." But he then proceeds to analyze Jennie's actions in terms that can only be construed as representing success. In the absence of "the power to strike and destroy" and the ability to "fall upon a fellow-being, tearing that which is momentarily desirable from his grasp," Jennie has been denied only bitterness, brutality and feverishness—"what a loss!" The epilogue ends: "Jennie loved, and loving, gave. Is there a superior wisdom? Are its signs and monuments in evidence? Of whom, then, have we life and all good things—and why?" (pp. 432–33). The intellectual problem with the novel is certainly this mixed message. For example, when Jennie philosophizes on the Egyptian ruins, Dreiser through Lester seems to hold all moral standards to be relative, yet at the same time he seems to underwrite through Jennie "goodness of heart." While the determinism Dreiser displays much of the time in *Jennie Gerhardt* lessens the novel's moral toughness, his irresolute employment of it denies the book amoral consistency as well. His unwillingness to forthrightly fix blame in *Jennie Gerhardt*, admirably understanding though it may be, lessens the tragic dimension of the novel. If only goodness of heart matters, then Dreiser cannot logically invite us, as he does, to condemn the perpetrators of the yellow journalism that exposes Lester and Jennie's secret liaison to public view in order to sell papers, nor can he rationally entice us to disapprove of Lester's eventual preference for comfort over commitment to Jennie. Moreover, he cannot plausibly direct implicit criticism, as he does, against the kind of bigotry shown by old Gerhardt and Pastor Wundt or the class cruelty practiced by the Kane family, which surely represent the crux of Jennie's predicament. On the other hand, one need not be entirely capricious to read *Jennie Gerhardt* as an illustration of the advantages of materialism, since Dreiser fails to answer decisively the question, What does it profit a man if he gain his soul and lose the whole world? After all, Jennie's goodness has apparently reaped for her only a long, lonely vista. Yet, the softest spot in Dreiser's heart is obviously for Jennie precisely because she lives the "virtues" that most cannot sustain—kindness, loyalty, affection. At one point in the novel, Dreiser even defines virtue as "the wishing well and the doing well unto others" and "that quality of generosity which offers itself willingly for another's service" (p. 93). Surely, Gerber is right in his contention that the "tenderness which characterizes every paragraph of Jennie's tale" shows that he has more affection and respect for the traits she displays than for Carrie's.[5] Although he devotes many lines to a defense of Carrie's "good nature," he clearly admires Jennie's "goodness of heart" more.

Dreiser attributes Jennie's "virtue" to her affinity with the natural world, which is "not ungenerous" (p. 93). This affinity is most clearly seen in her habitual giving, linked by Dreiser to "certain processes of the all-mother." Jennie's motherly yearning toward her child is at several points contrasted to the lack of such instincts in lesser women. She is compared again and again to the wood-dove and often to flowers like the "delicate arbutus" that "unfolds its simple blossom, answering some heavenly call for color" (pp. 98–99). Dreiser notes in the same context that nature displays "no outside"—that is, no predisposition toward judgment (p. 93). In another mood, however, he might recall and either despair over or rejoice in nature's tendency to breed destructive species. Nature, after all, conceived not only the wood-dove and the arbutus but also the hawk, and the deadly nightshade.

At any rate, Dreiser apparently saw no connection between "goodness of heart" and Christian precepts. *Jennie Gerhardt* clearly reveals one of the besetting problems of his early fiction—the tendency to equate the conventions observed by society with Christian morality. Again, the difficulty can be illustrated neatly by Dreiser criticism, which often duplicates the novelist's point of view. For example, Charles Child Walcutt points out, in his classic study of American naturalism, that one of Dreiser's purposes in *Jennie Gerhardt* is to indict the moral code that would condemn a good woman like Jennie for what were called her "sins." He then maintains that "the effect of the story is to show how utterly inadequate are standard Christian ethics for the judgment or guidance of conduct in a world that does not, as Dreiser sees it, correspond to the notion of reality upon which that ethical code is based."[6] But this view is, in large measure, misleading. Dreiser does attack with considerable vigor the use of religious ethics in judging another's conduct—especially sexual conduct—through Old Gerhardt, Pastor Wundt, and Lester's family. Nowhere in *Jennie Gerhardt*, however, is there to be found an invalidation of genuine

Christian values in moral guidance, although Dreiser seems to have thought otherwise. In telling Jennie's story, he is surely extolling a way of life based on love, tenderness, and purity of heart, and these virtues are the base for true Christian ethics. Again, Lehan in attempting to put Jennie's story in perspective reproduces Dreiser's thoughts: "As long as Christian laws prevail, what happens to Jennie is inevitable."⁷ But there are no Christian laws dictating old Gerhardt's exile of his daughter for her "moral lapse," nor does any precept of that faith call for Lester's family to disinherit him for preferring a woman beneath his class. Surely, forgiveness, compassion, and understanding represent the highest Christian injunctions, ideally informing the application of all lesser laws. What neither Dreiser nor many of his critics seem to have fully appreciated was that like so many "amoral" writers, his quarrel with Christians was primarily that they did not really practice Christianity. He evidently conceived the total view of life in *Jennie Gerhardt* to be antagonistic to "standard" religious morality. The fact that he always stresses extenuating circumstances in moral behavior attests not only to his antipathy to self-styled moralists but also to his own parting with religion in his youth, before more compelling explanations of complex ethical situations had been presented. This persistent quarrel with Christians colors a letter he wrote to an English reader of *Jennie Gerhardt* eighteen years after its publication. The man had complained to Dreiser that a passage in the novel focusing on the phrase "conceived in iniquity and born in sin" (p. 98) gave the erroneous impression that all "religionists" were warped because they believed sex was "dirty." Dreiser responded that the novel was an American work, reflecting the accepted American attitude toward sex, and then he tried to set his reader straight on theological matters:

> If the Church, as you state, considered natural conception as a beautiful, clean, uplifting achievement, then why the beatification of the Virgin primarily because of her "Immaculate Conception"? I am very much afraid that neither the Roman Church nor those of Anglican or Greek extraction look upon this close, intimate relationship as being anything except unholy and unclean—only raised to the standards of decency and a sacrament through the placing of the blessing of the Church upon it—and this in each and every individual case, not a blanket condonement ever.

Next, he punctuates his argument by quoting David in Psalm 51 saying that his mother conceived him in sin.⁸ The letter bears witness not only to Dreiser's somewhat dubious interpretation of the Scriptures, but also to the predominant attitude of his day among many "religious" persons who saw the sex act, not as sacred, sublime, and natural, but rather as a source of sin and an object for sniggering. This attitude did nothing to disabuse Dreiser of his misconceptions. Actually, his complaint in the passage from *Jennie Gerhardt* had been made against the "extreme religionist" whose "marvellously warped" views are validated by the world through its silence which "gives assent." But his English reader's letter triggered a less temperate response and demonstrated Dreiser's tendency for many years after the publication of the novel in question to impute to religious persons appalling ignorance and willful distortion of sexual processes.

The implicit moral judgments imbedded in Dreiser's partiality toward "goodness of heart" in *Jennie Gerhardt*, however, as well as his seeming preference for Carrie in her compassionate phase run counter to his more frequently adopted amoral stance. This discrepancy has not always been noticed by critics. In their traditional wish to subsume all of Dreiser's ideas under the rubric of naturalism, they have often been led into positions that literally duplicate the clash of ideas in the novels. Walcutt, for example, divides Dreiser's work into four stages, the first of which includes *Sister Carrie* and *Jennie Gerhardt*: "In the first stage Dreiser was expounding his conviction of the essential purposelessness of life and attacking the conventional ethical codes which to him seemed to hold men to standards of conduct that had no rational basis in fact, while they condemned others without regard to what Dreiser thought might be the real merits of their situations."[9] Since Walcutt let this analysis stand without further comment, it is reasonable to assume that he did not see in it the perplexing crosscurrents that render some of the ideas in Dreiser's early fiction intellectually disjunctive. For if life is purposeless, how can situations have "real merit?" In *Jennie Gerhardt*, Dreiser rejected the application of what he conceived to be religious standards in judging men who were simply unwilling pawns at the same time he affirmed what he thought to be a more noble code based on purity of heart and selfless giving. Walcutt was among the first Dreiser critics to show how the development of his work from darkly deterministic in *Sister Carrie* to reverent in *The Bulwark* and *The Stoic* bridged the "divided stream" of American naturalism and American transcendentalism. What neither Walcutt nor many critics since have suggested is that each of his novels before

The Bulwark is itself a divided stream. In each, one branch—the deterministic—is allowed to flow relatively freely while the other—the moral and religious—is clogged by old animosities and certain misconceptions.

Pizer is one contemporary critic who has noted Dreiser's simultaneous assumption of the conflicting attitudes of bitterness at mechanistic cruelty and affirmation of mechanistic beauty in *Jennie Gerhardt*. But he discounts the problem by asserting that Dreiser, seeing no discrepancy, felt that different temperaments might find an element of truth in both attitudes. For Pizer, Dreiser's "philosophy" of mechanism is secondary to its fictional role as a metaphor of life against which various temperaments can define themselves. [10] But this judgment neither lessens the reader's difficulty in deciding what his novels really say nor recognizes Dreiser's continuing struggle to decide for himself, within the framework of his fiction, whether the beauty might be accentuated and the cruelty diminished by the willingness to give.

Beyond the implicit morality of *Jennie Gerhardt*, there is a current of mysticism in the novel that has not often been remarked. A significant departure from *Sister Carrie*, it centers on the idea of material life as an illusion. Dreiser hints in several places that his characters may be pointed toward an afterlife. When Jennie is grieving over the loss of Vesta, Dreiser, in his wish to console her, interjects: "If only some counselor of eternal wisdom could have whispered to her that obvious and convincing truth—there are no dead" (p. 396). Although Brander's death is brought about in part by the loss of his Senate influence in a political fight and Lester's is hastened by the awareness that he will never enjoy the power his brother has appropriated with the inheritance of his father's carriage monopoly, Dreiser adds a curious dimension. Lester is persuaded to die by the ingrained race consciousness disposing a man to think that he is allotted the biblical "three score and ten." He does not realize, says Dreiser, that man is "organically built to live five times the period of his maturity," that "it is spirit which endures, that age is an illusion, and that there is no death" (p. 413). There are other ways in which the inexplicable impinges on the story. Jennie receives an omen of Lester's death. In a dream, her dead mother, her daughter, and Lester are floating about a mystic pool in a small boat. Within a few days of the ominous forecast, Lester dies. The incident derives from Dreiser's belief that his brother Rome was afforded a vision of his mother's death while far from the scene. These passages, however unconvincing they may be to many readers, attest to Dreiser's continuing concern about the limitations of his own mechanistic philosophy. They have also proved embarrassing to those of his apologists whose admiration is centered on his materialism. There are other implicitly religious parts of the novel that might prove disconcerting to that large segment of his reader constituency as well. For example, Dreiser's emotional attraction to liturgy is recast when Jennie attends Lester's memorial service. The service is held in the church where he has been allowed burial because "the family was distinguished," a fact that outweighs his lapsed Catholicism. Jennie, moved by the chant and the incense, finds the scene spiritually evocative and suggestive of "life in all its vagueness and uncertainty" (p. 427). In *Dawn*, Dreiser explained that Catholic ritual always impressed him deeply as "an artistic spectacle" (p. 480). The same emotions move Jennie at the very beginning of the novel, in a beautiful scene wherein Dreiser quite clearly shares Jennie's feeling. She is sitting among some grapevines with her younger sister and brother at dusk on a summer evening, wondering how it would feel to float among the clouds in the radiant western sky. Her brother points out a bee winging by. Jennie explains that, like all insects and animals, it is "going home." Overcome by the beauty of the evening and the tolling of the Angelus, Jennie is reduced to tears as a "wondrous sea of feeling in her . . . stormed its banks" (p. 17–18). Such passages occur sporadically in Dreiser's early fiction. The relationship of the displayed emotion to religious awe has not often been suggested. One is reminded here of the schoolboy in Emily Dickinson's "The nearest dream recedes unrealized." His frustrated attempts to capture a dipping, deploying, and, finally, soaring bee lead the poet to deduce that the boy is "homesick for steadfast honey," a "rare variety" that no earth-bound bee can produce. For both Dickinson and Dreiser, the recognition of the need for enduring substance signifies the longing for a transcendent reality. And in both writers, nature, not a church, prompts their implicitly religious emotions.

Despite many genuinely moving scenes, a loving portrait of the poor, and a noble attempt to correct readers' attitudes toward illegitimacy, however, *Jennie Gerhardt* is a less impressive achievement than *Sister Carrie* for a variety of reasons. Among its minor flaws is a certain sloppiness of detail, which was to become a Dreiser trademark over the years. For example, Jennie has supposedly passed Lester off to

Vesta as the child's uncle, yet she tells her in one scene: "Run to your papa." Vesta's age at different points in the novel does not mesh with the chronology of the action; Jennie's mother is alive when Vesta is five though she had died when the child was three and a half, and it is virtually impossible to determine Vesta's age at her death. Although many of the scenes between old Gerhardt and Vesta are beautifully written (Vesta is the catalyst for the regeneration of old Gerhardt's love), Dreiser displays his usual trouble in fictionalizing children. His lower-class background may or may not have kept him from under-standing the workings of the drawing room, as Norman Mailer has suggested, but there can be no doubt that Dreiser's considerable pow-ers of observation short-circuited when it came to creating believable children. Vesta, who is described as the "bright" child of Jennie's union with Senator Brander, learns to walk at age three and to talk at four, is still "goo-gooing" at five, and cannot distinguish an uncle from a father at seven.

But, aside from these minor matters and the difficulties within the philosophical framework previously discussed, the most vexing prob-lem in *Jennie Gerhardt* is the characterization of the heroine. Jennie's sacrifices for her family and her lovers are so conspicuous that they constitute a nearly fatal flaw in the novel, bending double the reader's willingness to suspend disbelief. Her every action from the opening lines until the final scene is dictated by her wish to help others, and she scarcely ever thinks of herself. This abdication of self was doubtlessly what led Oscar Cargill to compare her to George Moore's Esther Waters and to rank Jennie a distant second: "Esther has charac-ter and force—she lives for us; Jennie is so much dough . . . Dreiser did not really know Jennie."[11] To justify his comparison, Cargill might have pointed to Esther's nasty temper and her singular lack of remorse for her transgressions. Conversely, the evidence of Jennie's doughlike consistency is everywhere. She allows her father to abuse her for the slightest transgression; her strongest response is to color when old Gerhardt confronts her with accusations after an innocent walk with Senator Brander—but she says nothing. Moreover, unlike Carrie, who had not been above righteous indignation at her treatment by Hurstwood, Jennie actually helps Lester take advantage of her. She is given to pointing out to him women more beautiful than herself for his consideration. When Lester encounters his old flame Letty, Jennie stifles her jealousy, since that emotion would be "contemptible."

What little tension there is within her results not from the clash between her personal desires and her duties but rather from conflicting responsibilities, as when she must give up living with Vesta whose existence she had hidden from Lester in order to become his mistress and thereby indirectly aid her family. Cargill's accusation that Dreiser did not know his heroine is paradoxical, however, in view of his sister's and especially his mother's role as her models. But the charge is on target in the most important sense. Her character is a striking example of the truism which holds that it is one thing to know a subject and to feel deeply about it and quite another to realize it artistically. Whereas it could be argued that Carrie's comparative lack of ethical depth caused her to be atypically sensitive to every worldly temptation, Jennie's character becomes utterly flat because she is never really tempted; she never has an unkind thought. Whereas most of the players in *Sister Carrie* reveal, thanks to Dreiser's introspective method of characterization, that seemingly simple people can be bewilderingly complex, Jennie is one dimensional. By way of further contrast, Senator Brander, Lester Kane, and even old Gerhardt are rounded characters. Pizer's judgment that the expunged epilogue had been a botched job because it represented a "deflating simplification" of Jennie is indeed curious since she could hardly be more simple under any circumstances.[12] She is as difficult to empathize with as Adam and Eve before the fall in "Paradise Lost." That *Jennie Gerhardt* should soon through a surge of interest match the popularity of *Sister Carrie* among the reading public is inconceivable. Most contemporary readers probably would not find her programmed generosity either understandable or particularly attractive in these days of assertiveness training seminars. Dreiser in certain moods spoke of Jennie as his favorite creation, but the estimate of the novel he gave to the Indiana newspaperman and diplomat Claude Bowers around 1920 indicates that he was acutely aware of her shortcomings. Bowers had asked if it were true as he had heard that Dreiser liked *Twelve Men* better than any other of his books. When the novelist responded that only his portrait of his brother Paul in that book particularly appealed to him, Bowers pressed for a ranking of *Jennie Gerhardt* and was obliged: "'No, I don't like *Jennie* so much. I formed a dislike for it almost as soon as I had finished it. I wrote it in an emotional mood and liked it immensely in the process of composition, but almost immediately afterward I concluded that I had overdrawn Jennie. I think so still.'" When Bowers insisted that he had "'known some women after whom she might have been drawn,'" Dreiser responded: "'I can't say that I ever have.'"[13] In this instance, his judgment is more trustworthy than that of H. L. Mencken, who pronounced *Jennie Gerhardt* the greatest novel in American literature excepting *Huckleberry Finn*.

Jennie was, in fact, not originally conceived to be quite as angelic as she became. She is a more rounded and more credible character in the first draft of the novel, but after Dreiser had completed some forty chapters in 1901, he decided that an error in character analysis would have to be corrected.[14] Consequently he transformed her into the ministering saint of the published novel, dropping references to her sexual drive and material ambition. The few flashes of worldly desire which she displays in the novel survived from the original plan. In some ways, Dreiser changed the novel to make it more believable. At one point in the writing process, he had contrived a marriage for Jennie and Lester, a happy denouement which paralleled his sister Mame's in a similar situation. With the aid of some advice, he concluded that such a turn of events would detract from the tragic dimension of the story, and so he changed the plot. Actually, in some ways Lester and Jennie's "happily ever after" marriage would have been more appropriate to the work since its heroine is a highly romantic conception of natural goodness. In fact, the simplified Jennie falls short of a believable portrait, even of sainthood. Works like J. F. Powers's "Lions, Harts, Leaping Does" show that convincing characterization can be based on the lives of saints. Didymus, the Franciscan friar-hero of that instructive story, wages an enormously difficult daily struggle to conquer the self and is never completely successful. But when Dreiser wrote *Jennie Gerhardt*, he was a long way off from the recognition that goodness is not "natural," as he had also asserted in the case of Charley Potter in "A Doer of the Word."

Although at the end of the novel Jennie is dedicated to charity in a way that Carrie could never be, and although there is a greater recognition of guilt for violations of commitment to others exhibited in Lester and old Gerhardt than in any of the characters in *Sister Carrie*, troubling questions arise. How can man be expected to exhibit selfless devotion to others when his impulses are set free from moral discipline, as Dreiser seems to favor at times in *Jennie Gerhardt?* What accounts for Jennie's devotion to all others? The gloss of character formation offered in *Sister Carrie* will not suffice in *Jennie Gerhardt*. In the earlier novel, the environment from which a person develops was said to account for his actions. But in the later novel, the Gerhardt children other than Jennie, nurtured by the same strongly sympathetic mother and moralistic father, range in their maturity from indifferent to self-interested. What moves other characters in *Jennie Gerhardt*—the good doctor who visits sick family members out of sympathy or the grocer who extends Jennie's mother credit with little hope of being paid—to act so differently from Lester's destructive sister Louise or his coldly self-satisfied brother? And, were programmatic self-sacrifice as exhibited by Jennie attainable through rigid inner control, would it not prove destructive to the mental health even of those bent on canonization?

There has been both implicit and explicit debate among critics about whether the heroine of *Sister Carrie* displays growth in that novel, a debate that has most often ended in a hung jury.[15] The same question might be asked about Jennie. Up to a point, the pattern of her development follows Carrie's. Thanks to Senator Brander and Lester Kane, she becomes wiser in some worldly matters. But by the end of the novel she still has not learned that continuous denial of the self has rendered her "so much dough." There is no third man in her life, no spokesman to introduce her to "the call of the self" as Ames had introduced Carrie to the "call of the ideal." Lester in fact chides Jennie for lack of "defiance" at one point. But she continues to think almost exclusively of others. The single indication that she has even considered an alternative to complete sacrifice is the pleasure she takes at a later point in the knowledge that Vesta is growing into a "self-constructive" woman who "would be able to take care of herself" (p. 366). Perhaps Dreiser felt that Jennie had perfected her giving way of life and did not need a counselor to show her how to gain a new dimension. Or he may have been trying to avoid the kind of intellectual tangle that Ames's character had cost him in the earlier novel. But Jennie needs an anti-Ames to convince her that taking her own part, at least occasionally, might have led to a fuller life from which those who touched her could have benefited.

There are other ways in which Dreiser's second novel misses the mark set by his first. Because Jennie's desires are so few, her vision is narrower than Carrie's, Luxor and Karnak notwithstanding. Much of Jennie's interest in life focuses on a comparatively grim arena of domestic duties. She has no compelling dream to match Carrie's in the theater. Moreover, in this novel, Dreiser uncharacteristically passes up the chance to enrich the narrative with an extensively developed contrast between the lives of the poor and those of the affluent. Although we fully experience the Gerhardts' world, we see little of the Kanes'. Again, *Jennie Gerhardt* is relatively barren of evocative symbol and metaphor. *Sister Carrie* is alive with the sights and sounds of the great world; it is suffused with the refracted light of place and it echoes with American resonances. By comparison, *Jennie Gerhardt* suffers from a want of light and air. But that is not to say that it is without appeal. There is an undeniable attraction in the novel for those who have ever looked sympathetically into the faces of the poor.

Whatever the relative merits of *Jennie Gerhardt*, its reception was considerably warmer than that accorded *Sister Carrie*. Dreiser now felt justified in pursuing his fortunes with his pen. In the fall of 1911, he took a trip to Europe under the auspices of his English publisher, Grant Richards. He set down his impressions in *A Traveler at Forty*, published in 1913 but completed before *The Financier*. Valuable perspective on the direction of Dreiser's thought is provided by this first nonfiction book. In it, he assumes the role of visiting artist and intellectual, and a rather pretentious pose mars the writing. But there are important ideas here which play a role in Dreiser's ongoing struggle to choose between alternate courses of action. The reader is assured at the outset of *A Traveler at Forty* that its author has seen much of the world and accepts no foolish creeds. He then promulgates his own creed, which he later refined and extended: "I cannot view life or human nature save as an expression of contraries—in fact, I think that is what life is. I know there can be no sense of heat without cold; no fullness without emptiness; no force without resistance; no anything, in short, without its contrary" (p. 34). This is his first formal espousal of the theory of existence hinted at in *Sister Carrie* and *Jennie Gerhardt* and formulated in later books as nature's "equation." He found that it was now possible to describe some of the opposing forces which had always fascinated him, such as good and evil, wealth and poverty, strength and weakness, and of course, giving and taking, in terms of nature's desire for balance. The equation hypothesis, elaborated from the thought of Herbert Spencer, is Dreiser's attempt to resolve through an all-encompassing generalization the conflicts out of which his first two novels had been formed. At times in *A Traveler at Forty*, he seems intent on illustrating equation through the collision of his own antithetical ideas. At one point he asserts: "I trust the universe is not mechanical, but mystically blind. Let's hope it's a vague, uncertain, but divine idea. We know it is beautiful. It must be so" (pp. 18–19). Yet a few pages later he asserts, "I indict nature here and now, as I always do and always shall do, as being aimless, pointless, unfair, unjust" (p. 42). The same law of "equation" allows him to include chapters which demonstrate equal approval of Saint Francis of Assisi and the Borgias. Dreiser critics have most often been content to subordinate this kind of oscillation between opposites to the novelist's "uncompromising naturalism." Such an analysis does not, however, take into account his struggle to understand the meaning of life, and the related struggle to frame his developing understanding in fiction.

Although he spoke of the necessity for equation in *A Traveler at Forty*, Dreiser was clearly most attracted not to the equation itself, but to the extremes that defined it. In the summer before publication of the travel book, after finishing a draft of *The "Genius,"* he had begun researching a long three-part novel to be called *The Financier*. It was to be based on the career of Charles Tyson Yerkes. In the trilogy that would eventually develop from these plans, Dreiser would test the proposition that the ruthless acquisition of the objects of desire could make one happy. As he moved from *Jennie Gerhardt* to the Cowperwood trilogy, he shifted the focus from the Franciscan to the Borgian. Perhaps in unbridled indulgence of the will to power, one might make of his days not endless reiteration but infinite variety and enough.

4 / *The Financier*
and *The Titan*

I N *A Book About Myself*, Dreiser recalls his ambition as a very young man to be "president or vice-president or secretary of something, some great thrashing business of some kind" (p. 108). His later reading provided a context in which to place such ambitions, especially his reading of two German thinkers, Arthur Schopenhauer and Friedrich Nietzsche. Dreiser read Schopenhauer around 1900. The philosopher's concept of man as concrete craving meshed with the novelist's own self-evaluation and his observations of most others. Dreiser's first experience with Nietzsche's ideas was less direct. He initially encountered the theory of the "superman" in 1909 through H. L. Mencken's book about the maverick philosopher. He wrote Mencken after studying the outline of Nietzsche's thought in the introduction that "he and myself are hale fellows well met." Once deeply into the book, however, he told Mencken that he found Nietzsche less consistent and original than Schopenhauer. [1] But the idea of the "superman" made its impression, for Dreiser included in *A Traveler at Forty* a significant summary of human nature which shows the influence of both Schopenhauer and Nietzsche: "We are organized appetites, magnificent, dramatic, pathetic at times, but appetites just the same. The greater the appetite the more magnificent the spectacle" (pp. 459–60). The American perspective on the "magnificent spectacle" of amassed wealth and power was provided Dreiser through his reading of serious studies about native business moguls, most especially Gustavus Myers's *History of the Great American Fortunes*, published in three volumes in 1910. *The Trilogy of Desire* would record the drama and pathos created by one of the most voracious of all "organized appetites," the street-railway magnate and robber baron Charles Tyson Yerkes, fictionalized as Frank Cowperwood.

Dreiser first heard of Yerkes during the 1890s when both men were in Chicago and Yerkes was at the height of his power and arrogance. As Dreiser followed the tycoon's later career, his interest in him peaked, and so while casting about for a suitable protagonist for his business epic, he was irresistably attracted to Yerkes because of the audacity of his attempts to subject whole cities—Philadelphia, Chicago, London—to his will. He was also attracted by Yerkes's sexual magnetism, which had won him a legion of devoted women. After all, Schopenhauer had identified sex as the hidden motivation of all of man's actions. In Dreiser's mind, Yerkes's varietism, as well as his informed interest in art, set him above "dull bookkeepers" like Rockefeller. The street-railway king provided the novelist with an opportunity to study a character diametrically opposed to that of Jennie, one who used the power he possessed to acquire those things that were always highly attractive to Dreiser himself. Cowperwood's triumphs embody many of Dreiser's wishes. But at the same time, and more significantly, *The Trilogy of Desire* represents Dreiser's complex, mostly negative, appraisal of ruthless self-serving as a way of life.

The Financier (1913), the first volume of the trilogy, chronicles Cowperwood's business and romantic stratagems from his youth in Philadelphia to the close of the first phase of his career there. A natural leader by age ten, he is fond of questioning how life is organized. The definitive answer is provided by an odd drama he witnesses at a local fish market. For a number of days he watches a lobster and a squid which have been placed together in a tank. The lobster, after a period of relentless pursuit, succeeds in devouring the squid, a portion at a time. This natural brutality leaves its mark on the boy. Although he feels "the least touch of sorrow" for the squid, the lobster's mode of operation clears things up for him intellectually. He reads into it the justification for his own projected career in an often-quoted passage which establishes Cowperwood's conversion to Social Darwinism:

The [lobster-squid] incident made a great impression on him. It answered in a rough way that riddle which had been annoying him so much in the past:

"How is life organized?" Things lived on each other—that was it. Lobsters lived on squids and other things. What lived on lobsters? Men, of course! Sure, that was it! And what lived on men? he asked himself. Was it other men? [Pp. 13–14.]

Cowperwood concludes that men did indeed live on other men, as proved by the Civil War, then in progress. This insight does not set him to dreaming, like Carrie, of some "vague, far-off supremacy," but rather to working for the immediate possession of gold as a tool of dominance. He concludes his first business transaction at the age of thirteen, making nearly 100 percent profit on a case of Castile soap. After inheriting fifteen thousand dollars from his uncle, he sets himself up in business. In the jungle of finance he soon finds his own world view corroborated by the machinations of others, who do as they please despite the rantings of the public moralists. But he realizes that in order to succeed, he must appear to be what he is not, to deceive his victims: "The thing for him to do was to get rich and hold his own—to build up a seeming of virtue and dignity which would pass muster for the genuine thing" (p. 244). Despite such blunt descriptions of Cowperwood's devious self-serving, Dreiser manages to elicit understanding and empathy from the reader by painting the financier as a good-natured realist who sees through the shams of society. He defines the budding tycoon as "primarily your egoist and intellectual" with a "humane and democratic spirit" (p. 242). Cowperwood is most often straightforward and lies only when absolutely necessary. But he thinks only momentarily of the human rights issue in the Civil War; he worries more about the effect of a Southern victory on business than about the plight of the slaves. His only bond of affection is with his father. His sympathies are only fleetingly engaged by associates in trouble. For his competitors he maintains consistent disdain. By following his genius and adhering strictly to his own self-interest, he becomes a millionaire through a series of exhaustively documented financial transactions.

In recasting Yerkes's financial career into fiction, Dreiser had access to the public record, scores of newspaper articles about the tycoon's serial rape of business rivals and citizenry alike. It took little imagination to ascribe motivation to him in this highly accessible part of his life. When it came to his private situation—his relationships with his wife and children, his attitude toward the collection of women with whom he had liaisons, his purpose in amassing art treasures—the public record was less helpful. In these matters, Dreiser was forced to rely on his own attitudes and experiences. For authenticity in recreating Cowperwood's domestic strife, he put to use his difficulties with his own wife, Sara. To characterize the succession of women in Cowperwood's life, he used as models his own lovers, including Kirah Markham and Thelma Cudlipp. To motivate Cowperwood, he gave him parts of his own emotional makeup. Thus, at age thirteen, the budding business giant becomes enthralled with girls. By nineteen he has "broken the Seventh Commandment" many times (p. 68). When he meets Lillian Semple, a married woman, she appeals to him as "the shadow of an ideal," the possessor of a number of qualities Cowperwood finds ultimately desirable. She is beautiful, mature, and aloof. Death claims her husband, who had not been able to give her the children she had wanted, and she is drawn to Cowperwood. Observing his motto, "I satisfy myself," Cowperwood marries her, though it never occurs to him not to have other women at the same time. Acquisition is the rule in all things for him. He is the most consistent taker in all of Dreiser's fiction. Indeed, when his two children are born, he experiences a feeling of "self-duplication" which is "almost acquisitive" (p. 116). But the seeds of his dissatisfaction with his lot have already been planted. Lillian is five years his senior. (One of the facts that interested Dreiser about Yerkes was his marriage, like the novelist's, to an older woman.) She also has a "placid, retiring nature" which, though part of her original appeal, is not calculated to satisfy for long a man of Cowperwood's dynamism. Although they remain technically married for twenty years, the financier's dissatisfaction surfaces much sooner and especially when he begins comparing Lillian to younger women. When he is twenty-seven and she thirty-two, he encounters the first, fatal younger woman. Aileen Butler, the sixteen-year-old daughter of a political ally, is the most successfully delineated of Cowperwood's string of mistresses. F. O. Matthiessen, in fact, finds that "Aileen's character is far more coherently realized than Carrie's, and of a bold vitality that was no part of Dreiser's intention in portraying Jennie."[7] Not only beautiful, she is also richly emotional and vivacious. She appears just as the more low-keyed Lillian begins to suffer fits of depression, and Cowperwood is prompted to wonder if a man is entitled to only one wife: "Sympathy and affection were great things: but desire and charm must endure or one was compelled to be sadly conscious of their loss" (p. 148). The tycoon had found that the "shadow of an ideal" with tangible problems was a contradiction in terms.

Cowperwood's promiscuity is explained early in the novel as the natural result of his sensitivity to beauty, but his relationship with Aileen is defined in terms of chemistry and physics. She is drawn to him "as a moth to a flame" and as "planets are drawn to their sun." Something "chemic and hence dynamic" clamors for expression in Cowperwood. Part of Aileen's appeal for him is her defiant nature, matching his own. Whereas Lillian had been "conventional as the driven snow," Aileen is a seeking younger woman, rebelling against a parochial school education and the narrow religiosity of her parents. Her kinship with Carrie in at least one respect is established through a passage in *The Titan:*

Aileen was fairly bursting with hope and vanity and longing. Oh, to be Mrs. Frank Algernon Cowperwood . . . to have a splendid mansion, to have her cards of invitation practically commands which might not be ignored!

"Oh, dear!" she sighed to herself, mentally. "If only it were all true—now."

It is thus that life at its topmost toss irks and pains. Beyond is ever the unattainable, the lure of the infinite with its infinite ache. [Pp. 19–20.]

Although she shares Carrie's "infinite ache," Aileen is no drifter. Her clear, aggressive, unblinking attitudes and actions, contrasting markedly with Lillian's approach to life, enchant Cowperwood. He speculates on the imprudence of missing the opportunity for "color and beauty" presented by Aileen's love for him, and they are soon running together "like two leopards." This time there is none of the conflict between duty and desire that had plagued Hurstwood and Lester Kane, since Dreiser assures us that Cowperwood has no more conscience in these matters than in his business affairs. While Dreiser intrudes into the narrative to underwrite the idea of divorce, Cowperwood concludes his extramarital arrangement without concern for his wife. The thing for an intelligent man to do was to avoid being discovered, since exposure would involve some personal discomfort. Dreiser puts his protagonist's dismissal of an "esoteric standard of right," in historical context by citing the amorality of Helen of Troy, Messalina, Madame du Barry, Madame de Pompadour, and Nell Gwyn. In such personalities, as well as in Cowperwood's, "the chemistry and physics of life are large," and in them "neither dogma nor fear is operative" (p. 261). Dreiser explains that for Cowperwood, there is only strength and weakness, not good and evil, which are "bound up in metaphysical abstrusities about which he did not care to bother" (p. 476).

While Cowperwood is wooing and winning Lillian and Aileen, Dreiser is engaged in documenting another of the financier's passions—art. His interest in paintings, especially those in which the artist serves as an interpreter of nature, begins in his twenty-first year and by his late twenties he has already assembled a distinguished collection. Throughout the trilogy, he pursues paintings and sculptures as relentlessly as he pursues women. Dreiser does not satisfactorily account for the interest in art objects of such a thoroughgoing pragmatist, except to say that far from being merely acquisitiveness, Cowperwood's interest in art is bound up with his worship of feminine beauty. Cowperwood's appreciation of the artist is set down in a key passage in *The Titan*:

Of all individuals he respected, indeed revered, the sincere artist. Existence was a mystery, but these souls who set themselves to quiet tasks of beauty had caught something of which he was dimly conscious. Life had touched them with a vision, their hearts and souls were attuned to sweet harmonies of which the common world knew nothing. Sometimes, when he was weary after a strenuous day, he would enter—late in the night—his now silent gallery, and turning on the lights so that the whole sweet room stood revealed, he would seat himself before some treasure, reflecting nature, the mood, the time, and the man that had produced it. Sometimes it would be one of Rembrandt's melancholy heads—the sad "Portrait of a Rabbi"—or the sweet introspection of a Rousseau stream. A solemn Dutch housewife, rendered with the bold fidelity and resonant enameled surfaces of a Hals or the cold elegance of an Ingres, commanded his utmost enthusiasm. So he would sit and wonder at the vision and skill of the original dreamer, exclaiming at times: "A marvel! A marvel!" [P. 382.]

Perhaps the inference to be drawn is that a related kind of vision is necessary to build a financial empire. In fact, Dreiser does imply elsewhere in the trilogy that any great financier is himself an artist who should be able to appreciate a fellow creative spirit. Yet such an explanation should not have contented him, since his selection of Yerkes as a model for Cowperwood was based in part on the very fact of his sensitivity to art, an unusual trait among businessmen. Moreover, the link between art and sex in Dreiser's mind, alluded to a number of times in the trilogy, is not satisfactorily explained in either *The Financier* or *The Titan*. The connection would be made much more clearly in *The "Genius."*

Both Cowperwood's art collection and his business empire are threatened with ruin, however, when he displeases powerful political forces in Philadelphia. Aileen's father, a politician who had been used by Cowperwood to obtain railway franchises, seeks revenge against him for ruthlessly ruining his daughter. He connives with his cronies to have the financier tried in federal court for a technical embezzlement. In a rehearsal of the trial scenes in *An American Tragedy*, Cowperwood is convicted by a corrupt justice system. The judge is a political hack. Although the district attorney thinks he would have done the same as Cowperwood under the circumstances, he is newly elected and has a record to make. The jury has been threatened with commercial ruin to see that it reaches a verdict of guilty. But for all the documentation and narrative skill of the trial scenes here, they lack the great impact of those in *An American Tragedy*. This lack is, no doubt, owing partly to the comparative want of compassion the reader feels for Cowperwood and partly to the nature of the charge against him. After all, the financier's failure to deposit $65,000 in a sinking fund hardly makes for the kind of courtroom drama that goes with the murder charge against Clyde Griffiths. But Dreiser's insightful condemnation of the judicial system is just as vigorous in *The Financier* as in *An American Tragedy*. Cowperwood's case before the appellate court is weakened by the breaking scandal of his affair with Aileen and lost when the judges involved decide against him in deference to political bosses and their own careers.

Up to the climactic point in *The Financier* when Cowperwood's Philadelphia venture begins to totter, Dreiser's objective delineation of his protagonist's programmatic self-serving maintains a high degree of consistency. For this reason, several critics have assumed that the novelist approved of the financier's remorseless taking. But later in the novel, after Cowperwood's conviction has been orchestrated, Dreiser attributes to him a curious softening not revealed in the historical record. At his sentencing, Cowperwood and his co-conspirator, the former city treasurer Stener, are led before the judge along with two housebreakers, a horse thief, and a negro being prosecuted for picking up what he thought to be a discarded length of pipe from a lumber

yard. The financier reflects on this sad assemblage and is led to understanding and an uncharacteristic sympathy:

He felt sorry now for this entire shabby row of convicts like himself, sorry for
all who were in jails, men who were here now or would be or had been. It is
a grim, bitter world we are born into, he reflected. Who was to straighten out
the matter of the unjust equipment with which people began? Who was to
give them strong minds in place of feeble ones, able bodies instead of
wretched ones? Where were they to get pure tendencies instead of impure
ones, as the world looked on these things. [P. 660.]

Although Cowperwood puts these musings in the context of the survival of the fittest, his feeling for the oppressed is not accounted for in
his Darwinian system. Moreover, when he is taken to prison, he is
grateful for the sympathy of Mr. Chapin, the kindly Quaker cell over-
seer who because of his mental weakness and inexperience believes in
an illusory human justice and decency. And Cowperwood receives
such tender compassion from his mistress that he is very much moved.
Under Aileen's soft ministrations he is treated like a troubled boy and
is brought to the verge of tears:

The depth of Aileen's feeling, the cooing sound of her voice, the velvety tenderness of her hands, that beauty that had drawn him all the time—more
radiant here perhaps within these hard walls, and in the face of his physical
misery, than it had ever been before—completely unmanned him. He did
not understand how it could; he tried to defy the mood, but he could not.
When she held his head close and caressed it, of a sudden, in spite of himself,
his breast felt thick and stuffy, and his throat hurt him. He felt, for him, an
astonishingly strange feeling, a desire to cry, which he did his best to overcome; it shocked him. [P. 728.]

Dreiser weaves these incidents into the narrative without comment.
Just why he deviates from the public record by imputing emotional
vulnerability to his superman is not entirely clear. Perhaps it has
something to do with his need to make Cowperwood's sensitivity to
art more believable. Or, he may have been using this material to pre-
pare the reader for the epilogue, which posits the ultimate mutability
of the most imposing human accomplishments when viewed in cosmic perspective. [3]

In all likelihood, however, he interjects the passages about Aileen's
mothering instincts because of his continuing fascination with the

ideal of giving. An earlier passage, which has gone unnoticed by critics, supports this explanation. In a section introducing Aileen, Dreiser points out that beneath her hot-blooded exterior is a tenderness which contrasts dramatically with Cowperwood's brazen self-aggrandizement. Then he interrupts the narrative to lecture the reader on the admirable qualities of mistresses and in doing so reveals not only his attitude toward unsanctioned relationships, but also his preference for those who give. He begins by regretting how unfairly the mistress has been portrayed in literature, wherein she is always described as "the subtle, calculating siren who delights to prey on the souls of men," when indeed in the "vast majority of cases" there is no "design or guile" involved. When the ordinary woman is in love, she is "no more capable of anything save sacrificial thought than a child— the desire to give; and so long as this state endures, she can do only this." Such a "sacrificial, yielding, solicitous attitude" is in direct contrast to the "grasping legality of established matrimony." Man must necessarily worship such a "non-seeking, sacrificial note" which "approaches vast distinction in life" because it relates to the "largeness of spirit" in art, appealing through its "giving, freely and without stint of itself, of beauty" (pp. 303–4).

This incongruous ode to self-sacrifice in the midst of an epic celebration of the superman shows Dreiser still pulled between the extremes of human possibilities, here curiously polarized by implication as male and female attributes. And now the giving nature, which had been designated as anomalous in Jennie Gerhardt, is the biological inheritance of the "average woman" when she loves. There are, of course, major flaws in the logic of this position. Dreiser apparently asks the reader to believe not only that women are naturally selfless but also that the institution of marriage has the power to change biology, to turn women's giving into grasping. Moreover, the theory of women's gratuitous giving expounded in Dreiser's long aside in no way accounts for the career of Claudia Carlstadt, "the ruthless and unconsciously cruel" as well as "avaricious" prostitute used by Cowperwood's confreres to blackmail a rival businessman in The Titan (p. 332). (Dreiser, like Schopenhauer, believed that the money exchanged in houses of prostitution dehumanizes sex because sex needs romance and a sense of beauty to validate it.) Dreiser's unconvincing attempt to absolve Claudia Carlstadt of blame for her actions involves a description of her early environment, which was not unlike that of

Jennie Gerhardt. And early in *The Financier,* Cowperwood reflects un-
favorably on the number of "sacrificial" women who "toiled and slaved
for their husbands or children or both." These women appeal to him
less than the self-sufficient ones who see through the hypocritical
praise of "virtue and decency" (p. 68). But Dreiser did not totally share
this preference, since his mother, for example, had been one of the
sacrificial type. Indeed, the excursus on womanly giving in *The Financier* undercuts his fascination with Cowperwood's opposing traits. Unlike Ayn Rand, Dreiser was not able to write novels that glorified un-
abashed self-interest. Far from making selfishness a virtue in the tril-
oogy, as more than one critic has suggested he does, he makes quite
the opposite point through his digression in praise of loving mistresses. [4]

Whatever Dreiser's feelings about the giving spirit of women, he
needed to continue the saga of the ultimate male dominator. After
Cowperwood's release from prison, he seizes the first chance to re-
sume his rapacious activities. The panic of 1873 provides the opportunity, and he is soon a remade millionaire at age thirty-six. He moves
to Chicago, quietly divorces Lillian, and readies himself for the second phase of his career. The final pages of *The Financier* are devoted to
a two-part epilogue in which Dreiser interprets the events of Cowperwood's career to this point. The first part of the epilogue is a description of the black grouper, a huge fish not unlike Cowperwood in its
voracious appetite and nonexistent conscience. Dreiser's analysis is
totally mechanistic, a "scientific" attempt to sanction the financier's
predatory business practices. Like Cowperwood but in its own environment, the grouper lies in wait at the bottom of the sea, simulating
its surroundings and gorging itself on unwary intruders in its domain.
In trying to read the cosmic meaning of the creature's behavior, however, Dreiser is led to put several questions to the reader:

> Would you say in the face of this that a beatific, beneficient creative over-
> ruling power never wills that which is either tricky or deceptive? Or would
> you say that this material seeming in which we dwell is itself an illusion? If
> not, whence then the Ten Commandments and the illusion of justice? Why
> were the Beatitudes dreamed and how do they avail? [P. 779.]

The contrast between the ideal of the Beatitudes and the actuality of
the survival of the fittest is meant to underscore Cowperwood's realistic Social Darwinism. Through the characteristic non sequitur of the

naturalist, Dreiser excuses the financier's machinations because he sees him as coequal to so-called "lower forms of life," but then he goes a step further by making Cowperwood's trickery synonymous with the will of God. For these reasons, the black grouper section of the epilogue to *The Financier* has been understandably popular over the years as a touchstone of Dreiser's determinism. But it should be remembered that the passage concludes with a series of questions for which Dreiser doggedly sought satisfactory answers all of his life. Only in his last novels did he record what many critics have called his surprising final answers to the questions he asked in the *Financier* epilogue. In *The Bulwark* he tried to show why the Beatitudes were dreamed and how they availed. In *The Stoic* he reasoned from the final evidence of Cowperwood's life that "this material seeming in which we dwell" was in fact an illusion.

Even at the conclusion of *The Financier*, Cowperwood's worldly triumphs are placed in a perspective that diminishes them. His inevitable disillusionment and defeat are forecast in the second section of the epilogue, "The Magic Crystal." Despite power, mansions, art treasures, endless riches, and glory, which are to come from his Chicago and London ventures, all will turn to "the ashes of Dead Sea fruit" because Cowperwood will become, in the final analysis, the victim of "an understanding that could neither be inflamed by desire nor satisfied by luxury; a heart that was long since wearied by experience; a soul that was bereft of illusion as a windless moon" (p. 780). In the very first volume of the trilogy, Dreiser could not resist remarking on the vanity of accomplished wishes, and on the reality that even lobsters must finally go the way of the squid. And this in spite of the fact that, as Pizer points out, the epilogue misrepresents the events to come in *The Titan* in which Cowperwood's "opposing force" is the "'mass' rather than his own nature."[5] If the selfless Jennie Gerhardt had at last been forced to face a future of meaningless sameness, Cowperwood at the outset of the most flamboyant stage of his great career is doomed to a future of unfulfilling variety.

The Titan (1914) follows Cowperwood's career in Chicago, the city that Dreiser believed offered limitless possibilities. The novel dramatizes Cowperwood's successful campaign to control the street-railway system and his eventual expulsion by jealous rivals and an irate citizenry. When Cowperwood arrives in Chicago, like Carrie, he is moved by the city skyline, and Dreiser interjects several exuberant passages of tribute to the vitality of the new metropolis and its pilgrims "hungry for something the significance of which, when they had it, they could not even guess" (p. 6). Chicago is a fitting backdrop for Cowperwood's climactic rise to power. Indeed, Dreiser is moved to praise its dramatic turmoil in contrast to the more staid Philadelphia. Once Cowperwood gains his transportation franchises through all manner of trickery and treachery, his fortune accumulates to twenty million dollars, his extensive art collection becomes the most important in the nation, and his power becomes virtually unchecked. Yet he remains unsatisfied for several reasons. First, he and Aileen are unable to break into Chicago society because of the scandal of his imprisonment and Aileen's lack of polish, this latter fact the more stinging when Cowperwood compares his mistress to the supreme poise of European socialites encountered during his travels. Second, his dissatisfaction with Aileen as she grows older sets him on a relentless search for the one woman whose combination of qualities suits her to become his ideal mate. Fully two-thirds of *The Titan* is dedicated to Cowperwood's romantic adventures. The famous quip by the New Humanist critic Stuart Pratt Sherman that *The Stoic* would probably turn out like the first two volumes of the trilogy to be "a sort of huge club-sandwich composed of slices of business alternating with erotic episodes" was much more apropos of *The Titan* than of *The Financier*.[6] And clearly, in *The Titan* Dreiser considered the erotic slices the juicier morsels. As the novel develops, his concentration on the business segments appears to wane, a prelude to the total loss of interest that caused him to put off completion of the trilogy for thirty years. On the other hand, dealing with Cowperwood the womanizer allowed Dreiser to expatiate on one of his favorite subjects. Since the public record stopped just short of Yerkes's bedroom door, Dreiser imputed to Cowperwood many of his own experiences with women—experiences he had already prepared for public exposition in the first draft of his autobiographical novel, *The "Genius."* Indeed, the restless pursuit of the elusive paragon of womanly perfection who promises ultimate fulfillment and perpetual delight was to become a major theme in Dreiser's middle novels. He was always fascinated with his women characters, but he gave his personal ideal of transcendent femininity its fullest treatment in the Cowperwood trilogy and *The "Genius."* In these works, he created for the first time male protagonists with sexual drive matching his own.

Cowperwood's search for the feminine ideal is rooted in his social ambitions. He feels keenly the rebuffs of high society, though he realizes that elite circles tend to shut out the new rich. Dreiser frequently excoriates the stupidity of such social pretensions in *The Titan*, but his own envy of exclusive wealth and respectability helped him to empathize with and motivate Cowperwood in his desire for a worthy woman whose credentials might still gain him entree. When his "bright young bird," Aileen, begins to age, his thoughts stray to younger women. Dreiser has Cowperwood realize that the sex drive of a strong man endures through old age, but it cannot be satisfied by older women. The novel deals mostly with the tycoon's affairs with a series of mistresses at least twenty years younger than he. Dreiser explains that these affairs are the product of a "chronically promiscuous nature" connected with an appreciation of art. Cowperwood needs "the novelty of a new, untested temperament, quite as he must have pictures, old porcelain, music, a mansion, illuminated missals, power, the applause of the great, unthinking world." One might explain this need by calling it a search for "the realization of an ideal," Dreiser tells us, "yet to one's amazement our very ideals change at times and leave us floundering in the dark" (p. 201). Like Eugene Witla's quest for the perfect woman in *The "Genius,"* Cowperwood's search is characterized by excessive expectation followed by disillusionment. Each time Cowperwood, like Eugene Witla, discards a mistress because she lacks some necessary trait, his level of expectation rises until he discovers the ultimate "all girl." And, significantly, they both differentiate the "all girl" from her predecessors by her spiritual superiority. The fervent quest for the feminine ideal in these middle novels interconnects with other of Dreiser's fictional themes of expectation and disillusionment that are derived from his own experiences in the secular city. This interconnection helps to make understandable the spiritual sublimation of *The Bulwark* and *The Stoic*, for no earthly woman could possibly repay the investment of essentially religious emotion involved.

Cowperwood's search begins to reap dividends after a series of short intrigues with totally insufficient temperaments. When he meets Rita Sohlberg, a twenty-seven-year-old former art student and the wife of a Danish violinist, he discovers qualities that help him define his ideal. She paints and plays the piano. Her moodiness is irresistible. Her role in the novel is to add artistic talent to the set of requirements Cowperwood is developing. Dreiser also portrays her as much more mentally aware than Aileen, though as is true of all the "ideal" women in the novel, he fails to dramatize her transcendence. The reader must be excused for wondering what it is about Rita that so enchants his hero. For example, when the financier is showing her through his art collection, they pause before a nude by Gerôme. She reveals that she does not care for Gerôme because of a certain artificiality in his work, though the painting is "very pretty." Unaccountably, Cowperwood finds this a "sweet insight which sharpened his own" (p. 118). Again, she observes that the blue of the old man's coat in "The Adoration of the Magi" is "be-yoot-i-ful." Cowperwood rewards this judgment with a burst of overwrought appreciation, calling her "clover blossom" and "sprig of cherry bloom" and "Dresden china dream" (p. 127). The reader is tempted to conclude that since Rita is younger, rounder, plumper, more seductive and elusive than Aileen, her art criticism may not be the real basis for her appeal.

A year into his affair with Rita, he sets up another liaison, this time with his secretary, Antionette Novak, a "fine dark, brooding girl," whose appeal is "mere sex attraction" (pp. 129–30). After Aileen discovers these two affairs she physically throttles Rita and secures Antionette's banishment, thus winning Cowperwood's admiration and temporary fidelity. But his search for the perfect woman soon begins anew, and after a series of relationships which Dreiser passes over as "names merely," he meets Stephanie Platow (Plateau?) a "brilliant" Russian-American Jew from the Southwest with a penchant for art, literature, philosophy, and music. Stephanie at eighteen has already developed the requisite "artistic moodiness." Furthermore, her body strikes Cowperwood as a rhythmic "S" in motion, and of course she is younger than Rita. She also surpasses her predecessor in sophisticated sex gratification. Having indulged in sex at a young age, she has developed generosity. Yet paradoxically, Cowperwood regrets that she is not a virgin. Since "the evil" had already been done, however, he chooses to overlook it until he discovers that Stephanie is having a simultaneous affair with a young poet named Forbes Gurney. The poet turns out to be an embarrassingly obvious Dreiser self-portrait.[7] Cowperwood, feeling hurt by Stephanie's unwillingness to devote herself entirely to him, confronts the "lying prostitute" along with Gurney in her room and advises her to stick to her profession and renounce free love. Having given up on Stephanie, Cowperwood is next enthralled by Mrs. Hosmer Hand, the wife of another financier. She is "young, debonair, sufficient—a new type" (p. 265). He appreciates her superior social graces, assertiveness, and ambition, but he is troubled by her shortage of "heart." Dreiser paints this and Cowperwood's preceding affairs with a degree of comic irony based on the financier's vulnerability and his application of moral standards in his mistresses' behavior that are totally missing in his own. At one point, for example, he has Cowperwood reflect on the way passion and love "make fools of us all." But this perspective is lost by the tycoon and abandoned by Dreiser when the ultimate embodiment of Cowperwood's ideal appears.

While on a business trip to Louisville, Cowperwood meets the keeper of a brothel, Hattie Starr, whose sexual passion had cut her off from her monied background. This combination of passion and background has helped to form in her daughter, Berenice Fleming, the composite of qualities for which Cowperwood has been searching. Berenice is based on Yerkes's long-time "protege," Emilie Grigsby, and on Dreiser's former love, Thelma Cudlipp. Indeed, the novelist's awed descriptions of Berenice testify to his lingering infatuation with Miss Cudlipp and to his ability to idealize his lovers into utter unreality. Cowperwood instinctively knows that she is his "pole star" when he sees a photograph in Hattie's room of the fifteen-year-old girl, a "delicately haggard child with a marvelously agreeable smile, a fine, high-poised head upon a thin neck, and an air of bored superiority" (p. 347). The paradoxical aloof approachability of Berenice, a quality that makes her a forerunner of such F. Scott Fitzgerald flappers as Judy Jones in "Winter Dreams," convinces him that she has the makings of a high-society thoroughbred. At school she has learned to walk with six plates on her head. Given to leaping into the stance of the "Winged Victory," she is utterly certain of her own superiority, though not a snob. She occasionally dances before a mirror on moonlit nights and frequently affects ivory-colored clothing. Berenice is seventeen, and Cowperwood fifty-two when they finally meet. Soon after, the financier builds himself a splendid house to be nearer her. The familiarity he gains by being closer to her grows into adoration as he discovers in her all of the qualities of his previous loves plus several that they lacked. She possesses the required youth and stunning beauty. Her social talents are limitless and her ambition needs only his money for its realization. But beyond these familiar attributes she has a complexity of mind which lies "deep below deep" (p. 466). Blessed with a transcendent, commanding presence, she does not need to use her considerable powers of conversation, singing, declamation, or imitation because she always impresses others, even with her silence. Also in her makeup is another ingredient that had been missing in the other women Cowperwood had known—her affinity with nature. She manages to lure him outdoors, that least explored territory in the trilogy, and there she transforms his interest in stocks and bonds into an appreciation of fields and fledglings and trees, formerly accessible to him only through pastoral paintings. When, on a summer outing, Berenice catches a young sparrow, Cowperwood knows that here finally is a woman "who could and would command the utmost reaches of his soul in every direction" (p. 394). Significantly, she is also credited with a large, kindly, mothering instinct.

The "spiritual equipoise" of Berenice is referred to again and again, though it is never demonstrated. Most of the critics find her character totally unconvincing. For example, Pizer calls the "unbelievability of Berenice" the "principal weakness in Dreiser's depiction of Cowperwood's personal life," while Gerber argues that Berenice does not achieve "a cubit of Aileen's stature as a fictional creation."[8] Such opinions are not surprising. Despite Dreiser's enraptured descriptions of Berenice's alluring personality and fabulous beauty, most readers probably find it impossible to imagine how a mere woman could ever satisfy Cowperwood in view of the dozens of idealized mistresses who precede her. Emilie Grigsby was only one of Yerkes's protégés at this point in his life, and so by deifying Berenice Fleming, Dreiser was in fact altering the historical record, and this alteration is revealing. Dreiser's deification of Berenice, matching Cowperwood's, indicates that he shared the financier's longing for feminine indefectibility and that his longing had religious dimensions. The ideal is perceived "within a chalice-like nimbus," and it consists of a "compound of the taste, the emotion, the innate culture, passion, and dreams of a woman like Berenice Fleming" (p. 470). Earlier Dreiser had described "a static something which is beauty," a quality "above sex and above age and above wealth that shone in the blowing hair and night blue eyes of Berenice Fleming" (p. 381). But a significant contradiction mars this portrait of Berenice's perfection, for we are told a little later that "beyond [her] was nothing save crumbling age, darkness, silence"

(p. 470). Cowperwood's urgent need to maintain youth, meaning "sexual power," is incongruous, for virility is unnecessary in the devotee of ideal beauty. One must respect Dreiser's attempt to understand his hero's motivation, but one is tempted to view Berenice as simply another creature of the novelist's erotic fantasy. There is, however, an essentially spiritual energy behind the groping attempts to dramatize her transcendence. Dreiser was testing the possibilities of a secular faith based on romance with the perfect woman as the ultimate object of worship and in doing so transmuted Yerkes's philandering into a mystical search. Because Dreiser shared his hero's subjection to female beauty, he seldom achieves in *The Titan* the tranquility necessary to objectify the overflow of his emotions. Consequently, his interpretive and explanatory intrusions most often dissolve into rhetorical haze.

At the end of *The Titan* Cowperwood believes he has found the perfect woman, but the forces opposing him frustrate his ultimate triumph. His troubles begin when he meets his match in Governor Swanson (patterned after the reform governor of Illinois, Peter Altgeld). Swanson vetoes a bill that would have provided Cowperwood with one hundred million dollars' worth of street-railway franchises. In the clash between Cowperwood and Swanson, Dreiser was again playing off taking and giving, and he makes no attempt to hide his admiration for Swanson/Altgeld's idealism. The governor finds the financier guilty of "greed, over-weening ambition, colossal self-interest as opposed to the selflessness of a Christian ideal and of a democratic theory of government" (p. 485). The two men represent uncompromising adherence to opposing principles, and for these principles they are both hated by many. Dreiser himself is characteristically torn between the taker and the giver, between his admiration for his brazen hero and his sympathy for the reformer dedicated to helping the masses suffering at his hero's hands. He seems to extend equal sympathy to both. But he points out in the last stages of *The Titan* that Cowperwood himself has become interested in giving, having resolved, for example, to donate a telescope to the city. True to the historical record, the governor denies the financier the franchises and thus precipitates the fall of both men from power. Even the election of a new, more pragmatic governor does little to help Cowperwood. When the Chicago city fathers pass an ordinance that further limits his options, he is forced to withdraw, tired and beaten. With some effort, he plans a takeover of the London street-railway system with Berenice at his side extending to him her warming sympathy as Aileen had after his Philadelphia failure. But it is too late. Thanks not only to the idealistic Swanson but also to a crowd of self-interested politicians, the masses have proved the superior force in Chicago and have brought about Cowperwood's downfall. Dreiser concludes *The Titan* by calling his theory of equation to the task of summing up the significance of Cowperwood's life to this point. In an epilogue titled "In Retrospect," God, the life force, or Nirvana is said to be nothing more and nothing less than a balance that is struck "wherein the mass subdues the individual or the individual the mass—for the time being." The significance and the limitations of any great man are impressed on Cowperwood, who now realizes that despite the fact that he did "for the hour illuminate the terrors and wonders of individuality," he must confront "the pathos of the discovery that even giants are but pygmies" when considered in a cosmic context (p. 551). Far from answering the question of whether it is more intelligent to give or to take, Dreiser uses the equation theory at the end of *The Titan* to beg the question. He suggests that Cowperwood's buccaneering is necessary, for without him the weak would lose their significance. But because Dreiser is unwilling in the end to impute fulfillment to a life of conspicuous material success, he leaves Cowperwood disillusioned and meditating on the strangeness of reality as opposed to illusion. He has just completed a New York mansion as a "monument to himself," and he still has a fortune. He has presumably found in Berenice the ultimate treasure. Yet, as his Chicago downfall and his projected London venture indicate, he has not attained "peace." In the rocking chair coda appended to the Doubleday, Page first edition of *Sister Carrie*, the actress sits, still dreaming of an undefined supremacy. At the close of *The Titan*, Cowperwood has achieved and lost supremacy. He is Dreiser's first strong protagonist, the first to drive not drift, but it is only his singular ability to actualize his ambitions which differentiates him from many of the others, despite Dreiser's attempts to demonstrate his imposing complexity. Drouet is the "merry, unthinking moth of the lamp" in *Sister Carrie*, and similarly, Cowperwood is a taciturn, thoughtful moth circling a somewhat brighter light fueled by the same energy source. The reason for the close relationship is not difficult to locate. Although the trilogy represents a departure for Dreiser by being semi-documentary, the fact remains that he was again relying primarily on his most trusted source of character motivation—introspection.

The differing interpretations of *The Financier* and *The Titan* attest to the fact that Dreiser's immersion in Yerkes's biography did nothing to lessen the confusion his own inner conflicts had caused in the conclusions of his first two novels. Some critics read in the Cowperwood books a justification of the robber baron, while others argue from the same evidence that both novels attacked the laissez-faire economic system in which the robber baron thrived. Matthiessen's judgment that in the end Dreiser failed to choose sides in his evaluation of Cowperwood remains closest to the truth. He points out that although in the trilogy Dreiser describes robber barons as heartless enslavers of the rank and file, "the reader never feels that Dreiser is wholly involved in this verdict." As a result, Matthiessen believes the novels end in a "curiously blurred dream" combining "Horatio Alger with Darwin and Nietzsche."[9] Although in much of the Cowperwood material Dreiser seems to be defending ruthless self-serving, he manages to do so only by downplaying the effects of such a policy on the poor who suffer at the hands of financiers and by painting Cowperwood's business rivals as far more vicious than he. Indeed, the cunning machinations of his protagonist, a self-confessed scoundrel, are accomplished with such great good humor that the reader is led to sympathize with him in his battles with less "humane" enemies who are, after all, doing the very same things. But in keeping with his indecision, Dreiser chose to end *The Titan* as he had *The Financier* with a set of questions instead of providing some answers as he had in *Sister Carrie* and *Jennie Gerhardt*. The section called "In Retrospect," at the close of *The Titan*, leads from the equation theory to a crucial inquiry:

> What shall we say of life in the last analysis—"Peace, be still"? Or shall we battle sternly for that equation which we know will be maintained whether we battle or no, in order that the strong become not too strong or the weak not too weak? Or perchance shall we say (sick of dullness): "Enough of this. I will have strong meat or die!" And die? Or live? [P. 552.]

The Cowperwood novels represent Dreiser's closest approach to a totally naturalistic fiction. Their moral is that when it comes to meaning and purpose, even the haves are have-nots. But in spite of the explanation provided by the equation, the question of how to make existential sense of one's life continued to vex Dreiser. The search for satisfying answers to the questions posed in this epilogue would help form his fiction for the next thirty years.

The critical appraisals of *The Financier* and *The Titan* have been as mixed as the interpretations. Perhaps the most telling criticism of the trilogy, however, focuses on Dreiser's shift of subject matter from the lower to the upper classes. Much of the power of *Sister Carrie* and *Jennie Gerhardt* derives from their dramatization of the longing lives of outsiders. A perceptive essay by John O'Neill notes the abstract disengagement from the physical world which defines the "truly imperial" Cowperwood. O'Neill observes that there is none of the encounter of the outsider with the fabulous city full of things which animates Dreiser's other novels. The hero "suffers losses with as little emotion as gains."[10] With the exception of the scenes that depict Cowperwood's unmanning by Aileen at the close of *The Financier*, this analysis is just. Indeed, one might argue that even the tycoon's womanizing is coldly intellectualized.

H. L. Mencken placed *The Financier* next only to *Jennie Gerhardt* among Dreiser's artistic achievements, and more recently John McAleer has ranked *The Financier* and *The Titan* just below *Sister Carrie* and *An American Tragedy*.[11] But others have ranked them at or near the bottom of the list. Generally, *The Financier* is more highly regarded than *The Titan* because of Aileen's stature as a palpable character in contrast to the ethereal Berenice, and because of the "human interest" dimension provided in *The Financier* by the struggle between Cowperwood and Edward Butler over the politician's daughter. Donald Pizer and Charles Shapiro evaluate the two novels in representative fashion. Pizer regards *The Financier* as the best book in the trilogy, Dreiser's "most elaborate and successful venture in large-scale fictional architectonics during his early career." Shapiro calls *The Financier* "splendid." On the other hand, Pizer judges *The Titan* a failure for "the apparently simple-minded but essentially profound reason that the novel fails to move us deeply in its characters and events." Shapiro is more caustic. He links *The Titan* and *The Stoic*, calling them "wearisome and inept" and "worthy precursors of *Cash McCall*."[12] An argument can be made, however, for a reversal of these rankings, if one considers how much of *The Financier* is taken up with boardroom details, carrying for some readers all of the vital interest of a Dun & Bradstreet report. Although Aileen's admittedly engaging character becomes less important as *The Titan* develops, the relative absence here of business minutiae might for many make this the more readable volume of the two. And if Cowperwood's pursuit of the perfect woman fails to move readers deeply, it probably does not often fail to interest them. Whatever the relative merits of the two works, they remain required reading for the devotee of the business novel. The most fully documented studies of the world of finance in all of fiction, they rank as a major achievement in the genre. Perhaps that is why Robert Penn Warren has confessed to a grudging "commitment" to these first two books of the trilogy despite his intermittent impression that each is "a total failure and a bore, crudely written and dramatically unrealized." Warren testifies to the enduring fascination of the Cowperwood saga: "no matter at how low a rate I have regarded the trilogy, it has stuck in my mind, and sometimes on coming back to it—at least, on coming back to the first two novels—I have been surprised to find myself plunging on, completely bemused."[13]

Because he had lost interest in Cowperwood after finishing *The Titan*, Dreiser decided to put off the completion of the trilogy in order to devote himself to other projects. In the next ten years he would publish a number of nonfiction books, including several autobiographical works, plays, short stories, and poems. But his first move following the publication of *The Titan* was to cut and revise the manuscript version of *The "Genius,"* which he had completed early in 1911. The novel that appeared in October 1915 is the most unabashedly autobiographical of all of Dreiser's fiction. In it, he dramatized his own "artistic" dreams of power and the perfect woman.

5 / The "Genius"

THE "*Genius*," substantially completed before *The Financier* and *The Titan* but not published until 1915, puts Dreiser's own ambitions, passions, fears, and guilt directly on display. The novel turns on a series of conflicts that tore at Dreiser again and again in his own life: his duty to his art as opposed to his material desires; his pursuit of feminine beauty as opposed to his duty to his wife as specified in his marriage vows; his compulsion to accept a deterministic explanation of existence as opposed to his need to believe in transcendent meaning. The thin veil that had separated several of Dreiser's earlier characters from their creator is transparent in *The "Genius."* Eugene Witla, the painter protagonist, is patterned after the author in almost every respect, and the events of the novel dramatize Dreiser's life up to 1910. His move from a small town to Chicago and then New York, his "neuresthenia," his magazine career, his marriage and extra-marital affairs, his dreams of the ultimate woman, and his relentless exploration of religion—all are set down in minute detail. If these ingredients make for a less than satisfactory novel because of Dreiser's comparative lack of objectivity about them, they also make for a more revealing self-portrait than a writer often presents to his public.

Eugene is endowed with all of Dreiser's traits. As a boy, he is shy, sensitive, and unsure of himself. These qualities do not, however, stem from a background of poverty. In one of the few alterations of the record, Dreiser provides Eugene with a middle-class upbringing—his father is a sewing-machine agent with whom he has a good relationship—probably because the novel focuses on the artist, not as a young man, but as a mature ponderer on life and love. Eugene is a dreamer, and his dreams center on wealth, fame, art, and women. He envies the wealthy and feels shabby when he compares himself to them. Appropriately overawed by his first glimpse of Chicago, he seeks work there as a newspaper artist: "you could feel what Chicago meant—eagerness, hope, desire. It was a city that put vitality into almost every wavering heart: it made the beginner dream dreams; the aged to feel that misfortune was never so grim that it might not change" (p. 39). When his search for recognition leads him to New York, his expansive longing is vivified by the seething masses in the streets and the infinite sea beyond. In New York, he achieves his first significant success when he sells a painting to *Truth* magazine for seventy-five dollars. But his startled discovery that artists are never "tremendously rich" leads him to doubt that he has chosen the right profession. After a prolonged siege of mental disorientation, he works his way up the corporate ladder to the position of art editor with a ten-thousand-dollar salary. But at this point, he chastises himself for having become more of a businessman than an artist, and he returns to painting.

Eugene admires a wide variety of artists including Doré, Verestchagin, Monet, Degas, Manet, Ribera, Monticelli, Corot, Daubigny, Rousseau, Turner, Watts, Millais, Rossetti, Winthrop, Aubrey Beardsley, Helleu, Rodin, Thaulows, and especially Bourguereau. His own painting places him in the so-called Ashcan School of artists who found beauty in the commonplace scenes of American cities. Dreiser was an admirer of W. L. Sonntag, George Luks, William Glackens, and Everett Shinn. He came to know their work in the days when they were magazine contributors, before their urban canvases were widely recognized. Dreiser describes Eugene's art as his own fiction had been described. He probably consulted his own notices in constructing the reviews of his hero's paintings. One reviewer finds in Eugene's works a "cheap desire to startle and offend" with a style that mimics "commonplace photography." Yet another praises his ability to endow his subjects with color and "a higher spiritual significance," and his willingness to see beauty "even in shame and pathos and degradation" (pp. 237–38).

But Eugene is moved less by the hidden beauty of city scenes than by the manifest wonder of womanhood, which becomes for him an object of secular worship. From his elementary school days on, he is enchanted by various girls and he begins early to refine the perception, which is to become fundamental to his artistic credo, that womanhood is creation's greatest glory. That insight leads to a series of breathless affairs, patterned as in the trilogy by an ascending level of expectation and eventual disillusionment until the one truly worthy of adoration is encountered. An adolescent game of post office spurs Eugene's burning longing for physical and spiritual sublimity in the arms of a "truly beautiful" girl. Thus, he initiates his lifelong search for the world's consummate woman—his principal occupation, aside from art, for nearly eight hundred pages. Dreiser knows from the outset that Eugene's dream is doomed. He advises the reader that although Eugene does not realize it, he is investing the girls he meets with "more beauty than they had" and that "the beauty was in his own soul" (p. 12). This perspective and a certain satiric element in Dreiser's treatment of Eugene's chaotic emotional makeup doubtlessly led to Phillip Gerber's judgment that the novel represents so strong an "indictment of romantic love" that it deals a death blow to "the moonlight-and-roses notion."[1] But it should be remembered that Dreiser's treatment of Eugene's career as a "fool of love" is a retrospective assessment of his own frenzied search for a satisfactory relationship, including his worshipful affairs with Sara White and Thelma Cudlipp.

At seventeen Eugene meets his first love and she sets for him a standard of physical charm, the ideal of "what womanhood ought to be, to be really beautiful" (p. 31). Stella Appleton is described as a "dream" who proves unattainable because she employs in addition to coquetry the ultimate womanly weapon, the resolution to resist Eugene's amorous advances. Her ability to say no, the compulsory characteristic for the woman who wishes to remain enshrined in ideality, keeps Eugene balanced on the edge of "tremendous passion." Stella's attributes, like those of the parade of idealized women who follow her, are listed rather than demonstrated. She comes across as a mindless flirt, aware only of her destructive power. When Stella chooses one of Eugene's rivals during the first round of another game of post office, Eugene's first romance is shattered. But soon he meets Margaret Duff, who possesses not only "some shapeliness of form" and "some comeliness of feature" but also "some generosity of spirit" (p. 44). This last trait, conspicuously missing in Stella Appleton, leads to his first physical knowledge of sex, and for several months the two are intensely involved. Eventually, Margaret's "simplicity of attitude" loses its charm, and Eugene, longing for a woman capable of discussing Emerson, Carlyle, and Whitman as well as performing sexually, begins the search anew.

At this point in the novel, he meets Angela Blue, the fictional representation of Dreiser's first wife. Angela is a few years older than Eugene, a small-town girl possessed of a "peculiarity of temperament which lingered with him as a grateful taste might dwell on the palate" (p. 64). He senses about her an aura of distinction, born of a thoroughly virtuous nature, restraining a deep current of passion. Her guileless innocence is answered in kind by Eugene's, who concludes on their first meeting that she represents the kind of woman capable of great love and sacrifice, the kind of woman best for him, "clean, honest, simple, attractive" (p. 67). Like other virginal ideals in the novel, she most often appears clad in white—Dreiser's favorite color in women's clothing to the end of his life.[2] Although Eugene has seemingly found what he is looking for, he is not disinclined to pursue other relationships, including an affair with Ruby Kenny, a nude model and "flower of the muck and coal yard" whom he meets at one of his art classes. Not only does she have the discrimination to bestow sexual favors only on those she likes, she contributes to Eugene's developing feminine ideal: "He sought in women, besides beauty, good nature and sympathy; he shunned criticism and coldness, and was never apt to select for a sweetheart anyone who could outshine him either in emotion or rapidity or distinction of ideas" (p. 75). At this point, Eugene's desired woman is an amalgam of Carrie and Jennie, while domineering women like Mrs. Hurstwood are anathema. His desire for dominance and perhaps a Pygmalion complex are revealed by his preference for a woman less intelligent than he.

Although Dreiser tells us that it was impossible that "one woman could have satisfied all sides of Eugene's character" at this point, the artist nevertheless proposes to Angela Blue and she accepts. Their marriage provides the principal source of dramatic conflict in the novel, since Angela firmly believes in the doctrine of "one life, one love" while Eugene loves only "beauty—not a plan of life" (p. 82). But he must have her, partly because she is more resistant than any woman he has known since Stella Appleton, partly because she is tender, sympathetic, and emotional, and partly because she appreciates music and thinks more than does Ruby Kenny, whose relationships with other men also disturb him. The lure of Angela, who possesses a lovely figure as well as spiritual sensibilities and who artfully eludes him while at the same time dispensing occasional encouragement, is well calculated to spur a panting anticipation that is doomed to disillusionment. When she insists that engagement and marriage must precede physical union, Eugene idealizes her all the more, linking his unutterable vision to her perishable breath:

> He curbed his desire and waited, but it made all the more vigorous and binding the illusion that she was the one woman in the world for him. She aroused more than any woman yet a sense of the necessity of concealing the eagerness of his senses—of pretending something higher. He even tried to deceive himself into the belief that this was a spiritual relationship, but underneath all was a burning sense of her beauty, her physical charm, her passion. She was sleeping as yet, bound in convention and a semireligious interpretation of life. If she were aroused! He closed his eyes and dreamed. [P. 90.]

As had been true with Dreiser and Sara White, Eugene and Angela postpone the wedding while he pursues his career. He goes to New York to paint and she returns to Wisconsin to await his success. But while in New York, Eugene encounters several other women whose qualities are added to his catalogue of the ideal, and they put Angela in new perspective. He meets through an editor friend two women whose appeal is irresistible. The first is Miriam Finch. Like Rita Sohlberg in *The Titan*, Miriam is the first of the women in this novel who are "artistic" as well as beautiful. She appeals to Eugene, not only because she is a professional sculptor and a gifted pianist and singer, but also because she thinks for herself and introduces Eugene to books and classical music. She adds further dimension to his ideal, since she represents "a better intelligence, a keener selective judgment, a finer artistic impulse than anyone he had ever known had possessed" (p. 141). Just what Dreiser means by "artistic" is never clear in any of his writing. At times he applies the term to a set of sensibilities that make a person a practitioner or an appreciator of the fine arts, at times he equates it with a sympathetic and compassionate nature, at times he applies it to physical characteristics, such as "artistic" hands, especially of women. And at other times, the meaning of the word is even more elusive. (Kerrigan, a ward healer in *The Titan* wears "artistic trousers," while one of Cowperwood's business rivals consults "a watch of inartistic design.") But Miriam, who is "artistic to the finger tips," also expects marriage before pleasure (at thirty-two she is said to

be beyond "the most delightful love period" anyway), and Eugene is
soon pursuing the equally artistic but decidedly more sensuous opera
singer Christina Channing. Although she is a twenty-seven-year-old
virgin, she has lately begun to wonder whether virginity should apply
to the artistic temperament. Eugene is quick to take advantage of her
uncertainty and arranges to take a hotel room near the cottage in the
Blue Ridge mountains where she is vacationing with her parents. During their passionate summer fling, Eugene finds Christina "so beautiful, so perfect physically, so incisive mentally, so full of a fine artistic
perception" (p. 159). These attributes add nothing new to his conception of the ideal, but another quality of Christina's does add a further
dimension. She provides Eugene with mothering, yielding herself
"sacrifically" to him while assuaging his fears and approving his artistic
ambitions. But since Christina had suggested that they regard their affair as a transient joy to be taken in the knowledge that it would pale,
she insists on her freedom and returns to her work at the end of the
summer. When Eugene receives a cool letter from her while she is on
an opera tour of Europe, he begins to appreciate Angela's contrasting
loyalty (she has been writing him daily from Wisconsin), and he adds
yet another virtue to his list of requirements.

But Eugene's sharpened appreciation for loyalty in others does
nothing to stimulate his own. He has been engaged to Angela for
three years when Christina ends her relationship with him. Angela
has been back in Wisconsin all of this time contemplating suicide because Eugene has not written to her. With Christina beyond his grasp
he returns to Wisconsin and, while fantasizing a blissful affair with
Angela's extroverted sister, Marietta, he at last physically consum-
mates his relationship with the more introverted Angela. Once she
yields to him, she promptly vows to either marry him or kill herself.
Eugene's "tender-hearted" nature asserts itself and he marries Angela.
But his joy in the wedding bed is marred as Dreiser's had been by his
previous physical knowledge of his wife, and there is "more of crude
desire than of awed delight in the whole proceeding" (p. 199). When
the newlyweds settle in Alexandria, Virginia, Eugene's infinite desire
is manifest again. Clearly, he wants to be both married and single, de-
lighting in his charming wife ready to serve him an array of tempting
food in a comfortable apartment but brooding over the end of his
privilege to be gay and alluring to Angela's sister and to other women.
Soon Eugene and Angela's marriage begins to totter because of their

unthinking overindulgence in sexual relations, "not based on reason and spirituality of contemplation apparently, but on grosser emotions and desires" (p. 260). Eugene immediately begins to recognize the mistake of his marriage, since he has now discovered that passion is the only thing he has in common with Angela and he cannot be satisfied with this. He begins to suffer the diminishing of his art, to the extent that he considers even "death a relief." But instead of choosing death, he begins to dream of a possible new liaison with a beautiful woman, and he is soon hypnotized by "shapely" and "vivacious," eighteen-year-old Freida George. Although Eugene wonders "how it was that the formation of a particular face could work this spell," it is clearly the girl's youth and his familiarity with Angela which leads him to identify Freida with the "unattainable desire—the holy grail of beauty" and to conclude that the world turns on the beauty of eighteen (pp. 284–85). Here Dreiser interpolates an analysis of Eugene's anarchistic sexual nature, linking him to certain types of protozoa that are physically attracted to their own destruction and comparing his sexual desires to the "irresistible attraction of an iron filing for a magnate." Although Eugene worries about the moral aspect of his quest, Dreiser explains his need through biology and physics. He points out the error of convention and underscores the supreme right of the genius to justify his actions. In addition, he asserts that Eugene never tries to "persuade a girl to immorality for the mere sake of indulgence" because his feelings are "invariably compounded of finer things," including "love of companionship, love of beauty, a variable sense of the consequences which must ensue, not so much to him as to her, though he took himself into consideration" (pp. 285–87).

When the pressures generated by marriage bring on a nervous collapse, Eugene decides to separate from Angela while he recuperates. In the small town to which he withdraws alone, he immediately becomes involved with a married woman who, like Angela, is in her thirties. Carlotta Wilson is not only lovely, with her "ivory complexion" and "raspberry lips," she is worldly wise and humorous, two more qualities Eugene must now have in his ideal woman. But Carlotta's mother uncovers the affair, and although the two lovers see each other occasionally after Eugene and Angela are reunited, "there is neither peace nor happiness in deception." Eugene becomes disconcerted by his "peculiar vice," his apparently immoral and anomalous behavior, and although he believes, in theory, that "the common laws of existence could not reasonably apply to an artist," he has found that his "burning joy at one time was invariably followed by a disturbing remorse afterward" (p. 365). (Dreiser's diaries were often devoted to detailed, boastful analyses of the physical aspects of his love life, sprinkled with passages revealing self-doubt. At one point in the diary he kept in New York during 1917 and 1918, for example, he called into question the whole direction of his chaotic sexual activity, writing that he felt at times that he was leading an incredibly full life while carrying on several simultaneous affairs but also expressing doubts.)[3] At any rate, Eugene concludes that his womanizing is deflecting him from success and decides that he must reform. At this point, he becomes a successful magazine artist and editor and is soon thrilling at the prospect of earning $25,000, renting a posh apartment, and basking in his accumulation of stocks and bonds. His distinguished success allows him to find and lose the great love of his life, Suzanne Dale.

Eugene meets the eighteen-year-old Suzanne through her mother, Emily Dale, the beautiful widow of a prominent banker. Suzanne embodies not only the requisite beauty, intelligence, and "artistic" nature, but also position, good breeding, and an air of high society superiority—the final wishes of Dreiser, the social outsider. (He complained at times about Sara White's futile hopes of becoming a woman of consequence.) Eugene idealizes Suzanne into utter unreality. She has "burst forth full winged and beautiful, but oh, so fragile, like a butterfly from its chrysalis, the radiance of morning upon its body" (p. 500). If an artist had attempted to capture her essence on canvas, "he might have done so showing her standing erect on a mountain top, her limbs outlined amidst fluttering draperies against the wind, her eyes fixed on distant heights, or a falling star" (p. 501). It would be difficult enough to believe in Suzanne's perfection given only the fact of a succession of idealized mistresses who have preceded her and all of whom have long since been found wanting, but Dreiser is either unable or unwilling to demonstrate her appeal. What little specific physical description of Suzanne is given is amusing rather than enlightening—utterly unconvincing. She is described as "plump," with a "fat" but "delicate" nose, and she laughs with a "rippling gurgle" (transcribed Tee! Hee!). Her supposed transcendency elicits some of Dreiser's most wretched rhetoric. Seeking a kiss from her, Eugene is transfigured: "'Open your eyes', he pleaded. 'Oh, God! That this should come to me! Now I could die. Life can hold no more. Oh,

Flower Face! Oh, Silver Feet! Oh, Myrtle Bloom! Divine Fire! How perfect you are! How perfect! And to think you love me'" (p. 541). Suzanne's dialogue in the novel (she is "without an earth-manufactured vocabulary") cannot nearly match the reader's expectations, and the only clue Dreiser gives to her fascination is her propensity to consistently say no to Eugene's entreaties and advances. Eventually she admits her desire for him, but she apparently never allows Eugene to physically consummate his love—the one time-tested method of remaining on the pedestal of perfection.

Dreiser never makes clear his attitude toward Eugene's quest for the ultimate woman. He may intentionally have drawn an unconvincing portrait of Suzanne because, as Gerber has suggested, he was attacking the conventional definitions of romance. Certainly, until Eugene meets Suzanne, Dreiser's use of the third-person narrative voice provides a perspective on Eugene's actions and allows for commentary on the futility of the quest for perfection in a single woman. In an early description of one of Eugene's dream objects, Dreiser uses the term "impossible she" from the seventeenth-century poet Richard Crashaw. He once even ridiculed the idea of a perfect woman, in an aside in *The Titan* designed to attack the social pretensions of Chicago's upperclass women.

To really know the state of the feminine mind at this time, one would have to go back to that period in the Middle Ages when the Church flourished and the industrious poet, half schooled in the facts of life, surrounded women with a mystical halo. Since that day the maiden and the matron as well has been schooled to believe that she is of a finer clay than man, that she was born to uplift him, and that her favors are priceless. This rose-tinted mist of romance, having nothing to do with personal morality, has brought about, nevertheless, a holier-than-thou attitude of women toward men, and even of women toward women. Now the Chicago atmosphere in which Aileen found herself was composed in part of this very illusion. The ladies to whom she had been introduced were of this high world of fancy. They conceived themselves to be perfect, even as they were represented in religious art and in fiction. Their husbands must be models, worthy of their high ideals, and other women must have no blemish of any kind. Aileen, urgent, elemental, would have laughed at all this if she could have understood. Not understanding, she felt diffident and uncertain of herself in certain presences. [P. 63.]

Despite this aside, the situation with Suzanne in *The "Genius"* is analogous to Cowperwood's loss of perspective in *The Titan* when

Berenice Fleming appears. In trying to understand Dreiser's attitude toward Suzanne Dale, one should keep in mind that he was under a spell similar to Eugene's when he was courting Thelma Cudlipp. His letters to her are laced with the same extravagant rhetoric that characterizes Eugene's to Suzanne. The truth may be that Dreiser was using *The "Genius"* to help distance his lingering love for Thelma Cudlipp, but when Suzanne comes stage center, Dreiser stops making cautionary interruptions and affects a narrative tone that often seems to corroborate Eugene's awe.

Eugene loses Suzanne in time to save his ideal when Suzanne's mother discovers his intentions, spirits her daughter off to a country retreat, and threatens the artist with exposure. Mrs. Dale's actions also save Suzanne from the rigors of living up to Eugene's expectations. These expectations, defined over the course of the novel, require a woman who is physically beautiful, perpetually eighteen yet experienced and worldly wise, passionate but virginal, sensuous though innocent, intellectual but less so than her lover, coolly aloof yet extroverted and vivacious, married to him while he remains single, unswervingly loyal to him when he is disloyal to her, independent except in her subservience to him, appreciative of music and the arts, sensitive, tender, companionable, humorous, a lover of the outdoors, sympathetic, good-natured, discriminating, motherly, well-bred, socially prominent and possessed of a large wardrobe of white clothing!

The "Genius" is a compendium of psychological insights into the personality of its author. Several critics have suggested without elaboration that Dreiser's legendary accumulation of mistresses and one-night stands betokened an anguished search for a substitute for his mother, whom he idealized quite as much as his amorous conquests, if in a somewhat different way. (He speculates in *Dawn* on the possibility that his mother may have taken lovers.) The evidence of Eugene's need for mothering is to be found throughout *The "Genius"* and is most often related to his mechanistic view of life. Early in the novel, he reads Spencer, Marcus Aurelius, Epictetus, Spinoza, Schopenhauer, Darwin, Huxley, Tyndall, and Lubbock and is led to the conclusion that life is animated by dark and aimless forces—that he is "nothing, a mere shell, a sound, a leaf" with "no general significance." This heart-breaking revelation along with his recognition of the fleeting nature of life and beauty spur his eagerness to find "a lovely girl's arms to shut him in safely always!" (p. 157). To fulfill this need he finds Christina Channing, the most significant of the women in his life other than Angela and Suzanne. Christina's warm mothering and lovemaking help Eugene temporarily to exorcise the despair brought on by his speculations about the meaninglessness of existence. But what she gives is not enough, for by the standards established in *The "Genius,"* she is beginning to age. And on the very next page after Eugene longs for mothering arms, there is a description of his need for "persistent youth and persistent beauty," qualities which no single "lovely girl" can sustain. Dreiser reveals through the characterization of Eugene his own need for a succession of younger women. These younger women could keep alive in him the illusion of his own youth but also provide him with mothering arms to help shut out the unbearable reality of an indifferent cosmos and inevitable decay and dissolution. Eugene, in his loneliness, always fantasizes about his next affair and "this thought with him—quite as the confirmed drunkard's thought of whiskey—buoyed him up, kept him from despairing utterly" (p. 274). In this context, the need to escape Angela (Sara White), a woman older than Eugene (Dreiser), is underscored. In this context also, Eugene's passion for his favorite painting, a warm tinted nude by Bourguereau, is explained. Canvas and pigment have far greater staying power than flesh and blood. (Dreiser assembled his own *Gallery of Women* frozen in prose.) Art, especially art that depicted beautiful young womanhood, could achieve a permanence unapproachable in real life. In *The "Genius,"* Dreiser explains the relationship between art and sex more successfully than he had in *The Titan.*

A perceptive critical essay written a decade ago by Ralph B. Hovey and Ruth S. Ralph applies Freudian insights to *The "Genius"* and focuses on the importance of mothers in the novel. Hovey and Ralph point out that in Eugene's more fully developed love relationships, there is always a mother involved who is an authority figure. They assert that the artist consistently, though unconsciously, woos the mother more than the girl, hoping for the mother's approval and inviting her punishment. This behavior is said to be indicative of Eugene's psychosexual conflict. His breakdown and failure as an artist are consequently attributed to his inability to resolve his wife's role as lover-mother, playmate-sinner, and jailer-punisher.[4] This interesting analysis meshes with some of Dreiser's self-confessed longings for women's approval, the final proof of which would be their willingness to grant him sexual acceptance. In *Hey Rub-a-Dub-Dub*, for example, he wrote: "I am not handsome, and therefore not attractive to women probably—at any rate I appear not to be—and in consequence am very much alone. Indeed, I am a great coward when it comes to women. Their least frown or mood of indifference frightens me and makes me turn inward to myself, where dwell innumerable beautiful women who smile and nod and hang on my arm and tell me they love me. Indeed, they whisper of scenes so beautiful and so comforting that I know they are not, and never could be true" (p. 2). Dreiser's sense of isolation and rejection in the midst of a love life that would have done credit to Don Juan is truly amazing.

Another speculation among some critics is that Dreiser's womanizing was the result of sterility and an obsessive need to prove his manhood. Despite his often incredible candor about himself, he never discussed his sex life in terms of abnormal psychology. But he did admit that he never found the one woman who could elicit from him an unswerving love and commitment. What emerges in *The "Genius"* are Eugene's conflicting needs in his sexual activities for the kind of permanence and perfection that is attainable only in art and also for the fluidity and change that characterizes real life. During his affair with Christina Channing, Eugene recognizes that the value of beauty lies in its very transience. Unchanging beauty soon pales and becomes deadly, and furthermore: "The call of the soul is for motion, not for peace. Peace after activity for a little while, then activity again" (p. 163). The perceptive Christina recognizes and encourages his emotional conflict by reminding him that despite his protestations, he actually wants his affairs to end, thus allowing him to preserve his late lovers in the amber of his nostalgia. All the while he is pursuing a succession of women, the possessors of transient beauty, he is being drawn away by the possibility that his next conquest will bring him ultimate fulfillment. Eugene must always be madly in love with someone in order to live and to paint, yet he "really could not be madly in love with two people at once" (p. 288). His discovery that Suzanne embodies the perfect woman and that he need search no further seems to conflict with his earlier speculations on beauty and change, but it could be rationalized that as long as he needs to focus his love on one person at a time, he must be capable of focusing on one person for all time. For Dreiser, who by his own admission found himself incapable of a love that could settle on one woman, Eugene's discovery of the perfect woman was a form of wish-fulfillment. Unlike his fictional counterpart, Eugene, he could not forever have regarded even Thelma Cudlipp as the embodiment of unspeakable faultlessness—even though he lavished on her the same rhapsodic terms of endearment Eugene bestows on Suzanne—for no human being possesses the ideality he was groping to express. But through Eugene, Dreiser wonders at the amazing if temporary power that resides in the "formation of a particular face,"—a power that was to puzzle him until late in life when he found what he believed to be an explanation in religion.

Until the last quarter of *The "Genius,"* Eugene lives an almost totally self-centered life, devoted to the pursuit of his talent and to money and women. But he begins to doubt the rightness of his self-centeredness when Angela develops an extended illness that will eventually lead to her death in childbirth. At first Eugene hopes that Angela will die, thus removing the major obstacle to his freedom and happiness, but he becomes more conscience stricken with each of Angela's worsening physical crises. He recognizes in the unwhimpering strength she brings to her ordeal a marked contrast to his own adolescent pursuit of pleasure. After her death, he is stricken with remorse for having added hatred to his mistreatment of his wife. Through the device of Angela's sickness and death, Dreiser introduces another excursus on duty, this time as it relates to marriage. One alternative title Dreiser considered for *The "Genius"* was *This Matter of Marriage, Now.* The novel opens with the passage from the marriage service in which Eugene promises to comfort and honor Angela in sickness and health. But until the final section of the book, Dreiser strives to convince his reader that a "genius" is too big to be confined by social responsibilities. When Angela's suffering is compounded by Eugene's selfishness, however, Dreiser does not deny the artist's guilt. Eugene promises himself that he will never again be a slave to beauty, a pledge made easier by his loss of Suzanne. And because of his own suffering and guilt, he sets out anew to find the answers to life's ultimate questions.

Dreiser imposes a curious metaphysical ending on *The "Genius"* by applying his recent readings in religion, philosophy, and science to Eugene's situation. He prepares his readers for this somewhat jolting denouement by pointing out that Eugene had always been attracted to liberal preachers (as Dreiser had been to Jenkin Lloyd Jones and Emil

G. Hirsch), that he had always been "metaphysically inclined," and that he had been influenced, not only by the naturalistic philosophers, but also by Plato, Emerson's "Oversoul," and the Sermon on the Mount. In the midst of Angela's illness, her sister introduces Eugene to Christian Science, and after a period of ridicule, he develops a grudging respect for the religion. [5] He is at first highly skeptical of its claims to healing, but he is impressed after hearing an adherent's testimony that through his faith he had been cured of his "vile" lusting after women. When Eugene decides to read Mary Baker Eddy's *Science and Health*, his reaction is mixed. He is annoyed by the Biblical quotations, although he does retain "a profound acceptance of the spiritual understanding of Jesus" (p. 693). The author's acceptance of the Immaculate Conception strikes him as silly, and he feels that she has a streak of quackery, but he is interested in her belief in the ultimate abolition of marriage, and he likes her definition of God as a principle manifested everywhere. He accepts the broad nondogmatic basis of her faith, which would leave his artistic freedom intact, and he appreciates the dubious reputation of her faith among narrow religionists and especially likes her explanation of evil as an illusion.

Eugene wavers between near belief and disbelief in the forty-page parenthetical treatise on Christian Science. Angela's suffering will not allow him to assent to the easy dismissal of evil. Still, he has never believed in sin, and this faith might offer him consolation. His difficulties and his wife's death make him doubtful about the existence of a benevolent Creative Force. Yet he feels life can be good at times, and perhaps evil is an illusion. He cannot firmly believe in a reality beyond the material. Yet he has never doubted the claims of astrology and palmistry. Thus is Eugene pulled apart by Dreiser's own uncertainties until he feels pursued like the narrator of Francis Thompson's "Hound of Heaven." For three years after Angela's death, he is subject to "all the vagaries and alterations which can possibly afflict a groping and morbid mind," and he oscillates between "*almost* a belief in Christian Science" and "almost a belief that a devil ruled the world, a Gargantuan Brobdingnagian Mountebank, who plotted tragedy for all ideals and rejoiced in swine and dullards and a grunting, sweating, beefy immorality." Finally, after conceiving of God as a dual personality or compound of the "most ideal and ascetic good, as well as the most fantastic and swinish evil"—a conception related to the "equation inevitable"—he returns to mental health and agnosticism (p. 726).

Eugene's investigation of religion in The "Genius" is based on Dreiser's own studies, prompted at least in part by the moral questions
inherent in his marital situation. Although Sara White had not died as
Angela does in the novel, she had been extremely ill and bedridden
when she was confronted by Thelma Cudlipp's mother. Angela's
death is only a more striking device than separation with which to
dramatize the conflict between duty and desire. Sara's righteous re-
criminations doubtlessly induced in Dreiser "a terrible sense of
wrong," to which Eugene all but admits in The "Genius." Dreiser's permanent separation from his wife began in 1912, the year after he
finished the first half of the novel. His acquiescence in the arrangement, which provided for lifelong separation from his wife as opposed
to divorce, may have been motivated in large part by his wish to use
his marriage as a hedge against demands by any future lovers for more
commitment than he was willing to give, as several critics have
suggested. But Dreiser may also have retained from his Catholic background a residue of guilt about divorce. Certainly his marital problems caused him some anguish, and his nagging guilt can be inferred
from his bombastic denunciations of marriage as well as from the
pathetic admissions of his semifictional "genius."

Once the sting of defeat and guilt is relieved by time, Eugene re-
news his interest in art and women, and Dreiser makes embarrassed
apologies for his having retreated into religion. He attributes the artist's interest in Christian Science to a temporary despair and intrudes
into the narrative to explain religion to his readers: "If I were personally to define religion I would say that it is a bandage that man has invented to protect a soul made bloody by circumstance; an envelope to
pocket him from the unescapable and unstable illimitable . . . the
need for religion is impermanent, like all else in life. As the soul re-
gains its health, it becomes prone to the old illusions" (p. 734). Like a
loving mother, religion comforts the soul in distress. And Dreiser
clearly found nothing more distressing than his own intellectual commitment to an earthbound determinism when measured against his
infinite longing. When Eugene returns to his painting after a long absence from it, his work is remarkable for its "brooding suggestion of
beauty that never was on land or sea," and the book ends with a quotation from Spencer on the unknowable and the wonder in the existence of space without cause or origin. Thus Eugene, though better
equipped than Carrie to speculate in metaphysical terms, still has the

elusive ideal ahead, still searches for the ultimate beauty that only unweakened religious belief had the power to adequately suggest. Like
Jennie with her adopted orphans, he is left with a child to care for. He
has come to delight in "Angela, junior," and plans to build a charming
home around her. Dreiser may have been collecting an old debt from
Frank Norris when he created little Angela. Norris's descriptions of
Chicago in *The Pit* apparently owe a good deal to *Sister Carrie*. "Angela,
junior" (she is called "Angela second" in the first draft of *The "Genius"*) is
reminiscent of the young beauty in *The Octopus*, Angela II, the exact
duplicate of her mother, who had died in childbirth after being raped
by the villainous "Other." And like Angela II, Eugene's second Angela
represents good coming out of the illusion of evil, out of the suffering
of the artist's wife.[6] One wonders if Dreiser may be suggesting that
Eugene's daughter is destined to become the "impossible she." In the
last scene of the novel, the doting father employs the telltale terms of
endearment: "Little flower girl" and "Sweet little kiddie."

Although Dreiser explains in *The "Genius"* that the need for religion
is impermanent, the novel bears witness to his continuing longing for
the comfort and peace of religious faith. And although he states that
Eugene has not been much changed by his speculations, Dreiser himself had clearly developed out of his burgeoning religious,
philosophical, and scientific reading an altered perception of existence, which led to *The Bulwark* and *The Stoic*. His most important discovery was that there need be no real conflict between science and
religion. Eugene is "spellbound" by two newspaper articles that describe the findings of George M. Gould and Edgar Lucien Larkin.
Gould believed that God resides in organic cells and Larkin that cosmic mind is evident in the micro-universe of organic and inorganic
particles. Eugene discovers through them that "the evolutionary
hypothesis did not after all shut out a conception of a ruling, ordain-
ing Divinity, as he had supposed" (p. 696). Moreover, he studies the
hypothesis of the English naturalist Alfred Russell Wallace concerning "hierarchies of being" and concludes with considerable surprise
that some of the deductions of the English naturalists are not far removed from those of Christian Science. Eugene's need of comfort is
clear in these passages, for even after regaining his "healthy" agnosticism, he returns periodically to confer with Mrs. Johns, a Christian
Science practitioner who had been "motherly" to him.

Although the quotation from Spencer on the Unknowable which

closes The "Genius" seems to imply a rejection of the possibility of faith in a Creative Force, the oscillation between near acceptance and rejection which marks the discussion of religion leaves the door open to further inquiry and investigation. In the next few years, Dreiser would welcome for consideration almost any theory of existence, even those of the lunatic fringe. He defended, for example, the possibility of truth in Charles Fort's book entitled X, which argued that a mysterious substance was emitting strange rays responsible for creation. In the late 1930s, Dreiser would preface the spiritual avowal of his last novels with an intensified study of science, this time through the microscope in addition to the printed page.

There is evidence that Dreiser's decision to make Eugene revert to agnosticism in the late stages of The "Genius" was reached only after he had abandoned an earlier plan to have his hero undergo a permanent conversion to a belief in God. The conclusion of the first draft of the novel was considerably revised for publication. In the "happy ending" holograph, Eugene corresponds with Suzanne after Angela's death and reveals that the tragedy has opened his eyes to his own selfishness and that he is devoting his life to his daughter and his painting. Some four years later they meet again, and after discussing little Angela (Eugene had earlier conjectured about Suzanne's mothering talents), they decide to live together. The coda called "L'Envoi," which ends the published novel, is also considerably different in the holograph. In the published version, the pagan Eugene, cut off from Suzanne, walks alone on a starry night, wondering where in all this "sweet welter of life" he and Angela fit—what their lives mean in cosmic context. In the manuscript, the time is six months after Suzanne's return to Eugene and they are happily married and "meditative, philosophic, introspective." While rummaging through some books, Eugene comes across Spencer's description of the Unknowable "which interested him because he felt it expressed something which in his case had been superceded by something better." The idea of the Unknowable can no longer trouble him, though it is "full of kindly wisdom," because he has "truly changed." His life is "calmer, sweeter" because he recognizes that there is a "ruling power" (Dreiser first wrote "God," then lined it out) which "is not malicious." Eugene walks out under the stars and recognizes that Angela is an idea that lives "in the universal, circumambient, intelligent control" (Dreiser first wrote "in God," then lined it out). The draft ends with Suzanne calling Eugene back to the house.[7] The continuing struggle to decide whether the selfish pursuit of personal desires is just, as well as the simultaneous need but inability to believe in a meaningful existence are underscored when the "happy ending" is compared to the published version of the novel. Sometime between 1911, when the first version was completed, and 1914 when the novel was put in final form, Dreiser became convinced of the improbability of Eugene's blissful marriage to Suzanne, much as he had had second thoughts about the version of *Jennie Gerhardt* in which Jennie marries Lester Kane. Robert Penn Warren speculates that the final version of *The "Genius,"* wherein Eugene snubs Suzanne when they meet on the street, represents Dreiser's attempt to "settle the hash of Thelma Cudlipp."[8] It just may bespeak the official cessation of his feeling for her and account for his self-incrimination in the earlier rhapsodic descriptions of Suzanne's transcendence. Probably Dreiser was equally hesitant about endorsing his hero's religious conversion as his happy marriage since there is no indication that he shared Eugene's cosmic optimism for very long. F. O. Matthiessen believes that it was Dreiser's immersion in the Cowperwood material which caused him to regard the "happy ending" as false to life. Burton Rascoe conjectures that Dreiser had a religious experience shortly before completing the first draft and later came to doubt it. Dreiser's original biographer, Robert Elias, probably comes closest to the truth of the matter in his belief that a new series of sexual entanglements between the two drafts convinced the novelist of the lack of sincerity in the earlier conclusion.[9] There is ample evidence that Dreiser grew uneasy about much of the religious speculation in *The "Genius."* He later vehemently denied that he was becoming religious, in part because of his fear of losing his status as an "intellectual."

Although Dreiser seems to have retained a degree of respect for Christian Science in later years, there were reasons for his dissatisfaction with it. Ultimately, the Christian Scientist's definition of God as a principle lacked the warmth that a man of Dreiser's rich emotional nature demanded. Unable to accept the tenets of traditional Christianity because of his emotional break with the Catholic Church, he could replace them with nothing that met his personal needs. Mary Baker Eddy's easy denial of evil must have struck him as unsound given his marital problems and his general sensitivity to human suffering. If he subscribed momentarily to the tenets of Christian Science, he could not have been satisfied for long with its easy mysticism which

left too many questions unanswered. Certainly, the personal proclivities he had used to motivate his fictional characters remained
undampened, whatever Eugene learns in the novel. Dreiser seems unable to make the choice about whether Eugene should be an artist or
a businessman, a choice which he had not definitely made about himself. His fascination with wealth was still intense and his accumulation
of women, although informed with considerably more insight, remained unchecked. He was a long way from being ready to trade the
material for the spiritual. But if Eugene cannot sustain his belief in
God, there is throughout *The "Genius"* a forecast of Dreiser's spiritual
avowal as set forth thirty years later in *The Bulwark*. One passage that
was cut from the original version particularly exemplifies this forecast,
that is, the starlit scene in which Eugene divines Angela's immortality
within the beneficient and safe confines of the universal ruling power.
In the concluding pages of *The Bulwark*, Solon Barnes reaches a truly
mystical experience in which he apprehends the immortality of his
dead wife, Benecia. The passage bears a surface identification with
Eugene's intimations of Angela's immortality. The crucial difference is
that the passage in *The Bulwark* rings with the conviction missing in *The
"Genius."* Again, some of the best writing in *The "Genius"* is the description of nature, especially of the countryside around Blackwood, the
pastoral Wisconsin home of Angela's parents. The feeling for the
earth revealed in these passages presages Dreiser's developing interest
in nature as a repository of clues to the meaning of existence.

For all of its interest as an index to Dreiser's developing thought,
however, *The "Genius"* is an artistic failure. It points up the dangers to
the fiction writer dealing with material that is too personal for objective treatment. Its deficiencies are so numerous that they lend credence to the old saw that Dreiser was "the world's worst great writer."
In his earlier novels, he had based his characters at least in part on
others, and this method altered his perspective sufficiently to insure a
suitable aesthetic distance. What Warren calls Dreiser's "so nakedly"
displayed "self-indulgence and self-vindication" in *The "Genius"* con-
taminate nearly every element in this novel.[10] Among the deficiencies
are the characterizations of Eugene's lovers, which are justly con-
demned by Matthiessen as "monsters of unreality."[11] The book is
twice as long as it needs to be, and there are surges of swollen rhetoric
that would have embarrassed Thomas Wolfe, and an orgy of self-
administered psychiatric therapy.

The vigorous attempts at squelching *The "Genius"* by the New York Society for the Suppression of Vice and other watchdog groups intensified Dreiser's hostility to religion, but did not stifle his interest in metaphysics. Between 1916 and 1923, he published eight books, none of them novels. His preoccupation with ultimate questions became an obsession during these years. In January 1921, a book reviewer named Edward Smith called Dreiser's attention to this growing concern in a letter which expressed the hope that the novelist was not falling into "the mystical latrine." Dreiser replied heatedly in a long return letter that he was only interested in a scientific way in the reasons for existence, and that he certainly was not religious:

I may watch, like a cat at a mouse-hole, for any clear suggestion anywhere, of a definite superior intelligence at work, anywhere, but that is not due to a religious, or as you might say, metaphysical streak or weakness. It has nothing to do with morality or any moralic or religious theory as to man's place in nature. In my humble estimation he appears to have a damn small place, if any, and his religious and moral theories are the bunk. But that, (aside from such swill), there may not be certain very intelligent and constructive processes, or, if not that, then certainly some very marvelous and beautiful, if accidental constructive necessities, I am by no means prepared to deny. . . . I tried to show just how it was that [Eugene Witla] came to dabble with Christian Science, and why, in the long run it failed to hold him. Having recovered a part of his mental strength he shed it, as a snake does a skin. I have never been under any illusion in regard to religion, morality or metaphysical fiddle-faddle. I had my fill in my youth. Today I want facts but I am not to be denied the right to speculate in my own way and I have no fear that I shall be led into any religious or moralic bog. I am much too sane for that. If you see any signs, kindly let me know. [12]

But despite this emotional disclaimer, the reviewer had seen the evidence clearly, for much of the work Dreiser produced during this period mirrors his desperate search for a religious reality and a set of guiding principles. His *Plays of the Natural and Supernatural* (1916) grope toward a world beyond the physical. *Laughing Gas*, a revealing piece in that volume, concerns a prominent physician who, while anesthetized on the operating table himself, ponders the mystery of life and death and concludes that man can read no signs in the heavens. In *A Hoosier Holiday* (1916), Dreiser interrupts his descriptions of a nostalgic trip to Indiana with inquiries about what might be behind man's existence, "an avatar, a devil, anything you will" (p. 28). There are frequent references to the possible logic of Christian Science and a formal rejection of a purely mechanical interpretation of the universe in the book:

I once believed, for instance, that nature was a blind, stumbling force or combination of forces which knew not what or whither. I drew that conclusion largely from the fumbling nonintelligence (relatively speaking) of men and all sentient creatures. Of late years I have inclined to think just the reverse, i.e., that nature is merely dark to us because of her tremendous subtlety and our own very limited powers of comprehension; also that in common with many other minor forces and forms of intelligence—insects and trees, for example—we are merely tools or implements—slaves, to be exact—and that collectively we are used as any other tool or implement would be used by us. [Pp. 343–44.]

These halting approaches to affirmation, stimulated by his correspondence with scientists like Jacques Loeb and others, are counterbalanced by doubts, including a doubt that we really exist at all.

Dreiser's internal war between his need to find meaning in existence and his inability to do so reached a state of absolute anguish in *Hey Rub-a-Dub-Dub* (1921). The collection of "philosophic essays" was called by a reviewer for the *Catholic World* "an inane book—poorly written, full of repetition."[13] Even the most ardent admirer of Dreiser would be hard pressed to refute the charge. Here, his obstinate hatred of religion and groping search for faith betray him into ludicrous positions. He argues on one page for an Intelligent Creator and on the next condemns those who accept such arguments. There are many of the old accusations against "religionists"—that they "look upon love and passion as a disturbing, unsatisfactory and almost unnecessary element in life" (p. 219), that they are, like Bottom in *Midsummer Night's Dream*, unconscious of their furry ears (p. 267), that Catholics believe that "unless the Buddhists, Shintoists, Mohammedans, et cetera, reform or find Christ they will be lost" (p. 8). There are a hundred labored justifications of the amoral way of life.

In *A Hoosier Holiday*, Dreiser wrote that he preferred life's ultimate questions left unanswered:

Supposing, for instance, that one could reason through to the socalled [sic] solution, actually found it, and then had to live with that bit of exact knowledge and no more forever and ever and ever! Give me, instead, sound and fury, signifying nothing. Give me a song sung by an idiot, dancing down the wind. Give me this gay, sad, mad seeking and never finding about which we are all so feverishly employed. It is so perfect, this inexplicable mystery. [P. 153.]

But this mood was offset at other times by exhaustion and the desire for peace and permanence. In *The Color of a Great City*, for example, he wrote of his need for respite from the rigors of the search. Observing the birds that inhabit New York, he combines expansive desire with a profound weariness of spirit:

To fly so! To be a part of sky, sunlight, air! To be thus so delicately and gracefully organized as to be able to rest upon the bosom of a breeze, or run down its curving surface in long flights, to have the whole world-side for a spectacle, the sunny roof of a barn or a house for a home! Not to brood over the immensities, perhaps, not to sigh over the too-well-known end! [P. 76.]

Despite the impression of intellectual and emotional anarchy left by much of Dreiser's writing, he was always making some progress toward resolving his conflicts. After the trilogy and *The "Genius,"* he never wrote in quite the same way about the superman, the egocentric artist, or the "equation inevitable." Nor did he ever again join a protagonist in breathless praise of the "impossible she." *An American Tragedy* (1925) would usher in a new phase in his development—one that would lead him tortuously toward affirmation. The approach would be both metaphysical and moral. Although the defense of his developing metaphysical interest that he incorporated in his response to Edward Smith had been somewhat embarrassed, it was nonetheless a necessary method of insuring the openness to evidence that would be crucial to his new scientific and philosophical inquiries. He had been studying the nature of responsibility and commitment for some time. A record of his concentrated examination of these subjects is to be found in a series of short stories about the marriage contract. Through stories such as those in the "marriage group," Dreiser worked his way toward larger questions of responsibility and culpability that would become the core of *An American Tragedy*.

6 / "The Marriage Group"

IN a series of short stories that first appeared in various magazines, Dreiser examined in detail the mostly harmful effects of marriage on both husbands and wives. Like Chaucer's "marriage group," the set of tales told by certain of the Canterbury pilgrims, Dreiser's stories focus on the need for balancing the interests of the parties to the marriage contract. For Dreiser, however, such balance is at best achieved only temporarily by two parties whose needs mesh at a given time. Since needs are constantly changing, the delicate balance cannot be sustained without the continual compromising of personal dreams and desires, but that effort at accommodation inevitably diminishes either the husband or the wife or both. The stories in Dreiser's "marriage group" turn on the conflict between one's duty to oneself and one's obligations to another which marriage imposes. They play an important role in Dreiser's continuing existential search, framed by his fiction, for ethical moorings. In the give and take of marriage, he found a paradigm of the larger conflict between self-interest and self-sacrifice that is at the center of all social relationships.

"Married," which first appeared in *Cosmopolitan* in September 1917, was an episode dropped from the manuscript of The "Genius" and somewhat altered for separate publication.[1] The most autobiographical of the "marriage group," it concerns a concert pianist named Duer and Marjorie, his wife of several months. The conflict in the story arises out of the differing values that the two bring to their marriage. Duer (patterned after Dreiser) is a connoisseur of the New York studio life, a man with a rich and volatile artistic nature, while Marjorie (patterned after Sara White) is a conventional and conservative farm girl from Iowa. The first indication of trouble in this marriage occurs when Marjorie becomes jealous of the women invited to the studio— women with "their radical ideas, their indifference to appearances, their semisecret immorality" (p. 324). Since she is thoroughly grounded in the doctrine of "one life, one love," she cannot understand her husband's attraction to such women, and when she reproves him for being flippant with one of them at a studio gathering, Duer begins to see the dimensions of his mistake in marrying. He dreads his wife's increasing censure and control, an encumbrance that was not in evidence before their marriage. But mindful of the concessions demanded by marriage and already disposed to compromise out of a sense of guilt for having failed to be faithful to his engagement vows, he chastises himself for being too free, for laughing and singing too boisterously. Dreiser's meaning is clear. With each such adjustment, freedom is eroded and personhood diminished.

When Duer and Marjorie are invited to a dinner party at the Plaza, they are thrust into the company of social types different from the artists. They meet a music critic, a museum curator, a wealthy opera sponsor, and their wives. Marjorie is attracted to these men with their airs of impressive business achievement and their wives whose interests cluster about children and housework. After the dinner, Marjorie comes to feel that Duer should choose such solid people for his friends. She believes that if he were limited to this sort of society, he could be remade into a "quiet, reserved, forceful man"—her idea of the perfect husband (p. 333). But he cannot give up his artistic friends, and when he neglects her at a studio party, the first marital crisis ensues. Marjorie, having been "unable to hold her own in the cross-fire of conversation, unable to retain the interest of most of the selfish, lovesick, sensation-seeking girls and men," throws herself on Duer's pity, pathetic in her humiliation (p. 341). Seeing that she is "feeling neglected, outclassed, unconsidered, helpless," which is "more or less true," he is led by his compassion for her to falsely deny that he finds her dull and conventional. Dreiser attributes Duer's lie to the demand in such a situation for "kindness, generosity, affection, her legal right to his affection" (p. 343–44). In a speech reminiscent of Ames's attempt to bolster Carrie, Duer tells Marjorie that she is "emotionally great" beyond the hopes of the studio types and that no common soul could have such depth of feeling. Duer partly believes what he says, for the quality that had originally attracted him to her had been her emotional side, developed through her closeness to nature on the prairie farm. But unlike Carrie, Marjorie has no artistic talent through which to channel her emotions, and Duer reflects that her self-portrait of dullness had been just. With sad resignation, he looks forward to the necessity for reassuring her with lies: "He would always be soothing and coaxing, and she would always be crying and worrying" (p. 350).

"Married" explores not only the tragedy of temperamental incompatibility of husband and wife, but also several of the negative aspects of what has recently come to be called the "closed marriage." Marjorie's jealousy of Duer's female friends, her assumption that she owns her husband, her unwillingness to allow him to be himself, her attempts to fit him into a mold of her own design—all of these things contribute to the undoing of the relationship. Instead of loving Duer for what he is, for his ability to function in his artistic circle, she loves him in spite of his interests and friends. His response is predictable—not an increase in love but a demeaning pity spurred by guilt and the first questioning about whether he has ever loved her at all. But neither Duer nor Marjorie is cast as the villain of the piece. The wife's point of view is as sympathetically portrayed as the husband's, the simple virtues of Midwestern life as admirable as Eastern sophistication. This inherent fairness was one of the reasons that Sherwood Anderson was so taken with the story. But if Duer and Marjorie come off reasonably well, the institution of marriage does not. The tragedy is that the structure of marriage often traps two very different people in a situation they are incapable of handling or escaping. Marriage calls for a legislated self-sacrifice which few spouses can achieve without a residue of resentment. Marjorie cannot understand or tolerate Duer's social dreams. Duer's very recognition of his obligation to be compassionate to and understanding of Marjorie detracts from the freedom that alone can purify those virtues.

"The Second Choice" appeared in *Cosmopolitan* in February 1918. This story concerns a woman named Shirley whose commonplace life is uplifted by the arrival of a brilliant and attentive suitor named Arthur. For a while they enjoy an idyllic affair together, and his buoyant personality and passionate nature put all of Shirley's previous acquaintances in a demeaning perspective. But Arthur's visits become less frequent and finally he writes to her that he is taking a job in Java and that he is too young to marry anyway. The romantic world Arthur had created suddenly crashes around her, and she is forced to consider marriage to Barton Williams, a "stout, phlegmatic, good-natured, well-meaning" and essentially boring admirer, whom she had been keeping at a distance while Arthur was seemingly available (p. 139). Since marriage is "her only future," she decides to take up with Barton again, but she cannot expunge the memory of what it would have been like to be married to Arthur or cease her conjecture about what would happen if Arthur returned to find her married to Barton. After reviving her relationship with Barton, she feels that she has been forced by something beyond her control to sever her ties to the romantic past. When the train taking her to her suburban home passes over a river whose destination is the sea which she and Arthur had loved so much, her infinite longing is stirred: "Oh, to be in a small boat and drift out, out into the endless, restless, pathless deep! Somehow the sight of this water, to-night and every night, brought back those evenings in the open with Arthur at Sparrows Point, the long line of dancers in Eckert's Pavilion, the woods at Atholby, the park, with the dancers in the pavilion—she choked a sob" (p. 158). When she arrives home she watches a neighbor preparing dinner in her kitchen while her husband reads the newspaper on the front porch, and she contemplates the flow of sad, gray years that lie ahead of her with Barton: "'My dreams are too high, that's all. I wanted Arthur, and he wouldn't have me. I don't want Barton, and he crawls at my feet. I'm a failure, that's what's the matter with me'" (p. 162).

"The Second Choice" concerns the tragedy of marriages of compromise, which most seem to be. Seldom, if ever, do two souls who share the same dreams with equal intensity marry one another. The implication in the story is that Arthur's aspirations were larger than Shirley's, just as Shirley's were larger than Barton's. Arthur wants the world, Shirley wants love and marriage, and Barton wants only Shirley. Caught in the middle, Shirley will be forced by society's irrational insistence on marriage—she capitulates to Barton in order "to save her face before her parents, and her future" (p. 161)—to compromise before she becomes too old to make any match at all. Dreiser's point is that a marriage based on such self-sacrifice cannot bring fulfillment to anyone.

"Free," first published in the *Saturday Evening Post* in March 1918, is Dreiser's finest story and one of the most compelling in American literature. A long narrative concerning the thoughts of a sixty-year-old New York architect during his wife's medical crisis, "Free" describes the conflicts of a man caught between his dreams of personal fulfillment and the obligation to forego those dreams for the good of his family. The architect, ironically named Haymaker, has devoted over forty years of quiet desperation to his conventional, socially sensitive wife and to his children, all the while lamenting the fact that he has never had the kind of woman that he really desires. The story opens with Haymaker, his eyes "weary and yet restless," brooding over the news from his wife's physician that she is in imminent danger of death because of a heart lesion. His wife's condition has revivified his longing to be free, to spend his last few years doing only what he really wants to do. But this longing is balanced by his recognition of his selfishness, and throughout the story he vacillates, alternately wishing his wife will die, and being ashamed of his thoughts. Haymaker is described like other Dreiserian drifters, "wondering if time, accident or something might not interfere and straighten out his life for him, but it never had" (p. 12). The drift is caused by the paralyzing curse of the thinking person—the ability to see all sides of a given situation. The more he longs to be free of his wife the more tender and compassionate toward her he becomes, all the while sacrificing his own fulfillment in his wish to see her and the children happy. But outside his home the call of desire induces in him the infinite ache, and on the way to his office, he longs to be one of the bustling young businessmen possibly destined for a rendezvous with a charming young wife. The spires of the city skyline evoke in him his unextinguished hope. He does not recognize that the young men he envies are doubtlessly headed for their own marital tragedies and that the city is a seducer dealing in doomed dreams. Instead, Haymaker longs still, even though he remembers that his marriage to his wife so many years before had been an ideal love match—that she had appeared to him "a dream among fair women" (p. 17). But like Dreiser, he had been unable to marry immediately, and between the first promise and the marriage, his point of view had been altered by larger experiences. Nonetheless, he had married because of his belief that "an engagement, however unsatisfactory it might come to seem afterward, was an engagement, and binding" (p. 18). His duty to go through with the marriage had been compounded by his duty to stick by it for the rest of his life, acting as if he were satisfied.

Of late, however, Haymaker had begun to wonder what the compensation for a life of such sacrifice might be. He sees in the possibility of his wife's death a last chance at fulfillment with a woman who could truly understand him, but his conscience will not allow him even now to contemplate with equanimity such a denouement. Haymaker has insight into his own futility and recognizes the remedy: "Unless one acted for oneself, upon some stern conclusion nurtured within, one might rot and die spiritually. Nature did not care. 'Blessed be the meek'—yes. Blessed be the strong, rather, for they made their own happiness" (p. 25). One such strong personality is Zingara, another architect and former friend of Haymaker's who had never married and had become a distinguished success in his field. Despite the fact that earlier Haymaker's wife had disapproved of Zingara's poverty and had forbidden Haymaker to associate with him, Zingara had pursued his profession indifferent to what might be said about him. But Zingara's life is meant to show that even those who live free cannot make their own happiness. He has spent his last years a "dreamy recluse," the equally sad destiny of those who, refusing to submit to fatal compromise, find themselves alone.

After Haymaker's wife's rally and relapse, which induce in him a variety of emotional responses ranging from hope to sorrow that she might not recover, she does, in fact, die. Haymaker is finally free, but a glance into a tall pier mirror tells him that his freedom has come too late, for he is "old, weary, done for!" The story ends with Haymaker musing on the innate cruelty of life: "'Free! I know now how that is. I am free now, at last! Free! . . . Free! . . . Yes—free . . . to die'" (p. 53).

"Free" is perhaps the most brutally honest story about the married state ever written. Haymaker's marriage, undertaken in a state of youthful idealism and transient sexual attraction, is portrayed as a tragic mistake, compounded with each passing day of self-sacrifice and burning longing to be free. But clearly, the architect's life would have been blighted even had he left his wife years earlier, because the guilt he would have felt over his failed obligation and responsibility would have allowed him no peace of mind. This is made clear at the end of the story when Haymaker, finally released by his wife's death, reproaches himself for having caused her to die with his thoughts: "So then his dark wishing had come true at last? Possibly his black thoughts had killed her after all. Was that possible? Had his voiceless prayers been answered in this grim way? And did she know what he had really thought? Dark thought. Where was she now? What was she thinking now if she knew? Would she hate him—haunt him?" (p. 51). Mrs. Haymaker's reach beyond the grave at the conclusion of "Free" may well have influenced Steinbeck's classic short story "The Harness." In that piece, the devoted husband and farmer Peter Randall, whose life is defined by his ministering to his sickly wife, decides at her death that he will cut himself loose from his past and live a new life unencumbered by care. But like Haymaker, he discovers that his self-denial has become so ingrained that he cannot change, and he is led to remark ruefully that his wife "didn't die dead."

Dreiser's analysis of Haymaker's sacrifices in "Free" is not altogether negative. He does not disparage the intimate feelings the architect has displayed toward his wife during their marriage. There is no reason to regard them as anything but genuine. The compassion and tenderness he shows for his wife is as close to love as one can approach in marriage, which is an institution based on the denial of the most fundamental law of life—the law of change. In stories like "Free," Dreiser uses marriage as a stage set within which the conflict between man's desire for both freedom and structure, for personal fulfillment and loving dedication to another, for the many and the one is played out with no resolution forthcoming. "Free" is especially disturbing since its considerable length allows for a full exposition of the crippling ambivalence that is the inevitable outcome of marriage for the man or woman who is introspective. In The "Genius," Dreiser had imagined himself confronted with the premature death of the wife he no longer loved. In "Free," he showed what life is like for the many who lack the courage to end a marriage that has been frustrating or disappointing.

"The Lost Phoebe" first appeared in Century magazine in April 1916. One of the most frequently anthologized of Dreiser's stories, it is also atypical in that it deals with a happy marriage. It concerns an old farmer named Henry Reifsneider, whose wife of forty-eight years, Phoebe Ann, has just died. Henry and Phoebe Ann had been devoted to each other, and when death separates them, Henry slowly loses his grip on reality until he hallucinates his wife back among the living. Spurred on by a vision he believes to be Phoebe Ann, the farmer is finally led over the edge of a cliff to his own death. Some readers have been tempted to see in this poignant story Dreiser's underwriting of the doctrine of "one life, one love," but it should be remembered that he attributes this enduring marriage to a want of imagination in both Henry and Phoebe Ann: "You perhaps know how it is with simple natures that fasten themselves like lichens on the stones of circumstance and weather their days to a crumbling conclusion. The great world sounds widely, but it has no call for them. They have no soaring intellect. The orchard, the meadow, the corn-field, the pig-pen, and the chicken-lot measure the range of their human activities." Hence: "Old Henry and his wife Phoebe were as fond of each other as it is possible for two old people to be who have nothing else in this life to be fond of" (pp. 114–15). In its rustic subject matter, "The Lost Phoebe" is as anomalous among Dreiser's works as Ethan Frome is among Edith Wharton's. But the story evokes the devotion of a simple man in such a moving manner that it deserves the critical attention it receives. And in it Dreiser reveals that if he could not devote himself exclusively and unlongingly to one woman, he could see beauty in the lifelong devotion demonstrated by Henry Reifsneider. "The Lost Phoebe" foreshadows the treatment of marital fidelity in The Bulwark, wherein Solon and Benecia Barnes abide in commitment and peace.

"Chains" first appeared under the title "Love" in the New York Times in May 1919.[2] A long stream-of-consciousness narrative, it recreates the thoughts of a businessman named Garrison during a train trip from a convention city to his hometown. The subject of his thoughts is Idelle, a woman half his age to whom he has been married for three years and to whom he is "chained" through his irrational need. He had met her by chance in the office of a physician friend of his, and he had fallen in love with her because she was so beautiful and because she reminded him of a former lover. In Garrison's mind, Idelle turned out to be like her predecessor in many ways—restless, selfish, cruel, and varietistic. "Chains" explores the resistless attraction some men have for women whom they know or perhaps wish can only hurt them. Garrison is portrayed as conservative and society-minded, but also as a self-destructive fool with a weakness for beauty and a need to show off a younger woman to his envying associates. The more Garrison gives to the relationship, the more he believes Idelle has heartlessly toyed with him. As the train carries him closer to his home, he rehearses all of his wife's lies and assorted transgressions (perhaps inventing some of them and perversely enjoying his own torture), and he resolves to leave her if she does not meet him on his arrival as promised. When he gets to the house he discovers that she has left him a note asking him to join her at a friend's house party. Intent on following through with his plan to leave, Garrison packs his bags but decides to join his wife at the party instead, unable to break the bonds of his peculiar passion. While Garrison is on the train, his stream-of-consciousness is frequently interrupted by the sights and sounds along the way. At one point, his musing is appropriately disturbed by "the crashing couplings" of the train cars, for this is the story of the helplessness of a man who may be seen as the self-willed victim of his own "crashing coupling."

Wray, the subject of "Marriage—For One," a story which first appeared in *Marriage* magazine in 1923, tries purposefully to avoid making the kind of mistake that ruins Garrison's later life in "Chains." With his "clerkly mind," he methodically sets out to find "a woman of sense as well as of charm, one who came of good stock and hence would be possessed of good taste and good principles" (pp. 287–88). She must be liberal and intelligent as well—in short, someone whom he can regard as his equal. And he takes care to seek out a woman he could genuinely love. Soon he meets a stenographer who seems to fit his requirements except that she has a rather conservative religious background. Unbeknown to her parents, Wray sets about remaking her in a more liberal mold. He succeeds in developing in her an interest in books and art to the point where he deems her worthy to marry him. Soon after the wedding, however, she comes under the influence of several "restless, pushing, seeking" New York women who so embellish her education in books and the arts that she begins to regard her husband as excessively narrow. When she leaves Wray, he is left to contemplate the ashes of his dreams until, on the advice of the narrator of the story, he induces his wife to return on her terms and convinces her that they should have a child. This proves not to be the solution, however, since the intellectual gap remains. Before long, the wife has found a more suitable man, and the Wrays have separated permanently.

It remains for the narrator of the story to gloss Wray's attempt at playing Pygmalion. When Wray comes to him for advice, he is hesitant to provide it because he realizes that "the mysteries of temperament of either [Wray or his wife] were not to be unraveled or adjusted save by nature—the accidents of chance and affinity, or the deadly opposition which keep apart those unsuited to each other" (p. 292).

He concludes that the couple had represented "two differing rates of motion, flowing side by side for the time being only, his the slower, hers the quicker" (p. 294). The more Mrs. Wray had come to despise her husband, the more her husband had loved her, and the narrator is "shaken" by this irresolvable situation. The story ends with the narrator brooding over "the despair, the passion, the rage, the hopelessness, the love" which the situation bespeaks: "He is spiritually wedded to that woman, who despises him, and she may be spiritually wedded to another man who may despise her" (pp. 299–300). In Dreiser's world, feeling within marriage is almost never reciprocal because men and women constitute "differing rates of motion," which by their very nature seldom "flow side by side" and only during brief interludes. The mutual needs that must be addressed if marriage is to fulfill both partners demand a brittle balance between giving and receiving which is nearly impossible to sustain.

"The Shadow," originally entitled "Jealousy," appeared in *Harper's Bazaar* in August 1924. The story is divided into two parts. The first is written from the point of view of Gil, a man who fears that his wife, Beryl, is guilty of infidelity because of his fleeting glimpses of a person he takes to be her in various suspicious situations. He eventually decides on the basis of circumstantial evidence that she is having an affair with a violinist, but her denials lead him to doubt the justice of his accusation. In the second part, the same situation is described from Beryl's point of view. We learn that she has indeed had an affair, but with a novelist named Barclay whose realistic portrait of a woman much like herself had inspired her to write to him. Her motivation is familiar. Gil is a clerk "with a clerk's mind and a clerk's point of view," whose love for Beryl exceeds her love for him. Beryl's dissatisfaction with the marriage is fueled by her husband's propensity to be "too affectionate and too clinging." She had married him primarily because he was "rather handsome" which had "meant a lot to her then." She had realized her mistake "only after she was married and surrounded by the various problems that marriage includes" (pp. 360–61). Like the wife in "Marriage—For One," Beryl had quickly grown past her husband. She gives up her affair and resolves to stay with him only because she realizes that if her indiscretion is discovered, she will lose her right to her three-year-old son, whom she loves deeply. Thus, the price she pays for her child is a married life of repressed hostility. The story ends on a note of Dreiserian irony as Beryl remembers that in

Barclay's novel, which had drawn her to him, "the husband had gone away and the architect had appeared" (p. 370).

If Dreiser's portrait of the institution of marriage in the fiction of his middle career was almost uniformly depressing, he was sometimes able to see some advantages in the married life, as he demonstrates in one of his unpublished essays, "Rebellious Women and Marriage." The essay was produced after he had been totally immersed in the question of individual responsibility while writing *An American Tragedy*.[3] It sets out to examine the modern woman's restless absorption with rights and freedom and the strain this puts on the traditional marriage. It begins with an analysis of the moral situation at the moment, an analysis in which Dreiser offers a self-revealing explanation of the temptations of modern society: "I myself think that in the matter of our emotions and our morals many of us are at loose ends. We are perhaps too much shaken by the passing of dogma, if not convention and most certainly we are considerably loosened by not only the vastly increased opportunities for social contacts and exchange, but the amazing and arresting lures to the same" (p. 26). But he cautions those who want sexual freedom: "one thing is sure and that is that apart from such passing pleasure or entertainment as there may be in either polygamy or polyandry or the varietistic attitude in general there is little or no genuine romance." The reason is: "Romance centers around two and two only" (p. 41). Although the so-called varietist does not consciously recognize his need, he is always desperately searching for real romance, which is necessary for personal peace: "without that capacity for love of one and one only—or a genuine understanding of and so harmony with one other, how is any single individual to be content, let alone happy in marriage" (p. 42). Dreiser goes on to say that he approves of divorce, but only as a necessary instrument through which the unhappily married person can renew the search for the one partner who can bring peace and bliss. But he is quick to point out that his recognition of the necessity of divorce does not lessen his respect for marriage: "I am for more marriages of an enduring character where they can be built on genuine understanding and sympathy and so mutual helpfulness—none more so" (p. 43). The rest of the essay constitutes some gratuitous advice to married couples, admonishing them to work at preserving their marriages. He suggests trying "all forms of compromise" before ending a marriage because, "as the years roll on, both sexes are certain to find that more and more they require a certain personal as well as social stability which they can never find in varietism and without it they are likely to prove mental as well as emotional tramps of the road—hoboes" (pp. 44–45). The effort expended in sustaining a good marriage is worthwhile because: "In the long run—the later and soberer years—how wise and even beneficial will seem the compromise." Dreiser seldom wrote in this vein before *The Bulwark*, but another instance occurs in the sketch of a woman he had known, fictionalized as "Reina" in *A Gallery of Women*. He portrays the profligate Reina as a lazy loafer married to a "workaholic" and excoriates her for taking no pains to fulfill her half of the couple's marital vows. But even in "Rebellious Women and Marriage," Dreiser recommends that if a person finds himself in a union in which there is no romance, he should immediately "move and seek the real thing" (p. 47). Indeed, in the midst of his discussion of the strengths of marriage, Dreiser interjects a set of questions that implicitly and contradictorily applaud his own proclivities and undercut his whole argument: "Have you the strength of the varietistic life? The real courage? If not, —then what?—" (p. 46½). The essay clearly demonstrates his characteristic need for the one and the many in his sexual relations—a need that he was never to outgrow. Throughout his life, he longed for and actively pursued the tempestuous exhilaration of sexual variety at the same time he desired the emotional stability of monogamy. Whatever attitudes Dreiser expressed about marriage in his essays, his fiction remains the repository of his deepest feelings about this as well as most other subjects. The short stories of the "marriage group" reveal that "genuine understanding and sympathy and natural helpfulness" within the married state are extremely rare. When two people join in a sanctioned and sustained relationship in Dreiser's stories, they form an unstable compound—each striving for control, seldom intersecting spiritually, socially, emotionally; changing and growing at differing rates; never achieving the elusive balance between giving to and receiving from the other that could create harmony and happiness. This unstable compound is inevitable since most marriages result from short-lived sexual passion or temporary individual dreams or social pressure. The many personal tragedies that follow are owing, not only to the relative inaccessibility of divorce in Dreiser's day, but also to the fact that divorce does nothing to ease the inevitable guilty self-questioning which often leaves permanent emotional scars.

Ironically, however, Dreiser achieved a harmonious and happy wedding of content and form in his short stories about marriage. The expression of certain writers' ideas is better suited to one genre than another. Sherwood Anderson, for example, was a master of the short story. But the ideas in his novels, stretched beyond the requirements of the single moment of character illumination, did not hold up well. On the other hand, Dreiser's lumbering style and gigantic, brooding imagination were best suited to the form of the novel. Not often was he able to narrow his focus and effectively encase his ideas within a short story. By far his most successful ventures into the shorter form were the stories in the "marriage group." They allowed him to concentrate on the dialectic which was at the very core even of his most sprawling and sometimes directionless novels—the dialectic between giving and getting, observable in the microcosm of marital relationships. His next novel would dramatize his deepest soundings yet of the human heart, torn between desire and responsibility.

7 / An American Tragedy and the Thirties

A N *American Tragedy* represents an artistic achievement of the most impressive dimensions. Moreover, it shows that Dreiser had made substantial progress toward the culmination of his long quest for moral direction and spiritual peace. In the crime that society calls murder, he found the irreducible equation with which to work through the problem of the self versus society. Indeed, the person with the motive, the opportunity, and the will to commit murder confronts the question of giving or taking in its essential configuration.

Since his days as a newspaper reporter, Dreiser had been fascinated by murders, especially those cases in which the killer's motives involved sex and success. At various times, he began and then aborted fictional works based on this formula. For example, in 1914, he decided to fictionalize the celebrated Roland Molineux case in a novel to be called "The Rake." Seven years earlier, Molineux had committed two murders by poison, the first to do away with a rival for the hand of his monied girlfriend. But Dreiser wrote only a fragment of the novel. He changed the circumstances to approximate those that he later used in *An American Tragedy*, but he became dissatisfied with his efforts and put the fragment aside to work on other projects. By 1920 he had decided to try the murder novel again, but this time his source was to be the Chester Gillette case of 1906. Gillette had drowned his pregnant girlfriend, Grace Brown, to clear his path to acceptance in his wealthy uncle's social circle and to make possible his bid to win Harriet Benedict, the daughter of a society lawyer. By 1922, Dreiser had completed some twenty chapters of the new novel, which was to be entitled *Mirage.* The purpose of this original title was to illustrate how life's illusions destroyed the protagonist. A year earlier, Dreiser had concluded his response to Edward Smith, the book reviewer who had accused him of lapsing into metaphysics (see pp. 110, 112), with the promise that this new novel would "clear the air once and for all." But when the book finally appeared under the title *An American Tragedy* in late 1925—cut from over 1,000,000 words to 385,000—it "cleared the air" in a much different way than Dreiser thought it would.

An American Tragedy is a documentary novel, although it does not keep to its public sources as rigorously as does the Cowperwood trilogy. Dreiser used the running account of the Gillette case in the *New York World* as the foundation for his novel. He chose the Gillette case from among several similar ones which seemed to him typical enough to warrant treatment as particularly American crimes. Through 840 pages, he meticulously documents the youthful environment, the dreamy ambitions, and the crime, trial, and execution of the fictional Clyde Griffiths, who roughly resembles Gillette. In the process of studying his material, Dreiser himself became inextricably tangled in the question of the extent to which Clyde is guilty of murder, and by extension the larger issue of the responsibility of the individual versus the responsibility of society. All of the novelist's resources were summoned for this gigantic novel, which critical opinion usually ranks as his finest work.

In reconstructing Clyde's youth, Dreiser invented some events which diverged from the actual circumstances of Gillette's life, and he also drew heavily from his own early experience. Gillette's parents were missionaries, and Dreiser portrays Clyde as the son of poverty stricken Kansas City evangelists. For Clyde, the lure of the great world soon comes in conflict with his parents' religion. Their solemn preachments concerning the damnation attendant upon sins of the flesh can do little to assuage his burgeoning desire, since his mind is "much too responsive to phases of beauty and pleasure which had little, if anything, to do with the remote and cloudy romance which swayed the minds of his mother and father" (1: 5). The sight of well-dressed boys escorting young beauties along the avenue leads Clyde to long for better days. The young dandies, typically resplendent in "dress shirt, high hat, bow tie, white kid gloves and patent leather shoes," help Clyde crystallize his resolve to escape. While he is working as a soda jerk, his observation of the trysts between young gallants and their girls leads to an epiphany:

a revealing flash after all the years of walking through the streets with his father and mother to public prayer meeting, the sitting in chapel and listening to queer and nondescript individuals—depressing and disconcerting people—telling how Christ had saved them and what God had done for them. You bet he would get out of that now. He would work and save his money and be somebody. Decidedly this simple and yet idyllic compound of the commonplace had all the luster and wonder of a spiritual transfiguration, the true mirage of the lost and thirsting and seeking victim of the desert. [1: 26.]

In his quest for fulfillment, he flees from his family to a job in Kansas City as a bellhop at the Green-Davidson Hotel, an establishment he views as the "quintessence of luxury and ease." The garish hotel, "because of the timorous poverty that had restrained him from exploring such a world, was more arresting, quite, than anything he had seen before" (1: 40–41).

Clyde's attraction to pretty girls relates to material necessities in the old Dreiserian way, and thereby the seeds of tragedy are planted:

Incidentally by that time the sex lure or appeal had begun to manifest itself and he was already intensely interested and troubled by the beauty of the opposite sex, its attractions for him and his attraction for it. And, naturally and coincidentally, the matter of his clothes and his physical appearance had begun to trouble him not a little—how he looked and how other boys looked. It was painful to him now to think that his clothes were not right; that he was not as handsome as he might be, not as interesting. [1: 15.]

Yet for one who believes himself so limited, his standards in women are exceptionally high: "The thought of being content with one not so attractive almost nauseated him" (1: 80). When he sees a hotel guest fondling a girl at a party (significantly, she is wearing a white dress and he sees her reflected in a mirror), Clyde feels as though he is "looking through the gates of Paradise" (1: 45). During a visit to a local brothel arranged by his fellow bellhops, he is thoroughly enchanted by the "Aladdin-like scene" (1: 65). He soon discovers, after his own initiation, that he is by nature chronically promiscuous.

Spurred by a series of minor romantic conquests, Clyde associates the role of fancy-free bellhop with "the good life." Not even his shabby treatment by his first serious infatuation, the cruelly selfish and bitchy Hortense Briggs, can dampen his ardor for the tawdry. (Dreiser's tone in his portrait of Hortense is intensely negative. She is cast in the same mold as Mrs. Hurstwood in *Sister Carrie* and Claudia Carlstadt in *The Titan*.) But when Clyde and some friends accidentally run down a child while driving in an automobile, he is forced to flee Kansas City to avoid punishment. He spends several years in Chicago, where he encounters his rich uncle, Samuel Griffiths, who decides to give him a job in his factory. The deprived Clyde had always viewed his uncle as a "kind of Crœsus, living in ease and luxury" (1: 14). Nursing a dream of affluence and supremacy for himself, Clyde decides to accept his uncle's offer and move to Lycurgus.

Clyde's first glimpse of Lycurgus high society further inflames his imagination, but he finds himself an outsider despite his relationship to the wealthy Griffithses. He is placed in the shrinking room of the collar factory as a common laborer, a telling touch through which Dreiser emphasizes the chasm between the haves and the have nots. Eventually, he is given a minor supervisory post. This still humble role satisfies him temporarily, because his desk commands a view of the stitching section which employs a number of girls and women. After a few minor flirtations with several of the girls, Clyde becomes embroiled in a serious affair with Roberta Alden, who like Clyde has been lured to the factory from a poor and narrow background. Characteristically, the seeds of Clyde's dissatisfaction with Roberta are sown the moment she submits to him sexually: "And if now Roberta was obviously willing to sacrifice herself for him in this fashion, must there not be others?" (1: 308), and he is immediately longing for new girls and a more prominent social position.

He soon meets the embodiment of his dream, Sondra Finchley, the socially prominent friend of one of Samuel Griffiths's daughters. Sondra introduces Clyde into her circle out of spite for his snobbish cousin Gilbert, who regards Clyde as an interloper. The swirl of society soon captivates Clyde, and he desires only social supremacy and Sondra, though he continues to see Roberta. The tragedy is triggered, however, when Clyde learns that Roberta is pregnant. He searches in vain for a solution to his problem, including attempting several times unsuccessfully to obtain an abortion for her. Gradually the idea of killing her impresses itself upon him until he is unable to fight off the dark thought. He chooses the method of her murder when he chances upon a newspaper account of a successfully plotted drowning of a girl at an isolated lake. After a period of planning, he manages to lure Roberta to the middle of Big Bittern Lake in a canoe, but at the crucial moment he cannot go through with the intended crime. At this point, chance decides the issue, for as Roberta comes toward Clyde in the canoe, he "accidentally" strikes her with his camera, and in the confusion, they both fall into the water. Clyde elects not to try to save her, partly for fear that her thrashing will drown them both. He swims to shore and makes his escape, but thanks to his bumbling attempts to conceal the planning of the crime, he is quickly apprehended. The remainder of the novel is devoted to Clyde's trial and execution.

Dreiser's purpose in *An American Tragedy* is to question the extent of Clyde's guilt and to underscore a number of social injustices—those that drive Clyde to the crime and those that lead to his execution. Part of the importance this novel has in the development of Dreiser's moral thought lies in his replacing the implicit acceptance of injustice, made necessary by the "equation inevitable," with a full-scale protest against some of the basic assumptions on which American society is based. This significant change has its most obvious expression in Dreiser's altered treatment of the relationship between power and poverty. Instead of defending Samuel Griffiths as a minor league superman, Dreiser lacerates the American version of the capitalistic system for allowing the disparity between poverty and wealth to exist. The primary message of the book is that America's destructive materialistic goals are fostered by the emulation of men like Samuel Griffiths, whose ascendancy is the result of opportunity, ability, and ruthlessness, all of which only a few possess. Much of its force results from the juxtaposition of the two branches of the Griffiths family. While Clyde is crawling through the fields to escape the police in Kansas City, for example, the Lycurgus Griffithses argue about which of their summer resorts is the more fashionable. The poverty of Clyde's dreams is contrasted throughout the novel with the Lycurgus Griffithses' power and prestige. Because of this unjustifiable stratification, Clyde is reduced to a personification of desire, living always in the past or future, depending on which contrasts more favorably with the wretched present. Although Dreiser's object is to use Clyde's poverty and repressive religious background to minimize his responsibility for Roberta's death, he recognizes clearly in *An American Tragedy* that there is substantial guilt on every side. This is doubtlessly why his frequent detractor, New Humanist critic Stuart Pratt Sherman, felt justified in reversing his traditional evaluation of Dreiser to credit him with growth and to praise this novel for its intelligence, truthfulness, and moral strength.[1] Critics often point to this turnaround as evidence of a change in Sherman, but Dreiser was surely more changed. In *An American Tragedy*, there is none of the labored self-justification and much less of the blatant denial of human responsibility that Sherman had attacked so violently in the past. Furthermore, the recognition of society's guilt and the agonized questioning of Clyde's share in it at the end of the novel constitute a logical prologue to the assertion of individual responsibility in *The Bulwark*.

In attempting to shift the largest measure of guilt from Clyde to society, Dreiser stresses his protagonist's weakness. His defense attorney makes an eloquent plea for acquittal on the basis of moral cowardice, contending that Clyde had been "bewitched" in his pursuit of "beauty, love, wealth," and that he was powerless to resist temptation (2: 274). Dreiser demonstrated that he shared this view by making many of his own intrusions into the narrative. When Clyde is considering doing away with Roberta, for example, Dreiser interjects that he is brought to consider such a desperate proposal precisely "because of his own mental and material weakness before pleasures and dreams which he could not bring himself to forego" (2: 51–52). When the time for the actual deed arrives, it is not conscience which stays Clyde's hand but a "chemic revulsion against death or murderous brutality that would bring death" (2: 76–77). During the entire episode on the lake, Clyde is in a kind of trance that blurs his senses. Further evidence of moral cowardice is supplied when he tells lies on the witness stand and avoids confessing his real intentions until after his final appeal has been denied. For these reasons, Clyde is often called the weakest protagonist in American fiction. But there is no evidence that Dreiser approved of Clyde's cowardice or even that he thought it inevitable under the circumstances. Indeed, the tone of those passages that explore Clyde's motivations and morality is uniformly unfavorable.

In attempting to supply deterministic explanations for Clyde's actions, Dreiser obviously found the planning of the murder the most difficult part of the situation to handle. The language he employs to describe Clyde's intentions is charged with moral discrimination. When Clyde comes across the newspaper account of the summer boating accident that inspires his plot, he himself characterizes his first temptation as a "devil's whisper" and an "evil hint of an evil spirit" (2: 24). Try as he might to discount such thinking, Dreiser cannot avoid a negative judgment of Clyde's plan. In an intrusive passage just after Clyde conceives of the murder as a possible solution, Dreiser attributes his temptation to the tottering and warping of his reason which renders him vulnerable to "mistaken or erroneous counsel." At this point, he introduces the mystical Efrit which accompanies Clyde up to the climactic scene at the lake. A metaphor of Clyde's subconscious, the Efrit argues for his "diabolic wish" which arises out of his "darker or primordial and unregenerate nature" (2: 48–49). Again and again, Dreiser speaks of Clyde's "darker self." The language of these passages reveals Dreiser's debt not to Darwin but to Dostoevsky, whom he had read and greatly admired in the years between *Sister Carrie* and *Jennie Gerhardt*. Despite his working hypothesis, which theoretically rejected moral categories, Dreiser found the taking of a human life an evil which no amount of deterministic theory could excuse. On the surface it appears that Clyde is the embodiment of all the traits necessary for the naturalistic pawn. His impoverished childhood environment has molded his personality. He seems to be without a significant will of his own, as if the events of his life were strictly ordained by fate. Yet if Dreiser substantially discounts Clyde's responsibility for Roberta's death, he does not condone either the planning or the commission of what he could only regard as a moral transgression against humanity.

On the other hand, Dreiser seems at times in *An American Tragedy* to blame cowardice or inadequacy for Clyde's failure to act on his resolve to murder Roberta. Many critics have simply echoed this point of view. Charles Child Walcutt, for example, contends that "Clyde's inability to commit the deed in cold blood is indicative of his general weakness of will." Donald Pizer argues in a similar vein that Clyde's failure to rid himself of Roberta earlier stems from a "strain of emotional responsiveness" which he nonetheless identifies with weakness. Clyde is said to lack the "negative virtue of cruelty."[2] Thus, his one demonstration of moral potency is made to seem a further sign of weakness. This kind of argument, typical of the brand of criticism that is applied to Dreiser's work, stems from the compulsion to read his novels as consistently naturalistic. It also tends to obscure the fact that although Dreiser may have originally intended to fully absolve Clyde from guilt on the basis of his weak will, he could not finally do so. After the trial, Clyde is set to wondering about the extent of his sin. He can forgive himself much, on the basis of his wild fever for Sondra, but ultimately he cannot cleanse his conscience of possible responsibility:

> There were phases of this thing, the tangles and doubts involved in that dark, savage plot of his, as he now saw and brooded on it, which were not so easily to be disposed of. Perhaps the two worst were, first, that in bringing Roberta there to that point on the lake—that lone spot—and then growing so weak and furious with himself because of his own incapacity to do evil, he had frightened her into rising and trying to come to him. And that in the first instance made it possible for her to be thus accidentally struck by him and so made him, in part at least, guilty of that blow—or did it?—a murderous, sinful blow in that sense. Maybe. . . . And since because of that she had fallen into the water, was he not guilty of her falling? It was a thought that troubled him very much now—his constructive share of the guilt in all that. [2: 381.]

In truth, Dreiser's immersion in the material of this novel had led him into a labyrinthian consideration of the constructive share in the guilt borne by all parties, and far from absolving any one party, the results were, at best, inconclusive. He comes closest to ascribing responsibility to Clyde when he has him realize that he would have made every effort to save Sondra had she been tossed in the water—or even the Roberta of the previous summer.

The final section of the novel is, in fact, an elaborate treatise on guilt. It concerns the efforts of an unordained minister named Duncan McMillan to induce Clyde to embrace religion and confess his sins. McMillan is the most sympathetically treated clergyman in Dreiser's fiction. He is described as "a strange, strong, tense, confused, merciful and too, after his fashion beautiful soul; sorrowing with misery yearning toward an impossible justice" (2: 371). As the minister hears more and more of Clyde's story, he becomes more and more puzzled himself about the extent of Clyde's guilt. As he agonizes over the confusing, extenuating circumstances of the case, he comes finally to be no more enlightened than Clyde himself. F. O. Matthiessen views this treatment of McMillan as ironic, and Dreiser may have originally intended it to be so. Certainly, the once self-assured minister becomes confused about the real nature of sin. But Lionel Trilling, generally not a very perceptive critic of Dreiser, is closer to the mark than Matthiessen this time when he sees in McMillan a forecast of Dreiser's religious avowal in *The Bulwark.*[3] The minister becomes in part a spokesman for Dreiser, who ultimately shared his confusion about Clyde's measure of guilt. This is clearly illustrated in Dreiser's later statements about *An American Tragedy.* At one point, he spoke of Clyde, "through no real willing of his own," finding himself defeated and charged with murder. At another time, he indicated that his purpose had been to "explain, if not condone, how such murders happen."[4] Less than a year after the publication of *An American Tragedy,* Dreiser was approached for an endorsement by the League for the Abolition of Capital Punishment. He refused, stating that he was "by no means convinced that capital punishment is something that should be done away with."[5] Such uncertainty concerning the meaning of guilt, responsibility, and good and evil contrasts dramatically with the self-assured assertions that he often made about these subjects before he became enmeshed in Clyde's story. A few years earlier, for example, he composed a long letter in response to a man named Bauer who had written him about the nature of good and evil. Dreiser's rejoinder reveals the facile assumption of moral relativity that most often characterized his speculations before *An American Tragedy:*

Man is certainly a thing and a mechanistic device in nature who[se] import is certainly not so much individual as social. (See the essay "The Essential Tragedy of Life" in *Hey Rub a Dub Dub*). As for abstract *good* and *evil* and his ability to distinguish between—please note in the first place that you begin with *good* and *evil* and then in the next ten words confound them with *right* and *wrong.* I. e. Good = right Evil = wrong. How ridiculous. Good and Evil as well as right and wrong—four very different things by the way, may be and unquestionably are seen or pictured by differing individuals as very different. What is good in one climate, for instance, is not good in another. What is evil in one place is not necessarily evil in another. Equally so right and wrong—the savages and the intellectual concept of them being very different. Murder among the [unreadable word] is not wrong, although unquestionably it is an evil—to the individual and worthy of revenge. Murder may be and no doubt is very wrong in the mind of the average newspaper Editor or publisher but as an evil to him it does not exist. It is in short a positive good for it fills space, sells papers and entertains the public and so profits him in every way. Yet it is not only evil but wrong—when viewed from different angles by different people—but never evil and wrong to all people at once. Consider the attitude of the murderer himself—for one.[6]

In *An American Tragedy*, Dreiser considered murder from all angles and though his original intention was to absolve Clyde (to whom Roberta's projected death seemed neither evil nor wrong), he was led by his investigation to include him in a web of compound complicity.

Like *The "Genius,"* *An American Tragedy* concludes with a discussion of religion, and again Dreiser approaches the subject through a consideration of the morality of human actions. McMillan's significant role is in his attempt to induce Clyde to throw himself on God's mercy and sign a statement that he has accepted his punishment in a Christian spirit. Clyde teeters between near belief and disbelief much as Eugene Witla had in *The "Genius."* (Dreiser has few peers in the portrayal of religious doubt and ambivalence, the inheritance particularly of the twentieth century.) Not wanting to be frightened into religion as many of his fellow prisoners seemed to be, Clyde is at the same time "tortured by the need of some mental if not material support in the face of his great danger" (2: 379). In a kind of psychic terror, he signs a statement that he has found God. But when he is led to the electric chair, he is not at all certain that he has. The novelist displays a sure hand in resisting the temptation to convert his hero into a true believer. A last minute display of faith in a character like Clyde, as opposed to Solon Barnes in *The Bulwark,* would not be convincing. In a twentieth-century context, doubt is the only viable response to the question of the extent to which Clyde is guilty and to the possibility of religious recourse.

After witnessing the execution, McMillan, who opposes capital punishment, becomes physically and mentally sickened. Despite his considerable effort on Clyde's behalf, he feels that he did not expend himself completely and that therefore he shall never again know peace. He must carry forever the burden of his refusal to speak to the governor, a refusal based on his judgment that, though Clyde might not have been legally guilty, he did carry some real guilt in his heart. The clear purport of the final pages is that McMillan, in acknowledging his own share of the guilt, has experienced spiritual growth. Armed originally with abstract theories about the mercy of God and the reality of sin, he grows in personal compassion, for he is no longer willing to judge others. In the manuscript version of the novel, Dreiser had planned a more dramatic fate for McMillan. Near the end of the holograph, Dreiser inserted a headline reading "Clyde Griffiths' Spiritual Advisor Insane—The Reverend Duncan McMillan of Syracuse Taken from his Pastorate to An Asylum." The would-be newspaper article quotes the minister as having "declared that his early conclusions in connection with revealed truth had for the time at least been impaired by his work in connection with the Griffiths case and his mission and that he must find spiritual light or that he could not maintain his reason." The article continues: "One of his perpetual declarations was that the curse of life was gossip. Also, he was opposed to newspapers, capital punishment, liquor and wealth and often declared that the moment his father's fortune should fall to him he should proceed to distribute it among the poor as he needed nothing except his strength and two hands to sustain him." Dreiser thought better of this denouement, lined out "Insane" in the headline and substituted "A Suicide." He also lined out "Taken from His Pastorate to An Asylum" and wrote "Leaps from a Hospital Window to His Death."[7] But sometime between the completion of the holograph and the published version of the novel, he decided on a more hopeful consummation. Although McMillan is stricken with self-recriminations and doubts about Clyde's guilt and contrition, his last words are a profession of faith: "I know my Redeemer liveth and that He will keep him against that day" (2: 407). In assigning McMillan a renewal of faith rather than the despair he had originally intended for him, Dreiser was acknowledging the power of religion in times of adversity for those who are able to believe—a power he was to experience first hand toward the end of his life.

McMillan's spiritual growth is contrasted, however, to the blind belief of Clyde's mother in her son's obvious sin and ultimate salvation through contrition. She cannot view any of her son's behavior as other than wicked, and she understands only dimly the role of his early environment in his situation. Although Dreiser concedes that the narrow faith of Clyde's parents might bring them comfort, it lacks intelligence because "the necessity of thought had been obviated by advice and law, or 'revealed' truth" (1: 16). Clyde's parents approach in the most superficial way the conflict between desire and duty which is at the heart of all of Dreiser's novels. When Clyde is brooding about his guilt, the conflict resurfaces:

But then again, there was the fact or truth of those very strong impulses and desires within himself that were so very, very hard to overcome. He had thought of those, too, and then of the fact that many other people like his mother, his uncle, his cousin, and this minister here, did not seem to be troubled by them. And yet also he was given to imagining at times that perhaps it was because of superior mental and moral courage in the face of passions and desires, equivalent to his own, which led these others to do so much better. He was perhaps just willfully devoting himself to these other thoughts and ways, as his mother and McMillan and most every one else whom he had heard talk since his arrest seemed to think. [2: 378–79.]

Dreiser had often conjectured himself about the disparity between those like Clyde who were at the mercy of their longings and those like Jennie and the "Doer of the Word" who rose above personal desires and led admirably righteous lives. His puzzlement over these differences was not lessened by religious explanations. Early in *An American Tragedy* as a matter of fact, he registers his standard complaint against the easy answers of organized religion. In a passage describing Clyde's parents' beliefs, he scoffs:

In some blind, dualistic way both she and Asa insisted, as do all religionists, in dissociating God from harm and error and misery, while granting Him nevertheless supreme control. They would seek for something else—some malign, treacherous, deceiving power which, in the face of God's omniscience and omnipotence, still beguiles and betrays—and find it eventually in the error and perverseness of the human heart, which God has made, yet which He does not control, because He does not want to control it. [1: 20.]

Dreiser was unwilling to see only perverseness in Clyde's heart, and this unwillingness accounts for the protracted assessment of moral responsibility in the last few chapters of *An American Tragedy*. He could not accept the doctrine of Original Sin as a viable explanation of man's inhumanity to his fellows, since it ran counter to his hypothetical determinism and because it struck him as a vestige of religious superstition. Yet, if the reader is urged to question the extent of Clyde's guilt, he certainly cannot doubt society's or the Christian community's guilt. Dreiser strongly denounces, in the novel, a number of injustices besides America's social caste system.

These other injustices come to light when Clyde is brought to trial. The ignorant townspeople have no reservations about the totality of his perverseness. Their immediate desire is for vengeance, especially since there is the possibility of sexual immorality connected with the case. Once the newspapers have the story, the injustice is compounded. Doubtlessly recalling his own experiences as a reporter, Dreiser scores the kind of journalism all too frequent still. Clyde is convicted by newspaper coverage before the jury is assembled. In addition, the officials in charge of the trial are motivated by political considerations, especially Mason, the district attorney who regards Clyde's conviction as his passport to the governor's mansion. The jury that finally convicts Clyde, as much for his sex offense as for murder, has been unduly influenced by public opinion and their own prejudices and emotions. The result is inevitable. The eleven in favor of conviction intimidate the lone dissenter, who is "threatened with exposure and the public rage and obloquy which was sure to follow in case the jury was hung" (2: 329). Fearing the certain damage to his business, the dissenter relents.

Since Samuel Griffiths finds it inadvisable to come to his nephew's assistance, Clyde's mother is forced to seek help for an appeal of the case. She is turned down by all of the Christians whom she entreats and all of the Christian organizations which she asks for assistance. Because the Christians feel that they cannot aid such a callous sinner, Mrs. Griffiths is forced to rely on a Jew who immediately offers help. She might have anticipated such a reception from the Christian community, because early in the novel, her husband's mission in Kansas City had been frequented by this type of religionist. They "were always testifying as to how God or Christ or Divine Grace had rescued them from this or that predicament—never how they had rescued any one else" (1: 13).

The final protest against social injustice is Dreiser's angry denunciation of the conditions prevailing in the death house. The opening description of death row foreshadows the harrowing events that Clyde and the reader are to witness there:

The "death house" in this particular prison was one of those crass erections and maintenances of human insensitiveness and stupidity principally for which no one primarily was really responsible. Indeed, its total plan and procedure were the results of a series of primary legislative enactments, followed by decisions and compulsions as devised by the temperaments and seeming necessities of various wardens, until at last—by degrees and without anything worthy of the name of thinking on any one's part—there had been gathered and was now being enforced all that could possibly be imagined in the way of unnecessary and really unauthorized cruelty or stupid and de-structive torture. And to the end that a man, once condemned by a jury, would be compelled to suffer not alone the death for which his sentence called, but a thousand others before that. For the very room by its arrange-ment, as well as the rules governing the lives and actions of the inmates, was sufficient to bring about this torture, willy-nilly. [2: 352.]

As inmate after inmate is dragged to his death while praying to God for mercy, Dreiser builds a devastating case against this sanctioned slaughter. Finally, the reader watches Clyde being led through the doors of the execution chamber, still unsure himself whether he is actually guilty. Little wonder that this book became recommended reading for the forces opposed to capital punishment, despite Drei-ser's misgivings on the subject. Little wonder, too, that Clarence Dar-row so greatly admired the book. Dreiser had visited death row at Sing Sing in researching *An American Tragedy*. His descriptions bear the stamp of awful authenticity.

In condemning the social injustices that abounded in Clyde Griffiths's story, Dreiser sought to shift much of the blame from indi-viduals to the social system. A number of critics have dated his con-version to socialism from the publication of *An American Tragedy*, but such a conclusion is unwarranted. The socialistic implications of the novel are never really carried through. Although Walcutt indicates that in this novel Dreiser "demonstrates the evils of our society in a way that may lead the reader sometime to think about correcting them,"[8] it is not at all clear that Dreiser believed at this point that these evils could be corrected. He was by no means a convinced socialist, for there were still many conflicts in his approach. As late as 1927, during a visit to Russia, he could still argue society's need for the finan-cier, however unscrupulous. In the same year he asserted to the Rus-sian writer Sergei Dinamov that poverty would probably always exist and that he had no theories about life, or the solution of economic and political problems.[9] Yet there can be little doubt that Dreiser's moral indignation was aroused by the circumstances of the case that he fictionalized in the novel. The vengeance-seeking townspeople, the newspapers, and the hypocrites who refuse to help Clyde are con-demned with a sardonic irony. But the logic of Dreiser's indignation is weakened by the same determinism that he uses to discount Clyde's guilt. After all, were not the jurymen, the Christians, the prosecuting attorney, and the prison wardens, like Clyde, victims of the system themselves? With responsibility shifted to the system, the individuals must be forgiven their transgressions. Dreiser refuses in *An American Tragedy* to consider the possibility that no social system can exist apart from the individuals who sanction it. The problem is endemic to writers who combine naturalistic ideas with moral indignation. One is reminded of the way in which Steinbeck's spokesman, the preacher Casy, vitiates the novelist's righteous anger against "the banks" in *The Grapes of Wrath*. While Steinbeck heaps abuse on "the system," Casy reduces individual moral alternatives to actions that are simply "nice" or "not nice," categories that would have baffled Dostoevsky. Dreiser's reluctance to judge his fictional characters stemmed not only from his belief in determinism, but also from his negative reaction to those who were only too willing to judge their fellows. Despite Clyde's brooding over his "constructive share in the guilt," Dreiser was at least trying to believe that his crime was socially conditioned. That he could not quite believe him totally unresponsible was a negative decision which constituted a significant step toward the altered moral perspective of *The Bulwark*.

Other signs of a fundamental change in Dreiser's point of view appear in *An American Tragedy*. There is, for example, not only a greater moral discrimination in the book, but also a related new detachment. In reconstructing Clyde's youth, Dreiser had drawn upon much in his own life, as he had done in all of his other novels. Although he did not share Clyde's appreciation of brothels, which had always struck him as insufficiently romantic, he drew the rest of Clyde's values from his own personal store. But now he looked back at some of his desires with more distance than in any of his previous works. In assessing Clyde's dreams of wealth, which according to self-confession had been his own, he found them "extreme and mistaken and gauche" (1: 33). Through Clyde's dream girl, Sondra, he ridicules the quest for the "impossible she" in a way he would not have been capable of a few years earlier. Unlike Berenice Fleming of the trilogy and Suzanne Dale of *The "Genius,"* Sondra is clearly depicted as unworthy of adulation, inconsequential if alluring. Instead of defending Clyde as a vigorous self-seeking moth of the lamp, he blames society for lighting the lamp. Instead of relishing Clyde's animal nature, he derides society for treating him like an animal. Slowly, the fundamental conflict between the self and some call from beyond the self, evident in Dreiser's thinking from the beginning, was being resolved. Inexorably, the balance was shifting toward duty, responsibility, giving.

The reasons for these basic changes can only be surmised, but it appears that middle age had lessened Dreiser's personal involvement with the conflicts he had struggled so long to understand. Among the causes may also have been his new life with Helen Richardson, an actress whom he met in 1922. They could not be married until his first wife's death in 1942, but Dreiser's relationship with Helen introduced a stability into his life that had been conspicuously missing. Although his affairs with other women continued, he and Helen remained together until his death. In his early fifties, Dreiser was beginning to develop a sense of perspective. The next step toward the spiritual avowal of *The Bulwark* was taken when he began devoting himself to a personal humanitarianism.

As a consequence of the thought that Dreiser had given to social problems for a quarter of a century, there evolved in him a gradual reversal of social philosophy. Formerly, he had asserted that action on the part of individuals could only be ineffectual because men were pitted against forces that could be neither resisted nor questioned. Without consciously altering his basic philosophy, he came slowly to align himself with various social causes and parties that were implicitly antipathetic to many of the views he held. The immense popularity of *An American Tragedy* had made him overnight the champion of prison inmates and the oppressed generally, and it may have been the opportunity provided by this new fame that spurred him to social action. From 1926 to the early 1940s, he entered what might be called his public phase, abandoning the novel for social and political tracts, replacing inaction with allegiance to a number of causes. The bulk of the art published during this period consisted of sketches and poems composed before 1925. Between 1926 and 1930, Dreiser began addressing himself to selected humanitarian considerations. He attempted to improve conditions in a county poorhouse; he contributed to the American Civil Liberties Union; he joined attempts to secure pardons for convicted criminals; and he lent financial support to an emergency relief committee for Southern strikers and to a children's hospital. But he was still neither convinced that the individual was capable of having an impact on society, nor that poverty and suffering were not inherent in the social contract. In 1927 he accepted an invitation to visit Russia, and in the book that chronicles the trip he praised the Communists for their elimination of "that haunting sense of poverty or complete defeat that so distresses one in western Europe and America."[10] But being "an incorrigible individualist," he could not believe in the destiny of a system that rests on the elimination of individual greed. He could still argue the case for the world's need of financiers even as his political beliefs moved toward the left.

Dreiser toured America during the spring and summer of 1930, and as a result of what he saw, he became passionately committed to social reforms. His trip during the first year of the Depression yielded a strong conviction that the gulf between the rich and the poor was becoming wider. His recent visit to Russia had convinced him that something could be done to curb the power of the strong, and that it must be done in America. He felt impelled to become more vocal about injustice than he had been at any previous time. He chose to aid the underdog through his membership in various organizations and by espousing socialist and humanitarian causes. The most significant of his many activities of the next decade included: his chairmanship of the Committee for the Defense of Political Prisoners, which under his leadership assisted Tom Mooney and the Scottsboro boys; his investigation of conditions in Harlan County, Kentucky, where the coal miners' strike had focused national attention; his attendance as a delegate of the League of American Writers to an international peace conference; his efforts to enlist humanitarian aid for the Spanish people during their civil war; and his attempts to keep America out of World War II. The extent to which the impact of the Depression had begun to change Dreiser's philosophic outlook is evidenced in an article written in 1932 which completely reversed the Social Darwinism of a few years earlier:

Americans should mentally follow individualism to its ultimate conclusion, for society is not and cannot be a jungle. It should be and is, if it is a social organism worthy of the name, escape from the drastic individualism, which for some, means all, and for the many, little or nothing. And consciously or unconsciously, it is by Nature and evolution intended as such, and desires to avoid the extreme individualism of the jungle. In proof of which, I submit that it has indulged in more and more rules and laws, each intended to limit, yet not frustrate, the individual in his relations to his fellows. In fact, the dream of organized society, conscious or unconscious, has been to make it not only possible but necessary for the individual to live with his fellow in reasonable equity, in order that he may enjoy equity himself.[11]

Dreiser was beginning to see that limitation and frustration were not synonymous, and that self-abnegation, far from being an impossible ideal, was necessary for the maintenance of a just society. His work on behalf of others backed his words impressively.

As early as 1933, he began to speak of the need to eliminate the "capitalistic" class, and in succeeding years he became more antipathetic to the wealthy. Yet he did not abandon his allegiance to determinism, nor did he acknowledge a need to do so. He did not believe that socialism and determinism were mutually exclusive. Robert H. Elias wrote him in 1937 asking how he could square his deterministic assumptions with his arguments for social reform. Dreiser replied that he saw no conflict:

> Since I started in observing my world and writing about it, I have been interested in the effects of social systems on individuals. And although I didn't take any really active part in reform programs until the 1920's and after, my feelings have almost always gravitated toward sympathy with what I regarded as the underdog. At the same time, though I may sympathize with the unwilled, helpless, seemingly undeserved suffering which becomes the lot of the many, I am forced to realize that the strong do rule "the weak." Even determinists where and when sympathetic and taking part in social reform for the benefit of "the weak" are to some extent helpless. [12]

As questionable as the logic of this position may be, Dreiser continued to act on behalf of the oppressed. Whether or not he was certain that he was free to do so, he was now devoting almost all of his energy to social causes. In 1931 he explained the need for such work to a correspondent concerned about women's rights. In a civilization based on "selfishness and hardship," he found the governments organized in such a way that "everywhere, except in Soviet Russia, the masses are preyed upon by the so-called constructive geniuses at the top," a situation he deemed one of life's "outrages." The answer was that "equity [especially for women] can come about only by the vigilance of the common people and the supremacy of their interests over the selfish few who control the laws." [13] The way in which his social work was engendering political convictions is further illustrated in a letter to an admirer of "A Doer of the Word," Dreiser's early story of the saintly Charley Potter who gives all of his possessions to the poor. Thirty years after the fact, Dreiser saw that the story had not only a social, but also a political message: "'A Doer of the Word,' if you were to examine it more closely, is really a bellicose noise disguised as a soft word. In other words, it is an illustration of the vast inequity about which one single-handed man was trying to do something, and you will note that he was not an intellectual or a captain of industry or a senator, or a President or any ruling authority, outside of Russia, the World over."[14]

The motivation for Dreiser's social and political activities in the thirties has been called into question by several critics. In the very uncomplimentary section on Dreiser in *The Dream of Success*, Kenneth Lynn regards these actions as a bogus humanitarianism, which resulted from the novelist's loss of his own savings in the bank failures of 1929, and his subsequent animosity toward the bankers. Dreiser's motivations were always sufficiently complex that there may be some truth in Lynn's charges. He did begin to deride the rich with increasing vehemence during this period. A growing envy of the rich may account in part for his satiric portrait of Sondra in *An American Tragedy*. But to regard revenge as the sole explanation of his charitable activities is to disregard the entire trend of Dreiser's thought as it evolved after the publication of *An American Tragedy*. His ranting against the rich can more justly be attributed to his emotional commitment to the oppressed.

Lionel Trilling presents a more serious charge. He attributes Dreiser's compassion, the "great brooding pity" of which certain critics speak, to an excess of self-pity: "His pity is to be questioned: pity is to be judged by kind, not amount, and Dreiser's pity—*Jennie Gerhardt* provides the only exception—is either destructive of its object or it is self-pity."[15] Dreiser was, in fact, often given to speaking sadly of his own deprivations. Certainly there was an element of self-pity in his makeup. But just as certainly this personal element is present in the most praiseworthy humanitarians. Not only does Trilling miss the mark in his insistence that Dreiser's compassion represents only self-pity but also he grants the single exception to Dreiser's most obviously sentimental work. Dreiser's final vindication, however, must lie in his unstinting social campaigning during the thirties and early forties. For over ten years he devoted himself to this work, abandoning fiction, his vehicle for working out personal problems, and writing only when obliged by events. A man is not likely to give himself so actively for the benefit of others if he is wallowing in self-pity. Moreover, by the later thirties, his philosophy and his devotion to causes were beginning to converge. He may well have been sensitive to the relation of his own diminishing desires to the expansion of his social consciousness when he edited *The Living Thoughts of Thoreau* in 1938. He chose as his opening selection the Concord philosopher's statement: "Not till we are lost, in other words, not till we have lost the world, do we begin to find ourselves, and realize where we are and the infinite extent of our relations."

Although Dreiser was capable of genuine humanitarian service during the thirties, this is not to say that he had attained unalloyed wisdom. In several of his social tracts published during this period, he spread thin his analytical abilities, posing as a qualified commentator on economics, politics, education, finance, religion, international affairs, and a score of other subjects. As often as not, Dreiser's intelligence was compromised by bitterness. In *Tragic America* (1931), he attacked the wealthy with a silly petulance, praised Mussolini for his persecution of religion, called organized charity a vast racket, and castigated those who do not practice birth control as "among the most degraded representatives of society today, the poorest and the most unfit" (p. 267). In 1934 he defended an anti-Semitic article he had written for *The Spectator* by accusing the Jews of being "pagan," an adjective that he had used elsewhere to compliment his mother.[16] He also suggested that every Jew marry a Gentile in order to eradicate the "Jewish problem." One of the reasons for his resignation as co-editor of *The Spectator* was his shocked discovery that one of his colleagues was a Catholic. When he published *America is Worth Saving* in 1941, his blind hatred for "the English snobs" led him to accuse them of being far worse than Hitler. In reacting against bigotry, he often answered with his own blind bigotry, hardening his heart whenever his prejudices were threatened. That these old hatreds should not be diminished at a time when he was growing in humanitarian concern is a troublesome piece in what Granville Hicks once called "the Dreiser puzzle."

Despite the inconsistencies and petty prejudices that were sometimes embarrassingly prevalent in his arguments, however, he was nearly always during this period asserting the reality of human dignity, intemperate as some of his judgments may have been. He had conquered a good deal of the self-absorption that had reached its peak with the writing of *The "Genius,"* and he was now seeking meaning in the larger context of society. The importance of this development toward the altered perspective of *The Bulwark* and *The Stoic* is crucial. Dreiser was no longer himself the victim of an inflamed imagination. Because he was spending so much time on the many causes to which he had committed himself, he was much less absorbed by the restless search for fulfillment. During this period he had discovered that it takes action, not just compassion, to help the poor, and that action could help one escape the loneliness engendered by absorption in personal desires. It was a discovery that paved the way toward the greater spiritual peace of his last years.

At the same time that Dreiser was aligning himself to social causes, he began to study science seriously in the hope of finding the key to the always fascinating mysteries of existence. Ever since his parochial school days when he lamented the absence from the curriculum of chemistry, botany, and physics, he had been attracted to the scientific method. He became increasingly convinced in the late 1920s that science, especially the natural sciences, provides the only viable source of reliable information about man and his meaning. In 1928 he began to visit the biological laboratory at Woods Hole in Massachusetts, and the first question he put to the scientists was: "Do you believe in God?" In a letter to Mr. and Mrs. Franklin Booth, on 7 July 1928, he wrote that he had interviewed twelve of the two hundred scientists at Woods Hole, and that they did not believe in God: "They are all mechanists & in so far as life is concerned hopeless[.] It is a good show—sometimes—but ends for man here[.]"[17] Nine days later he wrote excitedly to Booth of what he had subsequently learned from other biologists and in his own studies with the microscope:

I have met and listened to and cross-examined some fifty men,—a fascinating group. They are not all mechanists, tell Franklin. Some are agnostics, some mystics, some of a reverent and even semi-religious turn. Personally I am awed and so amazed by the processes visible to the eye that I grow decidedly reverent.[18]

An article in *The Collecting Net*, a Woods Hole publication, notes Dreiser's visit and remarks on the charismatic intellectual curiosity which the novelist displayed whenever he was introduced to respected scientists:

Mr. Dreiser, who is intensely interested in present-day relations between religion and science, has spent his time since his arrival in talking with various scientists concerning their work, their aims, and their philosophies. He has that rare talent, developed in his earlier experiences as a newspaper reporter, of asking questions which require hours of enthusiastic monologue to answer. Silent scientists have burst into profuse verbiage at his questions, to explain themselves. Timid scientists with inferiority complexes have talked of biological ambitions for hours at a time. Ordinary, normal scientists have lifted their feet to the table, hunched themselves deep into their chairs, and discussed pros and cons, past and future. Mr. Dreiser sits, profoundly interested, and listens. [19]

The lessons of Woods Hole were fresh in his mind when, on 5 September, Dreiser wrote to Ruth Epperson Kennell, his guide on the trip to Russia and a professed atheist. He pointed out that she "should be aware of the vast difference between religion and dogmatic religion." The former, which Dreiser implied Miss Kennell ought to respect, constitutes "a response to as well as an awe or reverence before the beauty and wisdom of creative energy."[20] On 10 October, in the first of a long series of letters to scientists, he wrote to John Churchman of the Cornell Medical Laboratory of the "remarkable and mysterious activities of nature" which could be demonstrated through the microscope. [21]

Despite this early enthusiasm, however, Dreiser was far from being a convinced believer in a Creative Force. In the years between his first visit to Woods Hole and his changed perspective of the late thirties, many doubts persisted, and fundamental conflicts remained unresolved. In a statement of belief for the *Bookman* late in 1928, he asserted that his confusion seemed insurmountable:

> I can make no comment on my work or my life that holds either interest or import for me. Nor can I imagine any explanation or interpretation of any life, my own included, that would be either true—or important, if true. Life is to me too much a welter and play of inscrutable forces to permit, in my case at least, any significant comment. . . . In short I catch no meaning from all I have seen, and pass quite as I came, confused and dismayed. [22]

Dreiser was never satisfied with confusion, however. Indeed, his agitated search for answers to ultimate questions sometimes left him exhausted. In a letter to Emmanuel Morris late in 1929, Dreiser expressed relief that he had finally given up questioning the possibility of an afterlife: "I find acceptance of the idea of complete dissolution not so much comforting as restful. It means not a little to me to be done with bothering about the hereafter and so concerning myself with today."[23] The introduction to "Giff," a short story printed in *A Gallery of Women* in 1929, reveals his impatience with the slowness of science to provide ultimate answers. Dreiser felt that the clairvoyance of the gypsy fortune teller who is the subject of the story represented an instance of the kind that scientists were too hesitant to credit. "Beyond the material or electrical face of life—its remotest and most abstruse and to me mystical atoms or etherons or quantums—moves something which, if not less mystical, is still less divisible and quite possibly more real—an all-pervasive intention or plan, if not necessarily wisdom." Until someone humble enough to admit the validity of foreknowledge comes along, said Dreiser, we will have to be content with "chance" and "accident" in the explanation of phenomena (p. 262).

One of Dreiser's favorite plays was Eugene O'Neill's *Strange Interlude*, first produced and published in 1928. O'Neill, who later served briefly as a co-editor of *The American Spectator* with Dreiser, sent him a beautiful special edition of the stream-of-consciousness drama. The play's anguished characters, personifications of infinite desire, were well calculated to appeal to Dreiser. But it was the playwright's definition of human lives as "strange dark interludes in the electrical display of God" which must have especially struck him at this time. It was a definition that meshed with his own developing scientific-religious speculation. His general correspondence during the early thirties is sprinkled with appreciative references to the play.

A new willingness to be counted among those who could lend credence to religious explanations of existence is signaled in a letter Dreiser wrote to the English novelist Thomas Burke in 1930. Burke had written him to relate what he deemed a humorous incident he had witnessed in London's Hyde Park. An "earnest exponent of hellfire" had been haranguing the crowd when an interrupter had shouted that "'Theodore Dreiser says there ain't a God.'" When the religionist had expressed ignorance about Dreiser's identity, the interrupter had trumpeted his vindication indignantly: "'There y'are! He comes here pretending to teach other people, and he's so ignorant he don't know who Theodore Dreiser is.'" Dreiser ignored the humor in Burke's incident but troubled to lecture him: "I only hope that the assertion that I do not believe in a God in the old sense is not widened so as to exclude a creative energy which works well enough in certain ways although not as the believers in an all good being would have it."[24]

The theory of existence that Dreiser extrapolated from his biological research is included in "The Myth of Individuality," an essay he
wrote for the *American Mercury* in 1934. In it, Dreiser argued that some
mysterious force was working through man, living all life, and that individuality was a figment of man's imagination. He comes very close
here to defining the nature of the Creative Force he was ultimately to
posit, asserting that: "All creative thought, in man or animal or vege-
table, can but revert to the one, unoriginal, unindividual, almost
commonplace thing, the mystery of our existence, or the unified
reality behind it." Later he asks what force could produce natural cata-
clysms such as earthquakes, and he answers: "Only the eternal individual and none other, since from it—and none other—all life as well
as all 'thinking' on the part of life has proceeded, and from the very
first." "The Myth of Individuality," moreover, reveals the basis for his
changed social thought. Man "as a unit" cannot endure: "It is only as a
fraction of a multitude such as a race that he is able to exist as a so-
called unit." The essay ends with the assertion that life is "a good show
put on by something which seems to be dubious as to whether such a
show is worthwhile or not," a view not unlike O'Neill's at the conclusion of *Strange Interlude*. A quotation from Emerson's "Brahma" is
appended to "The Myth of Individuality."[25]

Dreiser's need for affirmation regardless of the evidence is made
clear by a prose poem he wrote in 1934 and sent first to the Reverend
Eliot White, and then, in a slightly different version, to Ralph Fabri
marked "for your private breviary." In the version sent to Fabri, Man is
portrayed as the only source of religious hope:

If only there were some kind God whose sanctuary were in a Church or many
Churches, or in the pure sweet places of the hills or the mountains! Yet only
in the vagrant heart of man is this dream of Him. Contemplating wild nature
as we must, the dream is groundless. There is none who in our extremity
cries, "Come unto me ye who are weary laden." Nature, machine-like, works
definitely and heartlessly, if in the main beautifully. Hence, if we, as individuals, do not make this dream of a God or what He stands for to us, real, in
our thoughts and deeds—then He is not real or true. If you wish a loving and
helpful God to exist and to have mercy, be Him. There is no other way.[26]

During 1935, Dreiser wrote numerous letters to biologists, professors of genetics, and physicists asking for their observations of life

forces. Most often his questions concerned the possibility of an ordered universe. For example, he wrote to Calvin Bridges, whom he had met at Woods Hole, asking:

Exactly what is meant by the principle of uncertainty in connection with microscopic processes, and does that principle imply a possibly irremediable disorder as opposed to order in the universe? I note the constant use of the phrase "ordered universe," and of course the word "cosmos" as representing the entire universe seems to imply a complete absence of disorder. Is there no room for the word chaos in connection with the universe? Even to the extent of a temporary chaos? Is there any evidence in sight so far that the universe has been partially, let alone entirely, chaotic?[27]

The same questions were put to Robert Andrews Millikan, who had won the Nobel prize in 1923 for isolating and measuring the electron. In 1936 he wrote Dr. George W. Crile requesting further information on the theory of existence expounded in his *The Phenomena of Life*. Crile had contended that life was the result of radiant and electrical energy.[28] Dreiser's habit now was to look for a religious dimension in the discoveries of science. When Joel Stebbins guided him through the solar system one evening at the Mt. Wilson Observatory, Dreiser greatly appreciated Stebbins's command of facts combined with his poetic appreciation of the phenomena of nature. He wrote to thank Stebbins for his "personal and poetic and affectionate response to the night sky outside, and . . . illuminating explanations and deductions." To Dreiser, Stebbins had represented the ideal man of science, as is illustrated by the compliment with which the novelist ended his letter: "Awe and reverence, as you well know, walk with deep understanding. I felt the three transfuse in all that you had to say."[29] In 1937, he wrote a long, unpublished essay about the scientists at Cold Spring Harbor which further illustrated his developing ideal:

Thus, after noting the character of these men and women, their work, their achievements, I am profoundly awed. How truly respectable. How honorable. Not that men should work for little or nothing in this world, unless they are deeply moved so to do, but that in the face of the greed and the clamor for wealth, show, parade, meritless notoriety there should be such as these willing to work day after day, year after year, until death suddenly overtakes them somewhere in order that some problem in connection with the mystery of life, some ill that besets humanity should be ferreted out—the how, not the why—and its possible cure."[30]

Two "mystical" events in the same year moved Dreiser closer to his climactic affirmation of a Creative Force. While walking in the woods in the summer, he had come across a puff adder, and believing it to be a harmful species, killed it. He later learned that it was harmless and felt remorse for his action. The next time he came across a puff adder he spoke to it reassuringly and sensed that it understood. From that moment dated Dreiser's conviction that man could hold communion with animals. The other event impressed upon him finally the reality of a universal order in nature. After spending a day in the biological laboratory at Cold Spring Harbor, he emerged and was struck by the beauty of a patch of flowers growing nearby, the same species that he had been studying under the microscope. He later wrote to Marguerite Tjader Harris of the importance of the incident:

Here was the same beautiful design and the lavish, exquisite detail that I had been seeing all day through the microscope. Suddenly it was plain to me that there must be a divine, creative Intelligence behind all this. It was after that, that I began to feel differently about the universe. I saw not only the intelligence, but the love and care that goes into all created things.[31]

In 1939, he wrote that "no intentional evil or cruelty" could be attributed to the Creative Force as he was beginning to understand it.[32] He was less certain about man's intention, and he questioned scientists about their theories on free will. In 1940, for example, he wrote to Gustav Stromberg, a physicist and mathematician at the Mt. Wilson Observatory, whose book *The Soul of the Universe* he had read. Dreiser wanted to know more about Stromberg's hypothesis on "partial free will." Two letters written within eighteen months of his questioning Stromberg indicate that he did not yet believe that man was either free or substantially responsible for his actions.[33] Whatever his doubts about man, he now believed in a benevolent Creative Force. He summed up this new feeling about the universe in an essay called "My Creator," written in 1943 and since published in the *Notes on Life*, the elaborate compilation of philosophical and scientific speculations which, along with his social causes, consumed much of his energy during the late 1930s and early 1940s. The essay sprang from Dreiser's appreciation of an avocado tree in the yard of his Los Angeles home. The beauty of the tree had led him to a new level of reverence for creation.

And so studying this matter of genius in design and beauty, as well as the wisdom of contrast and interest in this so carefully engineered and regulated universe—this amazing process called living—I am moved not only to awe but to reverence for the Creator of the same, concerning whom—his or its presence in all things from worm to star to thought—I meditate constantly, even though it be, as I see it, that my import to this, my Creator, can be as nothing, or less, if that were possible.

Yet awe I have. And, at long last, profound reverence for so amazing and esthetic and wondrous a process that may truly have been, and for all that I know, may yet continue to be forever and forever. An esthetic and wondrous process of which I might pray—and do—to remain the infinitesimal part of that same that I now am. [P. 333.]

Dreiser had come to affirm his faith in a Creator whose existence he had questioned yet sought to establish from his youth. The final embodiment of his religious thought is to be found in the posthumously published fruits of his last years, *The Bulwark* and the concluding section of *The Stoic*.

8 / The Bulwark

DREISER gave both his new faith and the principles he developed
from it their first fictional frame in *The Bulwark*. In the benevolent
Creative Force from which his Quaker hero, Solon Barnes, derives
solace and even joy in the face of family tragedies and his own imminent death, Dreiser had discovered an object commensurate with
man's capacity for longing. Moreover, his endorsement of the love-
service ethic, embraced at the end of the novel by Solon's prodigal
daughter Etta, signifies his final determination that dedication to giving, when chosen on the basis of mature experience, could offer an
enduring worldly fulfillment in contrast to the fleeting satisfaction of
self-interest. Yet, for all of the impressive evidence of logical development in Dreiser that *The Bulwark* contains, it was long his most mis-
understood book and it remains his most undervalued.

Because Dreiser's affirmation of spirit came about quietly in the late
1930s, the posthumous publication of *The Bulwark* in March 1946 was
greeted with considerable surprise and some consternation. He had
not published a novel or very much fiction of any kind since *An American Tragedy* twenty years earlier. What had reached the public in the
intervening years had been mostly intemperate political tracts. Only
a few of his close friends knew of his philosophic change of heart.
Primarily on the basis of his six earlier novels, Dreiser's reputation
among the critics was that of an uncompromising mechanist and
amoralist whose preference was for elaborate documentation and
gigantic canvases. Both the matter and the manner of *The Bulwark* are
markedly different. Lean in its structure and spare in its details, it
incorporates a message of tested faith and resolute optimism. The
new economy of method derived not only from its appropriateness to

subject matter but also from Dreiser's growing impatience with par-
ticulars and his wish to accentuate the final section of the novel in
which he dramatizes his own arduously reached belief in life's ultimate
meaning.

Part of the misunderstanding of *The Bulwark* grew out of the circumstances of its composition. Dreiser began the novel over thirty
years before it appeared. The idea for the story had come from a
young Pennsylvania Quaker woman, Anna Tatum, whom he met in
1912 and with whom he had a brief relationship. Anna Tatum told
Dreiser about her father's mostly unavailing attempts to preserve the
Quaker ideal of simplicity and stewardship against the encroach-
ments of the modern world, especially in his children's worldly ways
and his own business dealings. The conflict between the Friends' ideal
of selflessness and American acquisitiveness seemed to Dreiser the
raw material of formidable fiction. And in the religious patriarch
unable to transmit his values to his children, he also planned to reuse
his experiences with his own father. He began the novel in 1914, and
by 1916 John Lane had prepared a salesman's dummy in the expectation of its imminent publication. Then began a series of delays until
he suspended the work entirely in 1920 to begin *An American Tragedy*.
Although he always intended to get back to work on the Quaker
novel, it was not until the forties that he decided he would at last attempt to complete both of his long delayed projects, *The Bulwark* and
The Stoic. In 1914, however, he had conceived the title of *The Bulwark*
as ironic, masking a study of religious conviction as illusion, an ex-
posé of the mental poverty of the dogmatic and moralistic religionist.
Thus, the critics had been expecting for three decades a fault-finding,
antireligious novel. But by the time Dreiser induced his long-time
friend and sometime secretary, Marguerite Tjader Harris, to come to
California to assist him in completing the novel in 1942, he had decided to change the direction of the book in a way that would reflect
his own very different way of looking at life. Instead of holding religion up to ridicule, he sympathetically chronicles the lives of pious
Quaker parents and their children.

Dreiser had been fully introduced to Quakerism through his association in the thirties with Rufus Jones of the American Friends' Service
Committee. The two had worked together on behalf of the surviving
victims of the Spanish Civil War. Scattered references throughout
Dreiser's works indicate that he had taken some interest in the Society

of Friends much earlier. Carrie had been casually called a Quakeress. The kind but naive jailer who talks with Cowperwood during his imprisonment in *The Financier* is also a Quaker. In *Hey Rub-a-Dub-Dub,* however, Dreiser had accused the Quakers of suppressing sex. He had often spoken in the past of the impossible Quaker ideal. But when Rufus Jones induced him to read *The Book of Discipline* and John Woolman's *Journal,* the simple faith impressed him forcibly as an antidote to American materialism. In December 1938 he wrote Jones that he had come to regard Quakerism as "the direct road to—not so much a world religion as a world appreciation of the force that provides us all with this amazing experience called life."[1] One month later, he wrote Jones again and his enthusiasm was even more pronounced: "I feel the Quaker Faith is the only true exposition, and, in so far as it is carried out, realization of Christianity in the modern world. However, when I say Christianity, I mean social ethics and equity introduced into life according to scientific principles as I now, at last, understand those to be." He concluded that mankind "needs a revival of this kind and there is nothing else that it needs so much."[2] A week earlier he had written to a professor of biology at Whittier College that Woolman's *Journal* provided "the greatest service and encouragement to all seeking an intelligible faith." He especially appreciated the 1871 edition of the *Journal* which included an introduction by John Greenleaf Whittier, and he suggested a revival of that edition. Dreiser deemed the essay by Whittier, himself a most "distinguished" Friend, a moving and important Quaker document in its own right.[3] The incitement of the personality of Rufus Jones himself in Dreiser's attraction for Quakerism is suggested in an admiring letter which Dreiser wrote two years before his death: "When I think of you and contrast you with the average so-called Christian, I am inclined to use language that your temperament would not countenance."[4]

What Dreiser had come to appreciate were essentially those aspects described by the Quaker historian Frederick B. Tolles as "the four freedoms" of The Society of Friends: "freedom from materialism, from the reliance upon *things,* which deadens the soul; freedom from pride, from an unwarranted sense of superiority, which leads to unjust discrimination among men; freedom from self-centeredness, which denies our interdependence as men; freedom from hatred, which leads to violence and war."[5] His fiction had always exposed the falsity of material goals even though they might be irresistible and he had al-

ways protested the chasm between the rich and the poor. Lately he
had come to see that the materialism and the "sense of superiority" he
lamented were caused by the "self-centeredness" that he no longer felt
inevitable. And his rejection of violence took the form of humanitarian service during the Spanish Civil War and his efforts to keep
America out of World War II.

When Dreiser returned to the manuscript of *The Bulwark* in the
forties, he used much of the earlier version of the novel as the middle
section of the new version and sandwiched it between a new beginning which relates several incidents from Solon's boyhood and a new
ending which imputes Dreiser's own spiritual affirmation to his hero.
In documenting Solon's boyhood, Dreiser took several incidents and
background material from Rufus Jones's books about his youth, *Finding
the Trail of Life* and *A Small Town Boy.*[6] Like *The "Genius," The Bulwark* opens
with a scene from a wedding, but instead of using the words of the
ceremony as an ironic introduction to the story of an amoralist, this
time Dreiser borrows from the ritual the promises of love and honor
as a preface to a story of genuine, joyful marital stability. Solon Barnes
and Benecia Wallin promise to devote themselves to each other at the
Friends' meeting house in Dukla, Pennsylvania, but before Dreiser describes their lives together, he introduces a one-hundred-page
flashback which documents the history of the Barnes family up to the
time of Solon's marriage. His parents had been honest and industrious
Friends in a small Maine community, and thus Solon had experienced
a loving home in which "the fire of faith was ever alight" (p. 3). The
seeds of the potential destruction of that faith two generations later
had been sown when Solon's father had been called to handle the
estate of a widowed sister-in-law. An imposing house and sixty-acre
grounds called Thornbrough, which would eventually be willed to
Solon's father, went with the responsibility—causing him some difficulty because of the ostentation of the property in conflict with the
Friends' stress on simplicity. But he had decided to restore the house
little by little with money obtained by selling crops. Soon he had
begun to enjoy the echoes of social grandeur about the place. He had
retained his Quaker integrity, however, in his principal desire to help
others. When the estate and considerable wealth are willed to Solon
after his marriage to Benecia, the erosion of the Quaker precepts in
their children is swift and devastating.

Solon and Benecia, patterned after Dreiser's image of his mother, address themselves to the stewardship of the Lord's gifts which they believe the possession of wealth to oblige. Solon conducts himself with an almost savage integrity as an official of a Philadelphia bank. He is contrasted to his colleagues, who have a far more pragmatic approach to the bank's affairs, desiring more wealth and power for themselves. Solon is indeed an anomaly in the jungle of high finance. His staunch honesty is based in part on his devotion to the Quaker ethic; in part it is owing to his naiveté and narrowness. These last two traits are prefigured early in the novel when Solon as a boy in Maine witnesses a campaign waged by the Friends against certain saloons and houses of prostitution, which had sprung up in a poor section of town. Solon's sheltered and comfortable existence bars him from any understanding of the circumstances involved:

In Solon's case, having heard so much concerning good and evil as words, and having personally seen so little of evil in the form here displayed, he could not possibly look back of the surface appearance to the less obvious forces of ignorance, poverty, and the lack of such restraining and yet elevating influences as had encompassed his own life. He had no least conception of what from childhood had surrounded these ignorant people. He did not know life. Rather, to him, all those who had so sinned were thoroughly bad, their souls irredeemable. [P. 35.]

Solon's education in the way of the world is slow and painful. Trusting everyone, he is shocked at the slightest hint of dishonesty in his business associates. The first of the events that are to effect his awakening occurs when the son of a Quaker acquaintance, whom Solon has placed in the bank, embezzles money. Unaware of the impending tragedy in his own family, he cannot understand the boy's excuse that a narrow home life had caused him to yield to the temptation "to embark on a freer, happier existence" (p. 117). Thus Dreiser reiterates his contention that the narrowly religious person is often unaware of the more disturbing realities of life.

In Solon's relationship with his own children, moreover, he is ultimately betrayed by his lack of unspiritual experience. He cannot understand the lure of the great world for the generation of the twenties. Of his five children, he seems to understand only his priggish son Orville, whose circumspect behavior impresses him. The others cause him varying degrees of hurt. Isobel is plain, introspective, and decidedly unhappy. Dorothea is beautiful, but vain and interested chiefly in social climbing. Etta and Stewart, the two most eager for life, are to Solon the most painful enigmas. Both rebel against the confinements of their father's narrow precepts, but in different ways. Etta's is an artistic nature, given to romantic dreams, intuitive and poetic. She is a representative Dreiserian dreamer in the tradition of Carrie and Eugene Witla. After being told a beautiful story as a child, she creates "a realm of her own so beautiful that it was a thing for tears: halls and palaces of chalcedony and jasper rising out of plains where grew flowers more marvelous than ever any actually to be seen" (p. 130). She is clearly not a girl to be satisfied with a narrow conception of life, and when her father chastizes her for reading "immoral French novels," her decision to escape is complete. She steals her mother's jewels to finance her flight with a friend to the University of Wisconsin, where she hopes to study art and literature. Her father follows her with the idea of bringing her back, and the trip to Madison is another step in Solon's reeducation. On the train he meets a middle-aged teacher returning to the university for the summer session. He impresses Solon with his praise of the education offered there and his disclosure that even ministers are enrolled. Solon had regarded the school as a godless place, but the seemingly sincere stranger leads him to doubt his preconception. When he meets his daughter and she resists his entreaties to return home with him, he forgives her theft and allows her to stay for the summer. After the session at the university, however, Etta engages in a more serious project. She and her friend go to Greenwich Village, where Etta, unbeknown to her family, embarks on a love affair with an artist.

During this affair, events in the life of Solon's younger son precipitate the central tragedy of the novel. Despite the difference in their backgrounds, Stewart Barnes and Clyde Griffiths have much in common, and they suffer a similar fate. A comparison of Stewart's and Clyde's tragedies shows the growth during the thirties in Dreiser's conception of individual culpability. Solon's narrow outlook leads Stewart to rebel, as Clyde had against his evangelist parents. When he is told that all theaters are evil, he seeks out burlesque houses to flaunt his independence. He resents his father's religion, also, because it would hamper his "overwhelming hunger for physical sex gratification" (p. 244). He soon discards the Inner Light, the Quaker conception of the divine presence in every individual, and becomes embroiled in a number of escapades with school chums. They borrow a flashy car and pick up girls whom the boys know to be of easy virtue. Stewart, given only a token allowance by his father, steals to finance these forbidden pleasures. On one occasion, the boys attempt to drug a girl named Psyche Tanzer who has resisted them in the past. One of Stewart's companions, having stolen a sedative from his mother, administers the drug to the reticent girl, not knowing that she has a weak heart. The girl falls into a coma and is abandoned by the three boys, who soon find themselves apprehended and charged with murder. Although Stewart had not been directly responsible for the crime, he had consented with the others to abandon the girl, a decision similar to Clyde's allowing Roberta Alden to drown in *An American Tragedy*. But whereas in the earlier novel Clyde is portrayed as the victim of an unfair social system and hence absolved from total responsibility, in *The Bulwark* Stewart is "tortured to his very soul by regret and sorrow," and he realizes that he can "never escape the jury of his own mind, of his father's mind: the judgment of the Inner Light" (pp. 291, 294). Dreiser's sympathy for Stewart stops short of a dispute over the self-imposed guilty verdict. Pursued by conscience, the lad kills himself in prison.

Stewart's death triggers a number of events in the novel which further illustrate Dreiser's changed conception of individual responsibility. Etta returns to her family, blaming herself for setting the example for Stewart by running away and by lying about the innocence of her relationship with the artist. She asks her parents' forgiveness for her sins and vows to devote herself to making amends through loving care for them. Solon's cousin Rhoda is conscience-stricken for having introduced Dorothea to society and for unwittingly assisting in Stewart's downfall by supplying him with money against his father's wishes. She had directed Solon's children to the false goals of American society.

Most important of all is the effect of Stewart's death on his father. Of all Solon's experiences, this is the greatest blow to his religious convictions, and his own sense of guilt is acute. In the novel's most moving scene, he bends over the casket of his dead boy, peers down at the face, "so suggestive of eager desire," and questions himself:

As he viewed him, and all these features in turn, each curve and hollow place and sad, suggestive line, weeping in silence but in his heart only, his eyes dry, suddenly this thought came to him: What if, in so urgently seeking to sway him toward the right, he had, after all, failed to do all that he might have done—his full duty by him! Or perhaps (the thought was tormenting to him in this hour) might he not have been more gentle, loving, persuading, as the Book of Discipline of his faith so earnestly cautioned parents to be? Had it not been his bounden duty to exhaust the last measure of tenderness and liberality in seeking to save his son, rather than to drive him, spy on him, irritate him with his constant queries, trying to compel him, by sheer will and strength, to do this or that, when love—love and prayer—might have done so much more? Had not his own mother shown him that, and if so, why had he failed? Yet it was hard at times, as he now knew, to see exactly what to do and how to do it. [P. 298.]

Weeping before the casket, Solon experiences a "sudden and deep spiritual uncertainty." He questions why God has forsaken him. But his dark night of the soul has barely begun with Stewart's death. His beloved Benecia, stricken by her son's tragedy, dies and leaves the Quaker bulwark bereft of his life's greatest treasure. Solon is left to contemplate the extent of his guilt in the cataclysm that has struck his family, and at this point his spiritual growth begins. The result of his meditations is not despair, but an intense spiritual renewal and a growth in human tenderness which previously lay hidden beneath a stern morality. His daughters wonder at the profound peace he seems to have found, and it soon becomes apparent that the source of this peace lies in several of his "mystical" experiences which attest to the reality of the Inner Light. While walking near Lever Creek, a lovely stream that cuts through Thornbrough and on the banks of which he had first met Benecia, Solon suddenly apprehends the order of the universe. Dreiser transmutes his own epiphany when he discovered what he thought to be the universal design in microcosm in the patch of flowers outside the biological laboratory at Cold Spring Harbor into Solon's parallel discovery when he comes across a beautiful insect devouring a blossom:

One day, walking the paths around Lever Creek, Solon was arrested by the various vegetative and insect forms obviously devised and energized by the Creative Force that created all things in apparently endless variety of designs and colors. Here now on a long-stalked plant reaching up about four feet, and on the end of a small twig that bore a small bud, obviously a blossom of some type, was perched, and eating the bud, an exquisitely colored and designed green fly so green and translucent that it reminded one of an emerald, only it was of a much more tender and vivid texture. The green emerald, he now recalled as he looked at the fly, was a hard, unchanging stone, but this insect was changeful, in that it moved, now its minute feet, now its wings, now its head and mouth. It was industriously nourishing itself, at the same time that it was watchful—a variety of facts which for the first time in his life now arrested Solon, for although he had been about the fields of the region, as well as the lawns of his property, he had never seen one such green fly, and so had never paused to study one. And what was more, now that he did so, his mind was swiftly filled with wonder, not only at the beauty of the fly, but at the wisdom and the art of the Creative Impulse that had busied itself with the creation of this physical gem.

Why was this beautiful creature, whose design so delighted him, compelled to feed upon another living creature, a beautiful flower? For obviously, as it ate, it was destroying the bud of this plant, and in so far as he could see or know, the plant had no way of defending itself. Which was intended to live—the fly, the bud, or both? And now so fascinated was he by his own meditations on this problem that he not only gazed and examined the plant and the fly, but proceeded to look about for other wonders. And in so doing, he observed the various types of small fish in the water—the very type that years before he had sought to catch in a dip net for the young Benecia, now herself blended with these mysterious forces. And yet above him, among the limbs of the trees, the birds were flying, and in the air here and there was a butterfly that previously had been nothing more than a grub in a cocoon— yet designed to live and endure and more, fly like a wingèd blossom, but for a brief summer only.

Then, after bending down and examining a blade of grass here, a climbing vine there, a minute flower, lovely and yet as inexplicable as his green fly, he turned in a kind of religious awe and wonder. Surely there must be a Creative Divinity, and so a purpose, behind all of this variety and beauty and tragedy of life. For see how tragedy had descended upon him, and he still had faith, and would have. [Pp. 316–17.]

The message carried by the green fly is that the beneficent Creative Force dispenses a transcendent beauty based on transience which strikes the human observer as cruel and destructive. The passage reveals the novelist's profound debt to Thoreau. The extent of the Concord philosopher's influence is suggested by comparing Solon Barnes's experience at Lever Creek with the following entry in Thoreau's *Journal*: "It is remarkable that animals are often obviously, manifestly, related to the plants which they feed upon or live among,—as caterpillars, butterflies, tree-toads, partridges, chewinks,—and this afternoon I noticed a yellow spider on a goldenrod; as if every condition might have its expression in some form of animated being."[7] The green-fly passage in *The Bulwark* invites comparison with the epilogue

of *The Financier* in which Dreiser reads the activities of the all-devour-
ing black grouper as evidence of a possible malevolent intent behind
the mechanistic reality. This time, the key concept is purposeful
design as opposed to malevolent mechanism. Dreiser's affirmation
leads to Solon's apprehension of "the radiance" that tints not only the
"distant hilltops of the world," which Carrie had hoped to reach, but
also the very ground we tread.

Solon experiences another intensely spiritual moment which re-
fines his understanding of the Creative Force. Dreiser transfers his
own dialogue with the puff adder to his protagonist. The snake passes
knowingly over Solon's shoe, understanding that the man intends it
no harm. Some critics have used this snake incident as evidence of
Dreiser's naiveté or senility, but only recently animal researchers have
discovered that intention can be communicated from man to animals,
even snakes. Moreover, the incident has a valid relationship to the
main theme of the final part of the novel. The serpent, victim of a bad
press from the Bible to modern literature, is used here to illustrate the
infinite extent of our relations in a world animated by the benevolent
Creative Force. Earlier in the novel, in fact, the great Quaker thinker
George Fox is likened by Dreiser to the novelist's favorite saint, the
friend of animals, Francis of Assisi. Solon reads into the snake incident the same lesson that Dreiser had deduced from his recent years
of scrutinizing the Creative Force. He tells Etta the meaning of the
snake's behavior:

"I mean that good intent is of itself a universal language, and if our intention is good, all creatures in their particular way understand, and so it was
that this puff adder understood me just as I understood it. It had no ill intent,
but was only afraid. And then, my intent being not only good but loving, it
understood me and had no fear, but came back to me, crossing the toe of my
shoe. And now I thank God for this revelation of His universal presence and
His good intent toward all things—all of His created world. For otherwise
how would it understand me, and I it, if we were not both a part of Himself?"
[Pp. 318–19.]

Several critics have complained of the inclusion of these mystical elements in *The Bulwark*, but it is difficult to see how Dreiser could have
managed his message without them. Donald Pizer, for example, finds
that Solon's discovery of transcendental faith at the close of the novel
is not persuasive because: "fiction is a poor vehicle for the representa-

tion of religious miracles unless the psychological characterization and emotional texture of the work have prepared us to accept the reality of the supernatural."[8] The question of whether Solon's experiences with the green fly and the puff adder constitute "religious miracles" aside, the psychological characterization and the emotional texture of the novel are, in fact, eminently suitable to his rediscovery of faith. Despite his roles as a banker and a father, which Pizer thinks at least partially disqualify him as a mystic, he is, after all, a firm believer in the Inner Light and a pious Quaker throughout the novel. Pizer makes a more damaging, related point when he observes in the same critique that the language of Solon's response to nature is more appropriate to Dreiser than to the fictional Quaker.[9] There is a question of the violation of artistic decorum in Solon's references to the Creative Force, for example. By contrast, Etta's richly romantic nature is eminently suited to her poetic speculations about love and spirit. But the requisite emotional texture for the mystical conclusion of *The Bulwark* is established early in the novel when Solon's mother has several "supernatural" experiences. When her son as a child had been hovering near death as the result of an injury inflicted with an axe, she had gone into a trance while praying and had forecast that Solon would recover and render distinguished service to God. Later, she testifies at meeting about how her faith saved her child and thus effects the cure of another Quaker woman's son. Still later, she has a dream vision of Solon being thrown and injured by a previously docile mare, an event which foreshadows his impending tragedies. Even the matter of the seemingly gratuitous cruelty of nature in the green-fly passage is subtly related to the incident in which Solon as a child borrows a playmate's slingshot and, aiming for a pine cone, kills a mother catbird. The misfortune causes him to grieve intensely and his mother to ponder "the fact that so much ill could come about accidentally when plainly no cruelty or evil was intended" (p. 18).

Solon grows spiritually after his mystical experiences near the end of the novel, but his physical condition deteriorates. Soon it becomes apparent that he is dying of cancer. Etta gives up her affair with the artist and returns to minister to her father, whose last days are marked by an exemplary courage and a deep religious faith. All around him are greatly affected by the "spiritual beauty" that his dying days exemplify. But it is especially Etta whose life is transformed by her new relationship with her father. Her recognition of his spiritual peace, her own fulfillment in devoting herself to him and her reading of Woolman's *Journal* lead Etta to the formulation of a new point of view:

But now John Woolman and her father were helping her to understand something beyond human passion and its selfish desires and ambitions—the love and peace involved in the consideration of others—her father first and foremost. And so through her service to him she could see what it might mean to serve others, not only for reasons of family bonds or personal desires, but to answer human need. What love, what beauty might not lie there? [P. 331.]

Etta's discovery of the joy of fulfilling one's responsibilities to the human community was made possible because Dreiser had finally broken the tension between the selfish claims of the ego and the ideal of self-sacrifice in emulation of the pervasive benevolence of the Creative Force. In *Sister Carrie* he had tried with limited success to separate personal desire from an unworthy self-serving. In *The Bulwark*, he expresses his culminating belief that man's deepest longing is to love and serve his fellows. Etta Barnes makes this discovery. Recognizing her own need for affection and loyalty, she comes to see that she can evoke these qualities in others only by giving them herself. In the closing pages of *The Bulwark*, she discovers this infinite human connection and compares the love-service ethic to the restless seeking of personal pleasure about which Dreiser had so often written:

In this love and unity with all nature, as she now sensed, there was nothing fitful or changing or disappointing—nothing that glowed one minute and was gone the next. This love was rather as constant as nature itself, everywhere the same, in sunshine or in darkness, the filtered splendor of the dawn, the seeded beauty of the night. It was an intimate relation to the very heart of being. [P. 331.]

Thus, at the end of *The Bulwark*, Etta finds in selfless devotion and service the fulfillment that had eluded her in the great world, and Solon in his all-embracing love now sympathizes with, if he does not fully understand, the lure of material pleasures. It should be kept in mind, however, that each attains understanding through a process in which experience with worldly affairs is crucial. Etta moves from her Quaker background through romantic dreams to the actualization of her worldly desires and finally to a deeper commitment to the Inner Light and its moral imperatives. Solon's mature love of creation would not have been possible had it not been for his painful education in the way of the world, through Stewart's tragedy and Benecia's death, with which he must come to grips. *The Bulwark* shows that the world is desolate without the spiritual and that loving compassion must be grounded in an understanding of worldly temptations, this last a lesson which lifts the novel's principal players leagues beyond the other worldly heroine, Jennie Gerhardt.

Interpretations and estimates of *The Bulwark* have often been wildly divergent. In fact, the novel was suffused with controversy even before it was published. One of the most fascinating stories involving an American novel developed when Dreiser was completing the book in California. Having been unsuccessful in making significant progress on the project in 1942 and 1943, he arranged the following year for Marguerite Tjader Harris to move to Hollywood to assist him. Mrs. Harris had been associated with Dreiser sporadically since 1928, when she provided editorial assistance for *A Gallery of Women*. She had gone on to found the liberal journal *Direction* in the late 1930s, and Dreiser had contributed articles to the magazine. Helen Dreiser, who was enjoying her position as the most important woman in her husband's life, reluctantly approved of Mrs. Harris's new role as editorial assistant for *The Bulwark*. During 1944 and early 1945, Mrs. Harris helped Dreiser revise the material he had written between 1914 and 1920. Then she took his dictation of the sections from Etta's trip to Wisconsin through the end of the novel, and he cut the opening section which he had revised in the two preceding years.

When the work was completed, Dreiser decided to send the finished product to Louise Campbell, his editorial assistant for *An American Tragedy*, for possible additional editing. He also sent the manuscript to Donald Elder, an editor for Doubleday, Dreiser's contracted publisher. There then developed a complex debate by letter over the novel. By the time it subsided, a considerable correspondence had developed, and the participants had expanded to include Mrs. Harris, Helen Dreiser, and James T. Farrell. The subject of the controversy also broadened from that of excision and restoration of passages to the efficacy of Dreiser's religious ideas and even to the proper roles for the women in his life. Mrs. Campbell was of the opinion that the novel needed to be extensively revised—she was unaware of Mrs. Harris's editorial work—and asked Dreiser if she should proceed. He wrote her that she should send the manuscript to Farrell, a long-time fan of Dreiser's work, and a loyal friend in these later years. Meanwhile, Elder suggested making some cuts. Then Farrell responded in disagreement with Mrs. Campbell's negative attitude toward the novel. (She believed it was the product of a failing sensibility, although she did not tell Dreiser that.) But Farrell suggested in a long letter certain specific revisions. Dreiser then wrote Mrs. Campbell authorizing her to proceed with her own editing. When she completed the work, Dreiser sent it to Elder and asked him to return the earlier revision. But Elder was not entirely satisfied with Mrs. Campbell's job, feeling that she had cut too much. He asked and received Dreiser's permission to restore some of the material that she had cut. When he completed his work, he submitted his revision of Mrs. Campbell's revision for Dreiser's approval. He received not only the approval, but warm praise as well. By this time Dreiser was occupied with finishing *The Stoic*. Mrs. Harris was left to lament what she considered to be the damaging excision of some of the best religious passages. Helen had become jealous of Mrs. Harris. She felt that Mrs. Harris had exerted too much influence on Dreiser. [10]

The reviews of the published novel brought a new dimension to the divisiveness that the manuscript had engendered. The responses in the newspapers ran the gamut from ecstatic to abusive. For example, a reviewer for a Cleveland daily went so far as to contend that the novel "must inevitably take its place among the greatest books of our age," while a writer for a Dallas paper saw it as the work of "an artist destroying himself with a vengeance." Several newspaper reviewers implied that were not Dreiser the author, *The Bulwark* would have passed from the literary scene unremarked. (Perhaps the review Dreiser would have enjoyed most appeared in a small California paper. The reviewer, unaware that the novelist had died, made much of the fact that he was getting to be an old man. During his newspaper days, Dreiser had lost a job when he reviewed a theatrical performance that had never taken place because of a snow storm.) [11] The received critics were equally split in their evaluations. Robert Spiller judged the book to be "well conceived and carefully executed," representing its author in "his full creative power." Lionel Trilling, on the other hand, pronounced *The Bulwark* an emotional and intellectual disaster. [12] Many of the early responses were sharply divided even over basic interpretation. Some critics mistook Dreiser's intention as his original one of 1914, that of disparaging religion as a viable resource in the modern world. For example, John Lyndenberg wrote that at the conclusion of the novel, Solon is a "broken reed who has collapsed with his world."[13] This misconception persisted for a number of years, Charles Child Walcutt echoing Lyndenberg's judgment a decade later, for example: "Sister Carrie seeks a meaning in her experience which she cannot find. Solon Barnes has a meaning but he cannot live by it, and at the end of the book he is not unlike Carrie in wondering why events have happened as they have."[14] Leftist critic Annette Rubinstein also read the novel as an anti-religious tract and this interpretation has been maintained steadfastly by Dreiser's Communist admirers ever since.[15] On the other hand, George Snell early maintained that though Solon is "bludgeoned" by events, "he does not swerve from a belief in the ultimate certainty of divine truth," and thus remains a "bulwark of faith in a world tottering to ruin."[16] Robert Elias, who had the advantage of talking with Dreiser between 1937 and 1945, contended in his pioneering biography that Solon "instead of losing faith . . . gains a stronger one."[17] F. O. Matthiessen later called *The Bulwark* a religious novel about "Solon's rediscovery of Christian love."[18] This interpretation of Dreiser's intention has been generally accepted since the mid-sixties.

That those not familiar with Dreiser's development during the thirties should regard Solon as a "broken reed" is understandable. Like the Biblical Job, he has lost all that he has valued most in the world. When his daughters return to his side after Stewart's death, they notice the absence of his old moral conviction. When he dies, he seems on the surface to be despairing, for he murmurs to Etta: "'Daughter, what has become of that poor old man who was dying of cancer?'" (p. 332). But many of the early critics missed the significance of this question in relation to a previous incident in the novel. In the preceding chapter, Etta is reading a passage from Woolman's *Journal* which relates a significant experience in the Quaker saint's life. He had once been extremely sick, near death, when in a delirious state he had forgotten his name. During a vision, the voice of an angel had spoken to him, saying, "'John Woolman is dead.'" Later, he recovered and remembered the vision as well as his name, and he interpreted the announcement of his death as the dissolution of his will in repentance for sin. Solon's questioning of his identity, though mistaken by Etta as simply evidence that her father's mind is going, is surely meant to be an analogue of Woolman's vision. There can be no other reason for including the incident from the *Journal*. Furthermore, Solon's later statements are mostly rational, including a request to have a wall hanging which bears the motto so dear to his wife and himself—"In honor, preferring one another"—placed near his bed; several isolated statements made while his mind wanders, such as: "Men must be honest with God and with themselves"; "The poor and the banks!"; and "God talks directly to man when His help is needed"; and finally his last sentence to Etta, "If thee does not turn to the Inner Light, where will thee go?" (pp. 333–34). The statements reflect Solon's final acceptance of the doctrine of cosmic love. Further proof of Dreiser's attitude toward Solon is provided in the novelist's copy of Rufus Jones's *The Trail of Life in the Middle Years*. The Quaker humanitarian had sent Dreiser a copy upon his request for more information about the faith. In a passage devoted to John Woolman, Jones writes: "He carried farther than most have done the refining process which consumes the dross in the cleansing fire, and leaves the spirit pure and unalloyed, utterly humble, and freed from selfishness." Dreiser wrote in the margin: "Solon."[19] There is very little doubt that Dreiser regarded his protagonist as a real bulwark of faith, not as a "broken reed."

Beyond the question about the strength of Solon's conviction at the end of the novel, disagreement has surfaced from time to time over whether Dreiser really shared his protagonist's religious point of view. Although Solon's role as a spokesman for Dreiser was convincingly argued in Robert Elias's biography in 1948, some succeeding critics have insisted on divorcing the novelist from his creation. Charles Shapiro, for example, warns that Dreiser simply understood his protagonist and that those who would see in "Solon's unswerving religious devotions a reflection of Dreiser's ideas" are guilty of "a wonderful example of the 'intentional fallacy.'"[20] But Elias had drawn on his conversations with Dreiser to argue persuasively that "Solon undergoes a change in character that transforms him into a person whose attitude clearly reflects Dreiser's own."[21] This judgment seems incontestable in view not only of the testimony of those who knew Dreiser (including notably Elias, Helen Dreiser, and Marguerite Tjader Harris) but also by virtue of the logical progression of thought which leads inevitably if tortuously from *Sister Carrie* to *The Bulwark*. The essentially religious emotion evoked in Dreiser by the worldly attractions of Chicago and transplanted in Carrie were logically re-channeled in the thirties into the love of the Creative Force which Solon displays during his reaffirmation of faith. Furthermore, Etta's discovery of the love-service ethic fills the same need which Carrie addresses inadequately in opening her purse to the poor in the rocking chair coda added to the conclusion of the early novel. And the convictions espoused by Solon and Etta at the end of *The Bulwark* represent a consistent synthesis for Dreiser. A broad, nondogmatic faith, it rejoices in the beauty of the universe and the often tragic drama of human interaction. Belief requires little beyond a love and respect for humanity as a reflection of the love of the Creative Force—so little in fact that few people, regardless of their particular religious affiliation, would have difficulty accepting its tenets. Solon's wife defines religion early in the novel as "a warm feeling," and Dreiser's new outlook was little more defined. He appears to have conceived of the Inner Light solely as an emanation of the Creative Force. Indeed, Quaker critics have complained that he did not fully understand their faith; that Christ is not mentioned once in *The Bulwark;* that there is not a word about social reform. [22] Ultimately, Dreiser used Quakerism in the novel as a vehicle for expressing his own emergent exultation in the Creative Force. His discovery of what he believed to be order in the universe in his personal epiphany at Cold Spring Harbor readied him psychologically to dissolve his old objections to religion. But those critics who praise Dreiser for the courage and insight he displayed in the pessimistic materialism of his earlier novels should consider carefully before dismissing his affirmation as just an unreasoned bit of wishful thinking. Neither the dark determinism of his earlier work nor the spiritual avowal of *The Bulwark* were meticulously reasoned positions. Dreiser was always and preeminently a man of emotion, whether he was brooding over what he felt to be the cruelty of a meaningless mechanism or passionately praising what he had come to believe was a benevolent Creative Force.

Although the nature of Dreiser's relationship to Solon Barnes seems no longer to be a matter of dispute, a number of the other early negative reactions against *The Bulwark* have been echoed by contemporary Dreiser critics. These charges have cast doubt on the sincerity, the intelligence, and the courage that Dreiser displays in the novel, and even the extent of the change the book reveals.

Among the early critics who questioned the sincerity of *The Bulwark*

was Kenneth Lynn, whose attack on what he views as Dreiser's spe-
cious religiosity was typical and betrays a lack of understanding of the
trend of Dreiser's thinking from the beginning. He claims that Solon's
religious renewal lacks genuine conviction—that Dreiser seemed to
have "no real heart for what he was writing."²³ Besides the fact that *The
Bulwark* is a natural development of Dreiser's earlier ideas, there are
other matters which cast doubt on Lynn's judgment. For example,
Dreiser has always been praised by critics for his honesty. Thus,
Granville Hicks found him always "utterly faithful to his own vision of
life."²⁴ There is little reason to doubt the integrity of *The Bulwark*. It is
certainly a difficult novel for critics to cope with because it runs
against the grain of our national literature, whose genius is in attacking and negating rather than affirming. But evidence of Dreiser's
conviction can be discerned even in the very quality of its prose, particularly in passages that passionately evoke the Creative Force. The
surroundings come alive most fully, for example, when Solon is on
the banks of Lever Creek, a symbol of the Creative Force. Many of
the peripheral scenes, however, which would have interested Dreiser
immensely in the past, are dealt with in the most perfunctory manner.

Among the critics who find Dreiser's religious affirmation to be in-
sincere are some who interpret *The Bulwark* as the product of aging and
the fear of death. This is the position of John Lyndenberg in an early
essay that posited Dreiser's exhaustion and need for the comfort of
faith.²⁵ Lyndenberg's view has been echoed in one form or another by
a number of critics since. The charge has a certain ironic justice. Dreiser himself had often ridiculed faith as the last resort of a coward. In
The Color of a Great City, he ridicules his own early interest in Christian
Science in *The "Genius"*:

There is something about the type of soul which turns to religion *in extremis*
which is not pleasing. It appears to turn to religion about as a drowning man
turns to a raft. There is the taint of personal advantage about it and not a little
of the cant and whine of one who would curry favor with life or the Lord. [P.
206.]

All of his books up to *The Bulwark* display his obsession with youth,
and he had always felt that men become religious only when they are
old or otherwise fearful of losing the pleasures of youth. In *Tragic America*, he calls the Catholic Church to task for playing on fear:

Yet the Church plays up to the great fear—the fear of death—by offering people the supposed opportunity to live forever elsewhere by communion, by unction and the forgiveness of sins here. But contemplation of death is a sorrow at the loss of all the loveliness here, and should not be over-emphasized since our stay here may yet be made reasonably sufficient. More, courage and the desire to make life here worth while should be man's contribution to the society of which he is a part and whose functions he de-sires to improve if not perfect. [P. 361.]

There may have been an element of fear connected with Dreiser's avowal—the fear of the beckoning grave which might well have remained after Dreiser's contribution to society in the thirties was completed. In the past he had become religiously inclined only in times of great emotional turmoil. But in his last years, he merely came to appreciate what he and certain scandalized critics should have known from the start: that man's need for religious support is greatest in times of stress. C. S. Lewis supplies a terse reply to those who would discount this religion born of adversity:

There seems no reason for describing as hypocritical the short-lived piety of those whose religion fades away once they have emerged from "danger, necessity, or tribulation." Why should they not have been sincere? They were desperate and they howled for help. Who wouldn't?[26]

Moreover, the implication that Dreiser was merely a tired old man when he wrote *The Bulwark* is fundamentally misleading. The book does contain some chronological and other errors of detail: at times he gropes unsuccessfully for the right words to express feelings. But these deficiencies do not differentiate this novel from his earlier works. The fact that he could not perfectly formulate what he felt had never before been submitted as proof that he did not feel it. Further-more, a case can be made that *The Bulwark* represents the clearest ex-position of philosophical ideas he ever achieved. It certainly contains some of his most effective writing.

By far the most celebrated and influential attack ever made on *The Bulwark* was contained in Lionel Trilling's essay in *The Nation* published shortly after the novel appeared. Trilling assails what he calls a "failure of mind and heart," asserting that Dreiser was always guilty of such failure, but that the religious affirmation was especially "offensive" because of the "vulgar ease of its formulation, as well as in the comfortable untroubled way in which Dreiser moved from nihilism to pietism." The affirmation is portrayed by Trilling as the product of a mind at best unsophisticated and otherwise stupid. As evidence of this, he compares *The Brothers Karamazov* and the *Book of Job* with *The Bulwark*: "Ivan Karamazov's giving back his ticket of admission to the 'harmony' of the universe suggests that *The Bulwark* is not morally adequate, for we dare not, as its hero does, blandly 'accept' the suffering of others; and the *Book of Job* tells us that it does not include enough in its exploration of evil, and is not stern enough."[27]

It would be extremely foolish to argue that Dreiser was not limited as an artist, as a thinker, and as a man. But to compare him to Dostoevsky and the Bible and to rank him third is not to evaluate his work in any constructive way. Moreover, Trilling's suggestion that Dreiser's affirmation was easy ignores the anguished search for meaning that the novelist conducted for over forty years. At the close of that difficult struggle, he professed a belief that was devoid of the disagreeable elements of authority and institutionalism. He made the leap to faith without having solved the problem of evil or having answered the many disturbing questions about the extent to which man is morally free. His knowledge of Quakerism was admittedly superficial; the similarity of such doctrines as the spiritual relationship of the Quakers and the Mystical Body of the Catholic Church he so hated would not have occurred to him. *The Bulwark* reveals his acceptance of all that he had questioned most in the past. Even science, thanks to its eternal variables, had not satisfied his need to believe in a truth that stands above argument. He had not resolved all of the inconsistencies in his thought. His need to believe had merely dissolved the importance of these inconsistencies to him. All of these things are true, but at its best, *The Bulwark* conveys a keen sense of the interrelationship of all men and the help that religious conviction can provide for some in times of tragedy.

Perhaps the most widely held view among contemporary critics about Dreiser's affirmation as revealed in *The Bulwark* holds that, regardless of his sincerity or the state of his mind, he did not really change his beliefs significantly during his last years. Woodburn O. Ross was the first to make this point, tracing Dreiser's sympathy for explanations of life beyond the materialistic to his early work and concluding that "there is nothing whatever in *The Bulwark* to indicate any change in Dreiser's opinions or in his ways of thinking, beyond a certain mellowness which is perhaps accounted for by the fact that he completed the book at an advanced age. "²⁸ Edward Wagenknecht also makes this judgment, writing that "his final attitude, though by no means consistent with all the views he had expressed in the past, represented no clear break with that past either." Wagenknecht cites his abiding interest in the nonmaterial and his admiration for virtue: "He loved goodness, despite all his immorality; in his mother; in Jennie Gerhardt; in St. Francis of Assisi, whose paean in praise of poverty made his hair tingle to the roots; in the Christ-like 'Doer of the Word' of whom he wrote in *Twelve Men.*"²⁹ Sophisticated variations on this theme have been offered by more recent critics who have argued for the continuity in Dreiser's work. Richard Lehan, for example, sees no "radical departure" in the thinking reflected in *The Bulwark*. To Lehan, Dreiser had "merely shifted the magnifying glass, showing the man of big business aware of a higher principle than money, showing Spencer's realm of antithetical forces being absorbed—contradictions and all—within Thoreau's Oversoul—that is, on a transcendent level of beauty and order." He further contends that the novel "may better reveal Dreiser's state of physical decline than a resolution to his philosophy."³⁰ Pizer infers that the change in Dreiser was less than dramatic, for it represents a "shift from a stress on the limitations placed upon man's understanding and volition by the mechanistic nature of life to an emphasis on the opportunities for insight and action within a mechanistic world."³¹ On the other hand, some early critics felt that a significant change could be discerned. Edward Drummond, for instance, argued that although Dreiser had not become a mystic, he was significantly different:

> Dreiser had not become a mystic nor turned to orthodox Christianity; in reality by the end of the book the "inner light" of the Quaker had been so interpreted that it would have been acceptable to a yogi; still this softened and somewhat Emersonian cast of thought (it had more of warmth and feeling and less of intellect than Emerson's) of Dreiser's last years was markedly different from what had gone before.³²

The problem here is partially semantic. What is needed is agreement on what constitutes significant change. I have argued here for a development rather than a continuity of ideas in Dreiser's work, a position supported by compelling evidence and one that assumes significant change. A number of elements in *The Bulwark* demonstrate a dramatic, absolute reversal in outlook. Perhaps the most obvious contrast is in the vast difference between the passage describing the black grouper in *The Financier* and Solon's discovery of the green fly in *The Bulwark*. This seems more than a mere mellowing could produce, and there are many other signs of change. The altered attitude toward religion and devout believers is obvious. Jennie Gerhardt's father had been likable *in spite* of his tenacious hold on his religion; Solon Barnes is admirable *because* of his. Dreiser even spoke of dedicating *The Bulwark* to his father, a man he had formerly described as undeserving of affection. The Barneses' fellow Christians rush to the aid of the family in its hour of need in contrast to the Christians in *An American Tragedy*, who forsake Clyde. In a touch which reminds us that Dreiser had still not forgotten an important childhood incident, however, he impresses the reader with the fact that Stewart is not denied a Quaker burial as the novelist's mother had been denied a Catholic one. Throughout *The Bulwark*, Dreiser celebrates the things at which he had formerly scoffed, particularly the doctrine of one life, one love. Moreover, even Solon's plain but loving daughter, Isobel, marries and finds happiness. This is the first time that Dreiser has even hinted that there is anything in life for a girl without physical beauty. Roberta Alden's sister in *An American Tragedy* had been plain, and Dreiser spends several paragraphs in that book explaining the consequent futility of her life. And after all, even Jennie Gerhardt had been beautiful! In *The Bulwark*, Dreiser recognizes that beauty of the spirit is of first importance. Again, the extent of his transformation is to be measured by the things that now interested him. *The Bulwark* has none of the exhaustive naturalistic documentation of his earlier fiction. With an unmistakable significance, he puts his characters in a new perspective—one that both diminishes the importance of their worldly concerns and increases their human dignity. Although all of his talk of nature's equation in the past did imply a balance and a certain order in the universe (he uses the term "equation" once in *The Bulwark*), it did not elicit the religious awe before creation which is imputed to Solon Barnes and which Dreiser clearly shares. Such considerations doubtlessly influenced Rufus Jones's reading of the final section of *The Bulwark*. Jones spoke to the Library Associates of Haverford College regarding the passages from the return of Etta to the conclusion and though he was generally critical of the novel (especially its exposition of Quakerism), he did not doubt that Dreiser had changed markedly:

"The author is at his best in his account of the death of his main character—the father, with the returned prodigal Etta reading Woolman's
Journal to him. One feels that this fine ending reveals a new stage of
the author's life. Here he reaches a new level of insight and sees at last
the deeper significance of life."[33]

Again, the violations of the human connection—in Stewart's rebellious self-gratification, in Etta's stealing from her mother to finance
her larger life, in Solon's failure to live up to the compassion demanded by the Inner Light—all lead to a mature sense of guilt which
differentiates the characters from all the others in Dreiser's fiction.
Lester Kane, Eugene Witla, and Clyde Griffiths experience guilt of a
sort, but theirs is weak because they do not really understand human
commitment. Lester is really more sorry for himself than for Jennie.
Eugene soon recovers from his guilty morbidity. Clyde's guilt is measured against the greater guilt of society. But Solon, Etta, and Stewart
experience a real, individual guilt. Solon and Etta are the only fully
rounded characters in Dreiser's fiction because they undergo truly
transforming growth. They are not mere puppets, assembled to be
smashed by chance. Thus, Robert Spiller was right in his assertion
that *The Bulwark* is unique among Dreiser's novels because "the moral
issue and the forces of which it is composed are clearforces of which it
is composed are clearly defined and never for a moment forgotten."[34]
Finally, Dreiser thought of himself as significantly changed. Just before his death, he said to Robert Elias about his altered conception of
existence in *The Bulwark:* "'It's funny,' . . . 'how a fellow can go along
for years and not get it. . . . And when it's there all the time.'"[35]

Dreiser clearly came to recognize individual culpability, not only
as a result of his research into "the mechanism called man," but also
through introspection, his long-favored method of studying human
nature. There is evidence that years before writing *The Bulwark*, he had
begun to be troubled by the consequences of some of his own practices. For example, he carried on a rather surprising dialogue by mail
with a Catholic priest for nearly two decades, and in one of his letters
alluded to the possibility that he might one day turn up at his correspondent's confessional. Despite his bitter antipathy toward Catholicism, Dreiser found in the priest a welcome confidante. The Reverend
Paul Lacosky (né Laskowski) was a diocesan priest, one-eighth Polish,
born near the Vistula in 1886, and an American citizen since his childhood. He first wrote Dreiser in 1919, after he had read with appreci-

ation *Free and Other Stories.* A sporadic but revealing correspondence developed. It endured until 1937. Dreiser, who had told Lacosky that he was interested in Catholic priests intellectually, wrote in 1925: "If some day a weary author heavily laden with sin arrives at your confessional—absolve him if for no more than the reality he sought—in vain, I fear—to portray." Lacosky's response reveals the humanity beneath the cloth which must have spurred Dreiser to pursue the correspondence for so many years:

You, I think, could gain a lot if you could take my place in the "box" for a year. What we don't hear! And how we must steel ourselves—I do at any rate—to remain calm, kind, the wise counsellor. So whenever I am tempted in my nervous dispositions to fly off the handle at some sinner not because he is more laden, or laden more heavily than the rest, but because he shows so little sign of compunction, of the realization of his guilt and appears only to come because he feels he has a chore to do, I recall these words of yours, and I say to myself, Keep cool! Perhaps this is Mr. Dreiser; perhaps the next man may be Mr. Dreiser, and you must treat him right. [36]

In January 1933, Lacosky, who took Dreiser's allusion to confession as a serious compulsion, wrote to grant his absolution beforehand and to ascribe the novelist's felt need to "a latent conviction left over from something—the ashes of something burnt out" as well as "a determination for a future action." [37] Although Dreiser never confessed to the priest, he did confront his own sense of guilt six months after Lacosky's letter. Robert Elias records that one day in August 1933, Dreiser confessed to Arthur Davidson Ficke "a deep feeling of unworthiness." Ficke told him that he must learn to forgive himself. Dreiser was visibly shaken by his friend's advice and repeated it several times during the day. He apparently regarded self-forgiveness as a "tremendous thought," and "enough to change a man's whole life!" Elias was told by Dreiser that *The Bulwark* was to be not only a tribute to the Creative Force, but also an act of reparation: "As Dreiser thought over his own life, he felt he was now atoning for what seemed like irreverent attacks on God." [38] Dreiser's admission to Elias of his reversal in attitude presents more persuasive evidence of a genuine change in his outlook on the world. Helen Dreiser's recollection of her husband's brooding over his protagonist offers a further insight:

I noticed whenever he talked of his principal character, Solon Barnes, his eyes would fill with tears, and I knew he was thinking not only of his father but of what he considered his own shortcomings. I knew he was putting a lot of himself into this story of the Quaker, and I saw in his eyes the realization that his own life might end at any time and that he felt he might have done differently at times in the past. Often he quoted: . . . "this night thy soul shall be required of thee. "[39]

Although Dreiser clearly imputes individual guilt such as that he felt himself to the characters in *The Bulwark*, he does not judge them. There is no certainty, for instance, that Etta and Stewart or even Solon could have acted differently in the novel, for Dreiser appears to have finally cast his lot with the many philosophers and theologians through the ages who remained unsure of the extent to which free will is operative. Certainly, his long struggle to understand mankind and his own life bears witness to the inadequacy of intellect in explaining evil or measuring guilt.

Whatever the aesthetic merits of *The Bulwark*, Dreiser achieved both an intellectual consistency and a moral toughness which his previous fiction never approached. In *The Bulwark*, for example, he clearly rejects the primacy of self-interest in favor of the love-service ethic— whether or not man is fully free to choose it. There is a more mature sense of human responsibility in *The Bulwark* than in his earlier work. This new moral dimension derives from the increased dignity the individual accrues in this novel as a child of the Creative Force. The compassion for which Dreiser had always been justly praised is given for the first time a compatible philosophic context, for in a mechanistic system it had been merely gratuitous. The principal characters display a capacity for growth which dwarfs that of his earlier protagonists. The lives of Solon and Etta show that religion need not be merely "a bandage for the weak." They display a set of beliefs and principles that demand considerable strength and discipline to put into practice. In *The Bulwark*, the tenets of Quakerism are judged separately from the example of those hypocrites who profess to but do not live by Inner Light. No such discrimination between doctrine and observance is evident in his earlier treatment of religion.

In delineating the lives and characters of the Barnes children, Dreiser reintroduces former plots and themes, filtering familiar material through his altered perception of the world. And with impressive results. Stewart's blundering complicity in the death of Psyche Tanzer recalls Clyde's situation in *An American Tragedy*, but the recognition of individual culpability in this slim volume provides a tragic dimension which was only latent in its sprawling predecessor. The characters of Orville and Dorothea show that looks and social graces, which Dreiser had always previously overrated in his characters, are empty when divorced from sympathy and commitment. The portrayal of Cousin Rhoda's circle shows that the glittering world of society, which Dreiser had always envied even when he was attacking the economic system that permitted it, is utterly hollow. Solon Barnes proves that age provides one with a repository of experience out of which can come wisdom. In Dreiser's earlier fiction, age brought only the cessation of desire and the onset of despair. *The Bulwark* is one of only a handful of American novels with an aged protagonist and it is the most compassionate and understanding. Moreover, in the rapprochement between Etta and her father, Dreiser presents a prescription in microcosm for the truly humanistic society in which age is no barrier to mutual love, respect, and accommodation. And if he did not resolve the problem of evil, he insisted nonetheless on recognizing the darker side of life as always. The analysis of the persistent conflict between the Friends' ideal of simplicity and the temptations that accompany inherited wealth, Solon's concern for the exploitation of the poor by the banks, the searing scene in which Solon holds his vigil next to Stewart's coffin—all of these components of *The Bulwark* show that its message, though affirmative, is not easy.

Marguerite Tjader Harris recalls that Dreiser told her in the forties he had tentatively sketched out Anna Tatum's story when he first heard it in 1912 and had written the scene in which Solon mourns by Stewart's casket in order to test whether it contained "the germ of a great tragedy in it."[40] Ironically, he would never have questioned the tragic potential of Clyde Griffiths's experience, yet in classical terms, Solon, a man of nobility and moral stature brought low through his flaw of untutored naiveté, is much closer to the archetypal tragic hero. Indeed, in the final scene of the novel, which describes Solon's funeral, Etta's tears are not for herself or her father but for the pervasiveness of tragedy. When Dreiser offers this final vision of Etta crying for "life,"—the *process* through which the beautiful and the tragic ceaselessly intertwine, as the last sentence describing Solon's mourners returning to their carriages is meant to suggest—he offers the most mature world view to be found in his fiction: rejoicing in the sublimity of creation but accepting man's limited capacity to embrace it; affirming the dignity of personhood while admitting the individual's responsibility to community; recognizing design and trusting in a discernible human destiny, yet willing to let Nature answer the ultimate questions in its own good time.

When *The Bulwark* was published, its message of renewed faith ran counter to established taste just as *Sister Carrie's* American naturalism had in 1900. Its continuing neglect by critics has resulted from this still unfashionable hopefulness as well as its out-of-season technique. Moreover, the subjugation of the self by which Etta attains fulfillment is not likely to be a popular prescription with the present generation. But the passage of time may yet bring to the novel the wider scrutiny and regard that it deserves.

Solon Barnes's affirmation signifies the culmination of Dreiser's long quest for meaning. It remained for Berenice Fleming, the "impossible she" of the Cowperwood trilogy, to dramatize in the concluding pages of *The Stoic* the novelist's final message of faith and peace.

9 / The Stoic

DREISER acted on his resolve to push *The Stoic* to completion after his work on *The Bulwark* was finished in May 1945. He had originally planned to bring out the last volume of the Cowperwood trilogy late in 1914, six months after the appearance of *The Titan*. Other projects intervened, however, until 1932, when he finished some fifty-five chapters of a draft, but again he put the novel aside to pursue other interests. Finally, in July 1945, he took up the project once more, pushing on to the last few pages, which he was composing at the time of his death in December. The major difference between the novel published posthumously in 1947 and the one projected in 1914 and begun in 1932 is to be found in the closing section. Dreiser had planned to focus on the deaths of Cowperwood and Aileen, but shifted attention instead to Berenice Fleming's transformation into a devotee of yoga. The "impossible she" of *The Titan*, meditating on the elusive meaning of Cowperwood's life and career, is led to India to study under a guru. The lessons she learns about the responsibility to give and the peace afforded by belief are consistent with the religious renewal of Solon Barnes at the conclusion of *The Bulwark*. Moreover, the guru provides her with a spiritual context in which to place Cowperwood's chaotic sexual quest.

The first two hundred pages of the novel, which represent a slight revision and condensation of the chapters written in 1932, concern Cowperwood's efforts to gain control of the London street-railway system. The mixture of business and sex which structures *The Titan* also patterns this segment of *The Stoic*. While the financier plots the purchase of railway lines, he also contrives to bring together his wife, Aileen, to whom he has remained married only for the sake of appearances, and a gigolo named Bruce Tollifer. While Tollifer and Aileen are occupied with each other, Cowperwood dallies with other women including Arlette Wayne, a singer of great intellect and beauty; Caroline Hand, a society woman who had played a role in *The Titan*; and Lorna Maris, a sensual, nineteen-year-old dancer. But these affairs are carried forward in spite of Cowperwood's knowledge that only the unutterably perfect Berenice can command his absolute idolatry. Much of the tension in the first two-thirds of *The Stoic* is created by the financier's recognition of Berenice's superiority, his intellectual preference for fidelity to her, and his urge to test other temperaments. Dreiser ascribes Cowperwood's confusion to a "consuming and overwhelming force," the desire for "youth and beauty and sex" (p. 169). Despite his intellect, which argues for Berenice's preeminence, any "pre-determined course" is sidetracked because "there was something in sensual desire which superceded and therefore must be superior to reason and will" (p. 195).

There is a tension within Berenice as well. The infinite variability of her nature, the key to her hold on the varietistic Cowperwood, consists of contradictory qualities, principally her "seemingly non-material as well as mentally contemplative grace" and her "pagan modernity" with its "delight in luxury" (p. 137). Dreiser implies that these opposites are accounted for and subsumed by Berenice's affinity with nature, which is itself infinitely variable. At the same time, Cowperwood's perfect woman wishes to make of her life a work of art, thereby unconsciously striving for the immutability that Dreiser saw in painting and sculpture. The financier consciously seeks to blend the organic vitalism of nature with the permanence of art. His mansion is not only a repository of paintings and sculptures, but also an interior palm garden wherein flowers and fountains and "the cool greenness of the woods" insulate him from the "asphalt of Fifth Avenue" (p. 264). His plans for an elaborate tomb to house himself and Aileen stem from his desire to memorialize their former love. The plan is first stimulated by his visit to the graves of Eloise and Abelard. But when Berenice views the magnificent mausoleum that must ultimately stand for all of Cowperwood's achievements, she is forcibly struck by the transcendence of the man-made by the natural. Her final impression of the tomb as she leaves the cemetery carries Dreiser's message unmistakably: "Walking down the path some hundred feet, Berenice looked back to see the last resting place of her beloved, as it stood high and proud in anonymity, the name not being visible from where she stood. High and proud, and yet small, under the protective elms grown tall around it" (p. 274).

Early in the novel, Cowperwood begins to develop some perspective of his own regarding his acquisitiveness. At Berenice's bidding, for example, he vows that his London venture should be carried through on a higher plane of decency than his operations in Philadelphia and Chicago. Although he does resort to watering stocks and other trickery and occasionally muses on his Social Darwinism, the financier is somewhat mellowed. For example, he decides to endow a hospital and make a number of other charitable bequests. Later in the novel, after he is diagnosed for Bright's disease and given a year to live, his mellowing process is quickened. Dreiser transfers some of his own feelings to the financier. His last days are fulfilling in a new way as he develops a glowing friendship with his doctor, whom he comes to admire as a man of "goodness of heart and intention." He also intensifies his love for Berenice. On his final trip to New York, he admits to himself that "neither he nor any man knew anything about life or its Creator," viewed as a "great and beautiful mystery" (p. 247). In a touch which ironically parallels Dreiser's own last days, Cowperwood is disturbed by the atmosphere of intrigue around his sickbed, as Berenice surreptitiously visits him while trying to avoid Aileen. (Helen's jealousy of Marguerite Tjader Harris caused considerable friction during these last days and even led her to complain bitterly over Mrs. Harris's influence in selecting the clergyman to deliver the eulogy at Dreiser's funeral.)[1]

Near the end of *The Stoic*, an Episcopal minister provides the final commentary on the tycoon's career, just as the three witches from *Macbeth* had summarized Cowperwood's Philadelphia phase as well as the toil and trouble of his Chicago venture in the conclusions to *The Financier* and *The Titan*. Reverend Hayward Crenshaw selects a highly appropriate text to quote at the financier's funeral: "For man walketh in a vain shadow, and disquieteth himself in vain: he heapeth up riches, and cannot tell who shall gather them" (p. 273). Once Cowperwood is buried, his fortune is swiftly dissipated in the midst of legal wrangling, and when all of his possessions are auctioned off there remains only three million dollars, less than 15 percent of what he was once worth. But Dreiser was not content to leave the matter here. The last twenty-five pages of *The Stoic* follow Berenice in her attempt to construe Cowperwood's life with the help of Eastern philosophy. This "Berenice section" represents the novelist's longest interpretative coda.

Dreiser had long been interested in Hindu thought, although he believed that like Christian Science, it dismissed evil unrealistically. In 1933 he wrote a reply to George Vaughan, a professor of law at the University of Arkansas, who had sent him a letter asking if he thought that there would soon be an extensive religious revival. Dreiser's answer included his objections to Hinduism as a possible world religion:

> The Vedanta philosophy, particularly the last portion, the *Upanishads*, asserts, as did Mary Baker Eddy, who borrowed her idea from that source, that the ultimate spirit or self is in all material things as well as in the totality of space, in other words, is space, but that it in itself does not reflect the imperfections or degradations of the material world which we see. With that I disagree. Whatever may be said for illusions, and there is a great deal to be said for non-science or non-truth, there is still a body of moods and actions in the material phase of life which must be accounted for on some grounds, either on the ground of the dual nature of the great spirit, or on the ground of a devil warring with equal strength against pure mind. [2]

On the other hand, there are scattered debts to Hindu thought in the early novels. Eugene Witla had read the *Bhagavad-Gita*. In *The "Genius,"* his wonder at Angela's intuition leads him to "almost accept the Brahmanistic dogma of a psychic body which sees and is seen where we dream all to be darkness" (p. 366). And in the epilogue to *The Titan*, Dreiser had linked the "equation" to Nirvana. In the 1940s, he was willing to give credence to some other Hindu ideas, to which he was reintroduced by Helen in Los Angeles. She had taken up Oriental philosophy because everyone she knew was suffering from satiation with material comfort and luxury. Since the Indian religion supplied certain hypotheses about the plaguing problem of evil, Dreiser found it worthy of inclusion as a source of explanation for Cowperwood's desires and limitations and as a direction pointer toward world betterment and personal fulfillment. As has been true with the scores of other American writers fascinated by the religions of the East, the strangeness of the intellectual terrain, and especially Hinduism's preoccupation with desire, appealed to him. The fact that Hinduism was not a familiar religion in this country invested it with a certain romantic appeal. Moreover, there is precedent and some logic in Dreiser's progression from the Quaker background of *The Bulwark* to the Hindu ideas at the end of *The Stoic*. Emerson, the author of "Brahma," felt a parallel attraction for Eastern thought and the simple faith of the Quakers whom he believed "to have come nearer to the sublime history and genius of Christ than any other of the sects."[3] Indeed, Cowperwood alludes to his own parents' background as members of the Society of Friends in *The Stoic*. The broad and nondogmatic bases of Hinduism and Quakerism appealed to Dreiser. Ironically, he found a documentary rationale for using *The Stoic* as a vehicle for exploring the landscape of Eastern thought. Berenice's prototype, Emily Grigsby, had gone to India for her health after the death of Charles Yerkes, Cowperwood's real-life counterpart. There she had become captivated by the philosophy of yoga. The original notes for *The Stoic*, assembled in 1911, include the pronouncement: "Berenice goes to India for health."

After Cowperwood's death, Berenice seeks solace. Wishing to avoid the glare of public attention surrounding her career as the late financier's mistress and suffering from mental anguish because of the tragic end to the dreams she shared with him, she looks for a way to regain her spiritual equilibrium. She finds it quite by accident. Taking down a book from a shelf in Cowperwood's library, she discovers it to be the *Bhagavad-Gita*. Drawn to the religion "as by a magnet," she journeys to the Far East to study and returns to New York a confirmed practitioner of yoga. Dreiser's conception of Hinduism as revealed in *The Stoic* is very much colored by his own attitudes. The guru who teaches Berenice the fundamentals of the faith indicates that the great benefit of yoga is that the adherent "will lose the suffering that comes from desire" (p. 290). Earlier in the novel, Cowperwood's mistress had begun to question her own values:

Was her own life merely to be one of clever, calculating, and ruthless determination to fulfill herself socially, or as an individual? What benefit could that be, to her or to anyone? What beauty would that create or inspire? Now . . . here . . . in this place . . . perfumed with memories and moonlight . . . something was at her elbow and in her heart . . . something that whispered of quiet and peace . . . solitude . . . fulfillment . . . a desire to create something utterly beautiful, so that her life would be complete and significant. [P. 138.]

The ethical lesson the guru imparts to Berenice corroborates the moral message of *The Bulwark*. Berenice asks about the role of charity, and her teacher insists that we should do good works for their own sakes, since this is the secret of nonattachment: "'When you help the poor, feel not the slightest pride. Be thankful for the opportunity to give. To do so is your worship and no cause for pride. Is not the whole universe yourself? Be grateful that the poor man is there so that by making a gift to him you are able to help yourself. It is not the receiver that is blessed, but the giver'" (p. 297). Given this new direction, Berenice decides to devote herself to the poor, by using the money from her inheritance to found a hospital for the indigent. R. N. Mookerjee, an Indian critic of Dreiser's last novels, points out that *The Stoic* does not "represent the essence of Hindu philosophy." Clearly, Dreiser stressed those precepts which most fully accorded with his own views. This is nowhere more apparent than in the guru's emphasis on charity. Mookerjee rightly asserts that Berenice's own religious heritage "was more than sufficient to impress upon her the need of love, charity, and service to man which Christianity regards as supreme."[4]

When Berenice asks the guru about the lure of beauty which enslaves so many, as it had Cowperwood, his answer is well calculated to appeal to her and to Dreiser in his final phase:

"Even in the lowest kinds of attraction there is the germ of Divine Love. One of the names of the Lord in Sanskrit is Hari, and this means that He attracts all things to Himself. His is, in fact, the only attraction worthy of human hearts. Who can attract a soul, really? Only He. When you see a man being drawn to a beautiful face, do you think that it is a handful of arranged material molecules which really attracts the man? Not at all! Behind those material particles there must be and is the play of divine influence and divine love. The ignorant man does not know it, but yet, consciously or unconsciously, he is attracted by it, and it alone. So even the lowest forms of attraction derive their power from God Himself. 'None, O beloved, ever loved the husband for the husband's sake; it is the Atman, the Lord, who is inside, and for His sake the husband is loved.' The Lord is the great magnet, and we are like iron filings; all of us are being constantly attracted by Him, and all of us are struggling to reach Him, the face of Brahman reflected through all forms and designs. We think we worship beauty, but we are really worshipping the face of Brahman shining through. The Reality behind the scenes." [P. 297.]

This is the most convincing explanation of desire that Dreiser ever offered. To see his own infinite longing to embrace creation as a restless search for God has a persuasive inner logic. With this perspective, he might have discerned that much of his earlier writing had been remarkable for its undirected religious emotion—in the ceaseless evocations of ideal beauty in womanhood, or in a landscape, or in his descriptions of Chicago and New York in which urban sounds and sights replace the music of the spheres and the Beatific Vision. Berenice, with her new knowledge, even defends Cowperwood's promiscuity. Walking by his grave after her return to America, she receives a sudden insight into his romantic predilections, now understanding that "his worship and constant search for beauty in every form, and especially in the form of a woman, was nothing more than a search for the Divine design behind all forms—the face of Brahman shining through" (p. 305). Thus, the sexual desire Dreiser had first put in a philosophical context through reading Schopenhauer nearly half a century earlier is made to serve the cause of religion in *The Stoic*. Even his long-favored metaphor is given a new, religious significance—the "reality behind the scenes" becomes a "universal magnet."

The idea of the Creator as the source of all desire is no more foreign to Christianity than is the primacy of charity, although most Christian theologians would balk at Berenice's rationalization for Cowperwood's sexual promiscuity. C. S. Lewis speaks of the world as a mirror of the Infinite Mind: "The created glory may be expected to give us hints of the uncreated; for the one is derived from the other and in some fashion reflects it."[5] The Jesuit theologian and biologist Pierre Teilhard de Chardin refers in Christian theological terms to the same phenomenon that the guru outlines for Berenice. Teilhard de Chardin says:

We must not allow ourselves to be deceived by appearances. We must not let ourselves be disconcerted by the patent errors into which many mystics have fallen in their attempts to place and even to name the universal Smile. As with all power (and the richer, the more so) the sense of the All comes to birth inchoate and troubled. It often happens that, like children opening their eyes for the first time, men do not accurately place the reality which they sense behind things. Their gropings often meet with nothing but a metaphysical phantom or a cruel idol. But images and reflections have never proved anything against the reality of objects and of the light. The false trails of pantheism bear witness to our immense need for some revealing word to come from the mouth of Him who is. With that reservation, it remains true that, physiologically, the so-called "natural" taste for being is, in each life, the first dawn of the divine illumination—the first tremor perceived of the world animated by the Incarnation.[6]

Dreiser would have been much interested in Teilhard de Chardin's speculations had the two been contemporaries. The Jesuit's appealing combination of science and religion would have offered a corroborative Christian analysis to supplement the guru's teaching in *The Stoic*. But those teachings in themselves doubtlessly struck the novelist as an impressive explanation of life as he had lately come to view it. Did not men seek ideal beauty always and was it not logical that they would eventually seek out the Author of all beauty? Dreiser seems to have finally believed it to be so. Certainly his own pursuit of transcendence—evidenced even in the tactile oblivion of serial sex with its implicit longing for cosmic orgasm—had been lifelong.

His attraction to the brand of Hinduism preached by the guru in *The Stoic* is logical. Years earlier, while still under the influence of Darwin and Spencer, he had written in *The Titan* about Cowperwood's evolution of sensibility in his quest for the perfect woman. In one passage in the original manuscript of *The Titan*, he comes very close to defining that quest as the guru would in *The Stoic*:

Through many and promiscuous relations he was coming to see that what he had been seeking all this while and was still seeking was not so much one woman—or if so a paragon of beauty and ability—but that spirit of sex and temperament that lights up all women in fact, some possibly almost perfectly, although he had not encountered them. He was beginning to see that for him at least if not for other men, beauty spelled variability, that to satisfy the conception and the wonder of sex that was in him he should have to be permitted the privilege of browsing here and there, [if] taking up different temperaments he should encounter a warp and woof, the ultimate pattern of which should satisfy him. He must have beauty in all forms not the singular beauty of one woman but the braided beauty of many so that he could piece together in his own consciousness, the features of one, the hope of another, the nebulousness of a third, the artistry of a fourth, music from Rita, a smile from Cecily, art and posture from Stephanie—a spiritual and voiceless collection compounded in his own brain of thin air.[7]

The reason for his dropping this section is not clear, but it may well have been that he came to feel that the stress on the necessity of changefulness did not mesh with his later portrayal of Berenice as a paragon of perfection, sufficient in herself.

Whatever his attitude toward the "face of Brahman," Dreiser felt it necessary in *The Stoic* to attempt an explanation of evil. In India, Berenice learns that evil is an illusion, a somewhat different lesson from that learned by Solon Barnes. She wants desperately to believe that evil does not matter, but seeing the plight of the untouchables and the mass starvation in India makes it difficult. Nevertheless, she hits upon the solution to the problem in a personal epiphany that has much more to do with Dreiser's world view than that of Hinduism with its profound distrust of the possibility for amelioration in human affairs through social programs. Berenice is moved by divine inspiration to dedicate herself to social causes:

She was spiritually lacerated [over the suffering of the poor], and there sprang to her mind the assurance of the Gurus that God, Brahman, was All Existence, Bliss. If so, where was He? The thought stayed with her until it became all but unbearable, when suddenly there flamed the counter-thought that this degradation must be met and overcome. And was not the All in All God speaking and directing her thus to assist, aid, change, until this earthly phase of Himself would be altered or transmuted into the exchange of evil for good? She wished so with all her heart. [P. 301.]

Clearly, Dreiser could not accept with equanimity the Hindu cosmology even though its soothing assurances concerning maya probably played a major role in his attraction to the religion. A similar problem had influenced his ultimate rejection of Christian Science years earlier. (Berenice's experience with the guru bears a strong resemblance to Eugene Witla's conversations with the Christian Science practitioner in *The "Genius."*) In *The Stoic*, Dreiser lingers over the problem of evil long enough to reveal that the intellectual equilibrium he attained in *The Bulwark* was coming dangerously close to breaking up. Cowperwood's desires, for example, are said to be basically religious, yet the guru preaches that it is necessary to escape them through "non-attachment." The old conflict between self-serving and self-abnegation, so impressively resolved in *The Bulwark*, bubbles just below the surface of *The Stoic*. What of the havoc and heartache that Cowperwood's "religious" sexual proclivities have produced in the lives of his two wives? What of those laid low by his financial stratagems? *The Stoic* leaves these nagging questions unanswered. Whereas *The Bulwark* had introduced a new dimension in Dreiser's thought, *The Stoic* begins to backtrack. Moreover, as F. O. Matthiessen and others have suggested, Dreiser's Hinduism smacks of Helen's Hollywood connections. Only an enterprising Beverly Hills swami would bestow his blessing on sexual promiscuity the way Berenice's guru does, neglecting to emphasize that in Hinduism, the "Path of Desire" must be followed by the "Path of Renunciation." The final unconscious irony in *The Stoic* occurs when Berenice returns to New York from India a convinced mystic and proceeds to check in at the Plaza. This contradiction shows that Dreiser was not able to dramatize, with complete success, his heroine's resolution of the conflict between the "lure of the spirit" with the "flesh in pursuit."

Still, whatever its artistic and logical deficiencies, there is no evidence in *The Stoic* that Dreiser was having second thoughts about the beliefs expressed in *The Bulwark.* The guru's theology is consistent with that of Solon Barnes. The love-service ethic embraced by Etta Barnes is, in fact, the very lesson that Berenice brings home from India: "But now she knew that one must live for something outside of one's self, something that would tend to answer the needs of the many as opposed to the vanities and comforts of the few, of which she herself was one" (p. 306). The measure of Dreiser's change since *Sister Carrie* is to be taken by comparing its ending to the conclusion of *The Stoic.* Both Bob Ames and the guru function as counselors, each ministering to a beautiful, confused woman. Whereas the inventor fails to identify a reliable path to fulfillment, the mystic points out a certain way. Carrie remains bewildered and inert; Berenice resolves to work for the less fortunate.

Initially, the last chapter of *The Stoic* was to be in the form of an epilogue that would attempt to solve the problem of good and evil, a condensation of an article Dreiser did on the subject for the *North American Review* in 1938. But when he sent a draft of the novel to James T. Farrell for criticism, one of Farrell's suggestions was to drop the epilogue. A perusal of the essay fully justifies Farrell's misgivings. Badly written, it attempts to show that one man's good is another man's evil through several anecdotes, some of them light years removed from the subject matter of the novel. The examples include the contrasting views about good and evil of the starving man and the rich citizen he steals from; a boy who steals from a gas station to finance an affair with a beautiful girl, thus calling into question his free will as opposed to his "chemical and physical sensibilities"; the two spies for opposing countries in war who believe their spying to be good; the doctor's salary which he certainly deems good but which is based on disease and misery; the millionaire factory owner and the union that call on the same abstract principles of justice to bolster their positions. The essay ends with a proposed solution:

To be good you must have evil to contend with, or how would you know any-thing of your goodness? To be beautiful there must be that which is not beau-tiful about in order that your beauty will have a measure. Otherwise, how else would you or anyone know how beautiful you are? Again, to experience warmth, you must have known what cold is; life to be glorious must be con-trasted with darkness; strength with weakness; wisdom with ignorance; else, what would wisdom be? You might even say that evil is that which makes goodness possible—its other half or face. Be glad, therefore, if for the present you are not its victim; or worse, its very embodiment, feared or hated by all seeming good. [8]

Beyond the fact that the warmed-over application of the equation hypothesis to the problem of good and evil breaks no new ground, its connection with the meaning that Berenice discovers in India is at best tangential. Farrell suggested that the novel might be more effectively ended with a section in which Berenice reflects on her experience. Dreiser died before accomplishing the new ending, but Helen sup-plied his notes for the final chapter in an appendix to *The Stoic*. Accord-ing to these notes, Berenice was to visit a squalid New York slum, become physically sickened by the conditions, complete her resolve to build a hospital, and become a nurse herself. (Berenice represents Dreiser's final vision of the ultimate woman in white.) Discovering "a deep maternal instinct, hitherto unexplored," she was to adopt two blind children (her sudden affinity with Jennie Gerhardt is ines-capable), muse on the meaning of Cowperwood's career, and attempt to develop "a real and deep understanding of the meaning of life and its spiritual import" (pp. 308, 310).

Few critics have ever had very much good to say about *The Stoic*, either as a work of art or as philosophy. John McAleer admires the novel as the logical culmination of the trilogy, even arguing that the exposition of Hinduism is an "integral part" of the novel.[9] The most frequently employed criticism of the book, however, points to its broken-backed form—the final volume of a trilogy about a superman-financier becomes the story of a reformed debutante ministering to the rabble. The charge is just. One is reminded of the artistic failure of Frank Norris's *The Pit* after the considerable success of *The Octopus.* The second volume of the never completed *Trilogy of Wheat* suffered like *The Stoic* when Norris diverted attention from his Darwinian hero Curtis Jadwin's attempts to corner the grain market to the society beauty Laura Dearborn. One could argue that even the dazzling Berenice is of secondary importance in the later chapters of *The Stoic,* which become thinly disguised essays on Eastern thought. But, the discussions of Hinduism fail to impress because Dreiser had not studied the religion systematically. Moreover, Berenice is an inappropriate character to convey his message. Charles Shapiro complains that Dreiser's philosophical digressions in *The Stoic* would embarrass a college freshman, and James Lundquist argues that his haphazard education was nowhere more apparent than in the final section of this novel. [10] The most fanatical supporter would be hard pressed to defend against these charges. Dreiser was able to handle with some success the simple faith of the Society of Friends and to use it to express his own philosophy in *The Bulwark,* but he lacked both the knowledge and the patience to deal with the abstrusities of Eastern religion in *The Stoic.* All of these things are true, but at the same time *The Stoic* does represent a logical development in his thought. And at least in one way, the Cowperwood material was ideally suited to convey the message of Dreiser's late affirmation. Throughout the trilogy, he had been asking: What does it profit a man if he gain the whole world? The excursus on Hinduism punctuates the answer suggested by the dispersal of Cowperwood's fortune after his death and the crumbling of his plans for many of the monuments to his own memory. Dreiser's intellectual probing and his emotional needs meshed in *The Stoic* as they had in *The Bulwark.* But this time they produced an unimpressive if heartfelt performance.

While Dreiser was writing his last two novels, he attended various church services with Helen. Most of these were Christian Science services, although on Good Friday in 1945 he was moved to take communion at a Congregational church and, according to Mrs. Harris, was "deeply shaken by the experience."[11] Helen alludes to her husband's frequent Bible reading during his last months. Judging from her account, he returned most often to a long-favored text: "I would say that not ten days passed in which he did not quote from the Sermon on the Mount or some of the other sayings of Christ."[12] He became more and more friendly with a number of ministers during this last year. When his sister Mame said to him on her deathbed, "You know . . . Theo . . . all the men in the world, together, cannot create one blade of grass," he was moved to tears.[13] He became unusually demonstrative of his affection for his wife and friends. Dreiser's last days seem to have taken on a burnished glow which he must have attributed to the muted radiance of the Creative Force.

There remains only to account for the culminating political act of his last year, his application for membership in the Communist party. The relationship of this decision to his spiritual affirmation is direct. He felt that allegiance to the party would represent a significant gesture toward world brotherhood. His interest in radical politics had grown during the crusading days in the thirties; his visit to Russia in 1927 had interested him in the Soviet experiment. Always sympathetic to the masses, he had still not believed that greed could be eliminated. During the late thirties, he became convinced that some socialistic form of government was necessary to insure justice for the majority. When William Z. Foster, whom he regarded as a saint, took over from Earl Browder as head of the American party, Dreiser was induced by friends to join. In his admission application he stressed that "belief in the greatness and dignity of Man has been the guiding principle of my life and work."[14] Dreiser's conversion to communism was motivated by spiritual considerations in addition to political imperatives, as evidenced by the letter he wrote in 1943 to the Soviet news agency, TASS, in praise of Stalin's guidance of the world toward equity, "freedom of speech, freedom from want, freedom of worship, freedom of assembly."[15] His assessment of Stalin as the White Christ who had come out of Russia, though a classic case of political naiveté, was far from unique among American writers. Dreiser's reasoning about Soviet communism was as undisciplined as his understanding of Hinduism. Communism was for him a kind of secular religion, a theoretical, idealistic system with a belief in progress; a deification of the common man; a mystical brotherhood of all nations for human betterment—beliefs that led him to greatly admire Wendell Willkie as well as the Russian leadership. The internecine strife of party politics was far from Dreiser's mind. The way in which his spiritual avowal and his interest in radical politics had been merging for some time is apparent in the notes taken by Robert Elias to record the novelist's ideas as presented in several speeches and in conversation. In 1941, he had compared the Communists to "missionaries or Franciscans" and declared Lenin's social program "'the greatest piece of news since the Sermon on the Mount.'" In 1945, he said that the Dean of Canterbury was right when he had explained that the principles of communism were the same as those of Christ. [16] The fact that he simultaneously admired the individualism of Thoreau only underscores the depth of his idealism.

Dreiser died on 28 December 1945, and his small property holdings were left to his wife, with the stipulation that at her death they should go to a home for Negro orphans—a final giving gesture toward the Creative Force which had been the object of his lifelong yearning and his uniquely twentieth-century quest.

Conclusion

THEODORE Dreiser was very much an artist for his time, propheti-
cally in touch with the twentieth century. Having cut himself off
from religious beliefs at the outset of an increasingly skeptical,
materialistic age, he was nonetheless plagued by a gnawing need to
believe in some transcendent reality. His personal search and the art
that flowed from it represented an anguished attempt to find not only
a worthy worldly ideal but also a method of living that could guaran-
tee secular salvation in the form of fulfillment. His novels and stories
weigh the possibilities for happiness in money, possessions, power,
society, sex, art, beauty. The articles of faith implicit in the American
Dream have been subjected to no more thorough examination than
that which Dreiser conducted through his fiction. At the end of his
long struggle to understand, he came to feel that fulfillment was to be
found in the existential choice of sacrificial commitment over self-
seeking.

Dreiser created his major fictional characters out of the conflict
within himself between these two essential pulls. His work underscores the truth of F. Scott Fitzgerald's contention in "The Crack Up"
that "the test of a first rate intelligence is the ability to hold two
conflicting ideas in the mind and still retain the ability to function."
Instead of allowing the philosophy of naturalism to dictate every
stroke of his pen, Dreiser wrote books that measured the world by his
own performance—torn between the worldly objects of his "covetous
eye" and his compassion for those whose dreams were far less
audacious, yet equally doomed. His fiction validates the American
painter Edward Hopper's conviction that: "The man's the work.
Something doesn't come out of nothing." The dramatic tension in

Dreiser's novels and stories is nearly always supplied by the clash within the characters between the urge to take and the inspiration to give. If he had chosen to sum up all of his fiction, he might have reached back to one of the chapter titles in *Sister Carrie*: "The Lure of the Spirit, the Flesh in Pursuit." Out of this debate within himself Dreiser created formidable fiction. Yet if the struggle between taking and giving were the chief source of dramatic conflict in his work, it was also the source of disturbing contradictions which often marred his philosophical intrusions and his authorial attempts at construing the meaning of his characters' experiences. He was by no means a rigidly logical thinker, but if he was sometimes wrong, the importance and complexity of his subjects were never to be doubted. His love of life and immense emotional energy enabled him to penetrate and enliven the material world—to capture the way in which urban scenes overawe the senses of the modern seeker.

Frustrated by limits, he came in the later years to feel more and more urgently the need of some spiritual support, to identify the source of the light behind the varicolored life he celebrated. During the thirties, he hoped through his concentrated studies of biology and physics to bridge the gap between science and religion. Psychologically readied by his years of seeking, he finally came to affirm a new-found faith near the end of his life. Ironically, it was at the outset of World War II that he signed his separate peace, willing to trust that Nature's intention was benign and hoping to have a part in its continuity. The surprise and dismay registered by many of his formerly admiring critics signified their inability to recognize, even in his earliest work, which had been remarkable for its essentially religious longing directed toward worldly objects, the seeds of his later faith.

As an artist, Dreiser was very much the natural, with the natural's rough edges. Yet *Sister Carrie* is a world-class novel, deserving of a place alongside *Madame Bovary* and *Père Goriot*. *An American Tragedy* earns comparison if not parity with *Crime and Punishment*. *The Bulwark*, his most intelligent novel, represents a much underrated achievement. "Free" is one of the most ruthlessly realistic and disturbingly insightful portrayals of marriage in all of fiction. At its best his work reveals a power analogous to that of Mahler's symphonies, the felt force stemming from the grand sweep of the passion. When he wrote of man's restless desire for the infinite, he captured a little of the pure fire of the human spirit. Like all of those who truly seek the truth, he was allotted his portion.

Notes

Citations

All citations from Dreiser's books are from the following editions.

Sister Carrie (Philadelphia: University of Pennsylvania Press, 1981).
Jennie Gerhardt (New York: Harper, 1911).
The Financier (New York: Harper, 1912).
The Titan (New York: John Lane, 1914).
A Traveler at Forty (New York: Century, 1914).
The "Genius" (New York: John Lane, 1915).
A Hoosier Holiday (New York: John Lane, 1916).
Free and Other Stories (New York: Boni and Liveright, 1918).
Twelve Men (New York: Boni and Liveright, 1919).
Hey Rub-a-Dub-Dub (New York: Boni and Liveright, 1920).
A Book About Myself (New York: Boni and Liveright, 1922).
The Color of a Great City (New York: Boni and Liveright, 1923).
An American Tragedy, 2 vols. (New York: Boni and Liveright, 1925).
Chains (New York: Boni and Liveright, 1927).
A Gallery of Women (New York: Horace Liveright, 1929).
Tragic America (New York: Horace Liveright, 1931).
Dawn (New York: Horace Liveright, 1931).
The Bulwark (Garden City, N.Y.: Doubleday, 1946).
The Stoic (Garden City, N.Y.: Doubleday, 1947).
Notes on Life, ed. Marguerite Tjader and John F. McAleer (University, Ala.: University of Alabama Press, 1974).

With one exception quotations from the published writings of Dreiser are, in the absence of a standard edition of his work, drawn from the first editions listed above. For *Sister Carrie*, I have quoted from the recently published University of Pennsylvania edition, the first volume of the projected critical edition of Dreiser's work to be published.

All unpublished material cited either in the text or in the notes is in the Dreiser Collection at the Charles Patterson Van Pelt Library at the University of Pennsylvania unless otherwise noted. I have not distinguished in my notes between those letters by or to Dreiser in the Collection that are originals and those that are carbon or photoduplicated copies.

My notes do not adequately suggest the extent to which other scholars' work has helped to pattern my response to Dreiser's fiction. In order to avoid excessive documentation of secondary material, I have confined myself to citing instances of specific debt or disagreement.

1 / Before *Sister Carrie:* An Introduction

1. Kazin, *On Native Grounds* (New York: Harcourt, 1942), pp. 87–88.

2. Dreiser to Barbusse, 15 November 1934, *Letters of Theodore Dreiser*, ed. Robert H. Elias, 3 vols. (Philadelphia: University of Pennsylvania Press, 1959), 2: 705. Cited hereafter as *Letters.*

3. This perspective was provided by Vera Dreiser during an address at the Dreiser Centennial observances in Terre Haute in 1971. See also her book, *My Uncle Theodore* (New York: Nash Publishing, 1976).

4. Smith, *The Religions of Man* (New York: Harper, 1958), p. 92.

5. Bourne, "Desire as Hero," *New Republic* 5 (20 November 1915): 5.

6. *On the Nature of Things*, trans. Cyril Bailey (Oxford: Clarendon Press, 1910), p. 142.

7. "English Liberty in America," in Santayana, *Character and Opinion in the United States* (New York: Scribner's, 1920), p. 233.

2 / *Sister Carrie*

1. From his Preface to the third edition of *The Pilgrim's Regress* (Grand Rapids: Eerdmans, 1958), pp. 9–10.

2. Moers, *Two Dreisers* (New York: Viking, 1969), pp. 160–69.

3. The holograph version of *Sister Carrie*, the basis for the University of Pennsylvania edition, is some 36,000 words longer than the version first published by Doubleday, Page. In addition to details about Carrie's conscience and acting experiences as well as passages of sexual frankness that were dropped in the first published version, the second scene between Ames and Carrie in the Doubleday, Page first edition is considerably shorter. Dreiser telescoped the scene as part of his extensive revision of the last two chapters in the typescript prepared for submission to a potential publisher. Among the items expunged from the scene were the conversation between Ames and Carrie about Balzac and Hardy, Ames's explicit call for humanitarian action on Carrie's part, his linking of the actress's talents to those of great artists, and several other details. The editors of the Pennsylvania edition argue that Dreiser's rewriting of the novel's final two chapters resulted from the influence of his wife Sara and his novelist friend and advisor Arthur Henry. Both Sara and Henry worked closely with Dreiser during the

composition of *Sister Carrie* and through the process of revision and editing.

4. The scene in question from the Doubleday, Page first edition is reprinted in the University of Pennsylvania edition. See pp. 647–51.

5. Moers, *Two Dreisers*, p. 158.

6. "A Photographic Talk With Edison," *Success* 1 (February 1898): 9.

7. Ibid.

8. For a fuller discussion of the sources of Ames's character, see my note "Thomas Edison and *Sister Carrie*," *American Literary Realism* 8 (spring 1975): 155–58.

9. There are two versions of the coda appended to the holograph preserved in the New York Public Library. One version is in Dreiser's hand, the other in his wife's. Sara Dreiser was apparently asked to make a fair copy of Dreiser's version, and she may have made some changes of her own in the process. Ironically, it is the version in her hand that appeared in every edition of *Sister Carrie* until the publication of the University of Pennsylvania text. The editors of the latter edition have eliminated the coda by printing the holograph version of the final chapter, which ends with Hurstwood's suicide. Their contention is that Dreiser was probably reacting to the urging of his wife and Arthur Henry when he rewrote the chapter. Both Dreiser's version of the coda and that in Sara's handwriting are reprinted in the textual apparatus section appended to the University of Pennsylvania edition. See pp. 653–59.

10. Fiedler, *Love and Death in the American Novel* (New York: Criterion, 1960), p. 244.

11. A set of hastily scribbled notes is appended to the holograph along with the two versions of the coda. The notes are apparently also in the hand of Dreiser's wife Sara. They make two main points: that Carrie and Ames should not be thought of as potential marriage partners and that the novel should end with a portrait of Carrie, not Hurstwood. Whose ideas these were—Henry's, Sara's, or Dreiser's—is a matter for conjecture.

12. Interestingly, in Dreiser's version of the coda, the line that refers to Carrie's continued pursuit of "that radiance of delight" is written simply "that radiance." He apparently accepted Sara's addition of the word "delight" for the published version, thus intensifying the confusion about Carrie's state of mind.

13. Pizer, *The Novels of Theodore Dreiser* (Minneapolis: University of Minnesota Press, 1976), p. 72.

14. The chapter titles were added after the holograph was completed. They were a product of both Dreiser's and Arthur Henry's labors. Henry Lanier, senior editor at Doubleday, Page when the novel was submitted, urged that the title of the novel be changed from *Sister Carrie* to *The Flesh and the Spirit*.

15. Gerber, *Theodore Dreiser* (New Haven: Twayne, 1964), p. 68.

16. Lehan, *Theodore Dreiser: His World and His Novels* (Carbondale: Southern Illinois University Press, 1969), p. 79.

17. Ibid., p. xiii.

18. F. O. Matthiessen, *Theodore Dreiser* (New York: William Sloane Associates, 1951), pp. 59–60.

19. Lynn, *The Dream of Success* (New York: Little, Brown, 1955), p. 34.

20. See his Introduction to *Sister Carrie* (Indianapolis: Bobbs Merrill, 1969).

21. Robert Moskin, "A Conversation with C. P. Snow," *Saturday Review World*, 6 April 1974, p. 21.

22. *The American Diaries, 1902–1926*, ed. Thomas P. Riggio (Philadelphia: University of Pennsylvania Press, 1982), pp. 56, 57, 64, 72.

23. The account, now part of the Dreiser Collection at the University of Pennsylvania, is called "An Amateur Laborer."

3 / Jennie Gerhardt

1. *My Life with Dreiser* (Cleveland: World, 1951), p. 11.

2. *Dreiser*, p. 121.

3. Pizer, *Novels*, p. 115; Lehan, *Dreiser*, p. 81; Gerber, *Dreiser*, p. 84; and McAleer, *Theodore Dreiser: An Introduction* (New York: Holt, Rinehart and Winston, 1968), p. 96.

4. Lehan, *Dreiser*, p. 88.

5. Gerber, *Dreiser*, pp. 84–85.

6. Walcutt, *American Literary Naturalism: A Divided Stream* (Minneapolis: University of Minnesota Press, 1956), p. 194.

7. Lehan, *Dreiser*, p. 90.

8. Dreiser to George H. Warwick, 9 July 1929, *Letters*, 2: 491–92.

9. Walcutt, *American Literary Naturalism*, p. 187.

10. Pizer, *Novels*, p. 122.

11. Oscar Cargill, *Intellectual America* (New York: Macmillan, 1941), p. 118.

12. Pizer, *Novels*, p. 124.

13. "Memories of Theodore Dreiser," in his *My Life: The Memoirs of Claude Bowers* (New York: Simon and Schuster, 1962), p. 156.

14. See Dreiser to George C. Brett, 16 April 1901, in the Macmillan Collection, New York Public Library.

15. For a fuller discussion of the matter of Carrie's development, see my article, "A Measure of Sister Carrie's Growth," in *The Dreiser Newsletter* 11 (spring 1980): 13–23.

4 / The Financier and The Titan

1. Dreiser to Mencken, 6 December 1909, and Dreiser to Mencken, 16 December 1909, *Letters*, 1: 97–98.

2. Matthiessen, *Dreiser*, p. 140.

3. In April 1927 a revised edition of *The Financier* appeared. Dreiser had decided shortly after the publication of the first edition in 1912 that the book was too long but did not get to the task of cutting and revising until after the completion of *An American Tragedy.* In the short version, Dreiser in fact elaborated a few scenes and one of them, which appears in chapter 51, further "softens" Cowperwood. While awaiting imprisonment, he indulges in affection for his children, of whose very existence the reader needs to be reminded, so thorough has Cowperwood's and Dreiser's neglect of them been to this point in the novel. The financier's difficulties also elicit thoughts of his mother. They are now "about as tender and sympathetic as any he could maintain in the world." Remembering her "sympathetic care of him in his youth," he wishes fervently that he were able to spare her "this unhappy breakdown of her fortunes in her old age."

4. The way in which Dreiser's absorption in Cowperwood's exploits had increased his sympathy for the powerful and lessened his tendency to sentimentalize the poor, however, is revealed in a letter to Gustavus Myers congratulating him on his perceptive analyses of business tycoons. His admiration for Myers did not stop him from chastising him for his "repeatedly avowed belief that the common laborer—proletarian—possesses ¬ll the virtues which the middle class and the oligarch lack." Dreiser alludes to an earlier talk with Myers in which Myers had convinced Dreiser that he had changed his mind and now believed that "all men are more or less shot through with the universal threads of avarice as well as of mercy and tenderness." Dreiser hoped that for Myers's "own sake" he held the latter view. See Dreiser to Myers, 31 March 1916, *Letters,* 1: 208–9.

5. Pizer, *Novels,* p. 176.

6. "The Barbaric Naturalism of Mr. Dreiser," in *The Stature of Theodore Dreiser,* ed. Alfred Kazin and Charles Shapiro (Bloomington: Indiana University Press, 1955), p. 78. Sherman's essay first appeared in *The Nation,* 2 December 1915.

7. Stephanie Platow is based on Kirah Markham, the painter, actress, and intellectual, with whom Dreiser had a relationship.

8. Pizer, *Novels,* p. 193, and Gerber, *Dreiser,* p. 104.

9. Matthiessen, *Dreiser,* p. 158.

10. O'Neill, "The Disproportion of Sadness: Dreiser's *The Financier* and *The Titan,*" *Modern Fiction Studies* 23 (autumn 1977): 409–22.

11. Mencken's ranking is quoted in Matthiessen, *Dreiser,* p. 144. See also McAleer, *Dreiser: An Introduction,* p. 108.

12. Pizer, *Novels,* pp. 179, 199, and Shapiro's *Theodore Dreiser: Our Bitter Patriot* (Carbondale: Southern Illinois University Press, 1962), pp. 27, 44.

13. Warren, *Homage to Dreiser* (New York: Random House, 1971), pp. 72–73.

5 / The "Genius"

1. Gerber, Dreiser, p. 116.

2. I am indebted to Marguerite Tjader Harris for this bit of suggestive information. Mrs. Harris, Dreiser's long-time literary secretary and confidante, revealed to me in conversation that Dreiser not only made known his preference for women's white clothing, but also frequently insisted that Helen Dreiser and others wear white.

3. This particular diary was kept during Dreiser's stay in New York in 1917. American Diaries, pp. 147–256 passim.

4. Hovey and Ralph, "Dreiser's The "Genius": Structure and Motivation," Hartford Studies in Literature 2 (1970): 169–83.

5. Dreiser's sister Mame had become a Christian Science convert in 1898 and a healer in 1906. Grant Richards renewed the novelist's interest in Mary Baker Eddy's speculations during his trip to England in the fall of 1911.

6. Dreiser had also toyed with the idea of good coming out of evil in the trilogy, wherein Berenice Fleming emerges from Hattie Starr's Louisville brothel.

7. The so-called happy ending holograph is in the Dreiser Collection at the University of Pennsylvania.

8. Warren, Homage, p. 50.

9. Matthiessen, Dreiser, p. 161; Burton Rascoe, "Does Dreiser's Final Novel Reveal a Spiritual Creed?" Chicago Tribune, 24 March 1946, sec. 4, p. 1; and Robert H. Elias, Theodore Dreiser, Apostle of Nature (New York: Knopf, 1949), p. 157.

10. Warren, Homage, p. 50. Warren also suggests that Dreiser's choice of Yerkes as Cowperwood's model in the trilogy was motivated by the novelist's "self-indulgence and self-scrutiny" (p. 75).

11. Matthiessen, Dreiser, p. 166.

12. See the correspondence between Dreiser and Edward H. Smith, Letters, 1: 335–38.

13. Review of Hey Rub-a-Dub-Dub, in Catholic World 111 (May 1920): 260.

6 / "The Marriage Group"

1. "Married," "The Second Choice," "Free," and "The Lost Phoebe" appeared in Free and Other Stories (New York: Boni and Liveright, 1918). All subsequent quotations from these four stories are from that volume.

2. "Chains," "Marriage—For One," and "The Shadow" appeared in Chains: Lesser Novels and Stories (New York: Boni and Liveright, 1927). All subsequent quotations from these three stories are from that volume.

3. "Rebellious Women and Marriage" was written in 1926 during Dreiser's European trip. Both a manuscript and a typescript are among Dreiser's papers at the University of Pennsylvania. All subsequent quotations are from the manuscript.

7 / *An American Tragedy* and the Thirties

1. See Sherman's essay "Mr. Dreiser in Tragic Realism" in *The Main Stream* (New York: Scribner's, 1927), pp. 134–44.

2. Walcutt, *American Literary Naturalism*, p. 207, and Pizer, *Novels*, p. 255.

3. Matthiessen, *Dreiser*, p. 206. *The Liberal Imagination* (Garden City, N. Y.: Doubleday, 1957), p. 16. Trilling's essay, "Reality in America," in which this assessment appears was originally published in *The Nation*, 20 April 1946.

4. Dreiser to Harrison Smith, 25 April 1931, *Letters*, 2: 528, and Dreiser to Jack Wilgus, 20 April 1927, *Letters*, 2: 457–58.

5. Quoted by Vivian Pierce in her unpublished letter to Dreiser, 8 March 1926.

6. Dreiser to Bauer, undated, but in the 1920 correspondence file at the University of Pennsylvania Dreiser Collection.

7. The references to McMillan's earlier fates are at the end of the unpaginated holograph in a section headed "N. B." There are also two divergent typescripts of *An American Tragedy* extant. The holograph and the typescripts are at the University of Pennsylvania's Dreiser Collection.

8. Walcutt, *American Literary Naturalism*, p. 211.

9. Dreiser to Dinamov, 5 January 1927, *Letters*, 2: 450.

10. *Dreiser Looks at Russia* (New York: Horace Liveright, 1928), p. 26.

11. "Individualism and the Jungle," *New Masses* 7 (January 1932): 4.

12. Dreiser to Elias, 17 April 1937, *Letters*, 3: 784, 785.

13. Unpublished letter, Dreiser to Nazife Osman Pacha, 21 November 1931.

14. Dreiser to E. S. Martin, 4 September 1934, *Letters*, 2: 689.

15. Trilling, "Reality in America," pp. 15–16.

16. Dreiser to Hutchins Hapgood, 10 October 1933, *Letters*, 2: 651.

17. *Letters*, 2: 469–70.

18. Dreiser to Franklin and Beatrice Booth, 16 July 1928, *Letters*, 2: 471.

19. The *Collecting Net* article was sent to Franklin Booth. It is in the Dreiser Collection at the University of Pennsylvania.

20. Unpublished letter, Dreiser to Kennell, 5 September 1928.

21. Unpublished letter, Dreiser to Churchman, 10 October 1928.

22. *Bookman* 68 (September 1928): 25.

23. Dreiser to Morris, 25 November 1929, *Letters*, 2: 495.

24. Unpublished letters, Burke to Dreiser, undated, and Dreiser to Burke, 22 February 1930.

25. *American Mercury* 31 (March 1934): 337–41.

26. Unpublished letters, Dreiser to White, 23 June 1934, and Dreiser to Fabri, 12 July 1934.

27. Dreiser to Bridges, 16 March 1935, *Letters*, 2: 735.

28. Dreiser to Millikan, 16 March 1935, *Letters*, 2: 739, and Dreiser to Crile, 7 August 1936, *Letters*, 3: 776–77.

29. Dreiser to Stebbins, 30 August 1935, *Letters*, 2: 749.

30. The essay, dated 24 August 1937, is in the Dreiser Collection at the University of Pennsylvania.

31. As quoted in Matthiessen, *Dreiser*, p. 241.

32. Dreiser to Mary Elizabeth Thompson, 18 January 1939, *Letters*, 3: 833–34.

33. Dreiser to Stromberg, 14 May 1940, *Letters*, 3: 878–79; Dreiser to Dorothy Payne Davis, 18 July 1940, *Letters*, 3: 886–90, and unpublished letter, Dreiser to F. MacConnell, 12 July 1941.

8 / *The Bulwark*

1. Dreiser to Jones, 1 December 1938, *Letters*, 3: 822.

2. Unpublished letter, Dreiser to Jones, 27 January 1939.

3. Dreiser to Sheppard Arthur Watson, 20 January 1939, *Letters*, 3: 834.

4. Unpublished letter, Dreiser to Jones, 23 April 1943.

5. Tolles, *Quakers and the Atlantic Culture* (New York: Macmillan, 1960), p. 133.

6. Dreiser patterned the Quaker meeting at Segookit, of which Solon's parents are members, after Jones's boyhood meeting in China, Maine. He also drew on Jones's narratives for the schoolboy fight and Solon's infection after being cut by an axe. See Jones's untitled typescript dated 10 June 1946 in the University of Pennsylvania Dreiser Collection.

7. Henry David Thoreau, 21 August 1851, *The Journal of Henry D. Thoreau*, ed. Bradford Torrey and Francis H. Allen, foreword by Walter Harding (1906; reprint ed., New York: Dover, 1962), 2: 248b.

8. Pizer, *Novels*, p. 330.

9. Ibid., p. 325.

10. For a detailed history of the divisive debate over the manuscript of the novel, see Jack Salzman's article "The Curious History of Dreiser's *The Bulwark*," in *Proof* 3 (1973): 21–61. Salzman demonstrates that the final text of *The Bulwark* is essentially Donald Elder's version. There is a feeling among some Dreiser critics, though unspoken in their published critiques, that the novel does not so much represent Dreiser's thinking as that of Mrs. Harris, whose own conversion to Catholicism dates from the same period, or perhaps that it represents the thinking of Helen Dreiser, whose burgeoning interest in Hinduism definitely influenced *The Stoic*. But the overwhelming preponderance of the evidence points to the authenticity of *The Bulwark* as Dreiser's work. It should be remembered that he was always careless about editorial changes made by others after the fact of his completing a manuscript, and that he did approve and commend the final text of the novel as ultimately revised by Elder. See Dreiser to Elder, 22 December 1945, *Letters*, 3: 1033.

11. See Emerson Price, "Book Reviews," *Cleveland Press*, 26 March 1946; P. T. R., "Books—New and Old: Dreiser's Posthumous Novel: Work Written in Desperation," *Dallas News*, 24 March 1946; Orville Prescott, "Outstanding

Books," *Yale Review* 35 (summer 1946): 767; Lewis Gannett, "Books and Things," *New York Herald Tribune*, 21 March 1946, p. 23; and Fred C. Whitney, "Books in Review," *El Cajon Valley News*, 17 April 1946. All of these reviews are reprinted in Jack Salzman's collection *Theodore Dreiser: The Critical Reception* (New York: David Lewis, 1972).

12. Spiller, "Dreiser as Master Craftsman," *Saturday Review of Literature*, 23 March 1946, p. 23; and Trilling, "Reality in America," pp. 8–19.

13. Lyndenberg, "The Anatomy of Exhaustion," *Saturday Review of Literature*, 6 December 1947, p. 36.

14. Walcutt, *American Literary Naturalism*, p. 221.

15. Rubinstein, "A Pillar of Society," *New Masses*, 30 April 1946, pp. 23–24.

16. Snell, *The Shapers of American Fiction* (New York: Dutton, 1947), p. 247.

17. Elias, *Dreiser*, p. 301.

18. "God, Mammon and Mr. Dreiser," *New York Times*, 24 March 1946, sec. 7, p. 44.

19. Dreiser's annotated copy of Jones's book is in the novelist's personal library, preserved as part of the University of Pennsylvania's Dreiser Collection.

20. Shapiro, *Dreiser: Our Bitter Patriot*, p. 79.

21. Elias, *Dreiser*, p. 300.

22. See, for example, Carroll T. Brown, "Dreiser's *Bulwark* and Philadelphia Quakerism," *Friends Historical Association Bulletin* 35 (August 1946): 55.

23. Lynn, *Dream of Success*, p. 74.

24. Hicks, "Dreiser the Puzzle," *Saturday Review of Literature*, 4 April 1959, p. 16.

25. Lyndenberg, "The Anatomy of Exhaustion," *Saturday Review of Literature*, 6 December 1947, p. 36.

26. Lewis, *The Four Loves* (New York: Harcourt, 1960), p. 31.

27. Trilling, "Reality in America," pp. 17–18.

28. Ross, "Concerning Dreiser's Mind," *American Literature* 18 (November 1946): 243.

29. Wagenknecht, *Cavalcade of the American Novel* (New York: Holt, Rinehart and Winston, 1952), pp. 292, 284.

30. Lehan, *Dreiser*, pp. 233–34.

31. Pizer, Introduction to *Theodore Dreiser: A Selection of Uncollected Prose* (Detroit: Wayne State University Press, 1977), pp. 25–26.

32. Drummond, "Theodore Dreiser: Shifting Naturalism" in *Fifty Years of the American Novel*, ed. Harold C. Gardiner (New York: Gordian Press, 1952), p. 46.

33. See Jones's typescript, dated 10 June 1946, in the University of Pennsylvania Dreiser Collection.

34. Spiller, "Dreiser as Master Craftsman," p. 23.

35. Elias, *Dreiser*, p. 304.

36. The actual letter from Dreiser to Lacosky has been lost. The para-

graph in question is quoted back to the novelist in a letter from the priest. See unpublished letter, Lacosky to Dreiser, 1 November 1925.

37. Unpublished letter, Lacosky to Dreiser, 11 January 1933.

38. Elias, *Dreiser*, pp. 283, 304.

39. *My Life with Dreiser*, pp. 302–3.

40. Tjader, *Theodore Dreiser: A New Dimension* (Norwalk, Conn.: Silvermine Publishers, 1965), p. 156.

9 / The Stoic

1. See the unpublished letter from Helen Dreiser to H. L. Mencken, 13 February 1946. Mrs. Harris had apparently been given a letter by Dreiser authorizing her to make the funeral arrangements. She had commissioned the Reverend Allan Hunter to conduct the ceremony, much to Helen's consternation. Helen believed that Mrs. Harris was trying to promote Hunter. Helen viewed the whole situation as sad because now Dreiser had to be "interpreted as someone who was panting and thirsting for God." She was also upset because Hunter had not introduced Charlie Chaplin at the funeral. The complex relationship between Helen, Mrs. Harris, and Louise Campbell and their influence on Dreiser in these last years awaits a definitive analysis.

2. Dreiser to Vaughan, 13 September 1933, *Letters*, 2: 641.

3. *The Uncollected Lectures*, ed. Clarence Gohdes (New York: W. E. Rudge, 1932), p. 57.

4. Mookerjee, "Dreiser's Use of Hindu Thought in *The Stoic*," *American Literature* 43 (May 1971): 276.

5. Lewis, *The Four Loves*, p. 38.

6. Teilhard de Chardin, *The Divine Milieu*, trans. Bernard Wall (New York: Harper, 1960), p. 109.

7. The passage is from chapter 62 of the manuscript of *The Titan* in the University of Pennsylvania Dreiser Collection.

8. A typescript of the proposed postscript, entitled "Concerning Good and Evil" is preserved in the University of Pennsylvania Dreiser Collection. The quotation is from p. 12 of the epilogue.

9. McAleer, *Dreiser: An Introduction*, p. 115.

10. Shapiro, *Dreiser: Our Bitter Patriot*, p. 43, and Lundquist, *Theodore Dreiser* (New York: Frederick Ungar, 1978), p. 71.

11. Mrs. Harris in conversation with Elias, as quoted in Elias, p. 298.

12. *My Life with Dreiser*, p. 291.

13. Ibid., p. 297.

14. Unpublished letter, Dreiser to William Z. Foster, 20 July 1945. W. A. Swanberg, in his biography of Dreiser, casts doubt on the authenticity of this letter, believing it to have been written for him by a "well-drilled Marxist." Helen maintained, however, that Dreiser had approved and corrected the letter's contents.

15. Unpublished letter, Dreiser to TASS, undated, among his 1943 correspondence in the Dreiser Collection at the University of Pennsylvania.

16. Elias, *Dreiser*, pp. 275, 306.

Index

Ainslee's, 16
Alger, Horatio, 88
Altgeld, Peter, 86
America Is Worth Saving (Dreiser), 145
American Civil Liberties Union, 141
American Friends Service Committee, 154
American Mercury, 149
American Spectator, The, 148
American Tragedy, An (Dreiser): author's evaluation of, 126, 139–40, 195; compared to *The Bulwark*, 131, 134, 135, 140, 158, 159, 174, 175, 177–78; compared to *The Financier*, 76, 89; compared to *The "Genius,"* 76, 135, 140; compared to *Sister Carrie*, 129; compared to *The Titan*, 129, 140; compared to *A Trilogy of Desire*, 127, 140; critics' responses to, 127, 131, 132–33; culpability in, 130–35, 139–40, 158–59; McMillan in, 53, 133–36, 137; mentioned, 15, 53, 112, 123, 144, 153, 154, 165, 201n3; naturalism in, 130–33; plot of, 127–30; social injustices in, 137–39, 159
Anderson, Sherwood, 115, 125
Ashcan School, 92
Auchincloss, Louis, 42

Babbitt, Irving, 8
Balzac, Honoré de, 26–27, 30, 32, 198n3
Barbusse, Henri, 4
Bauer (Dreiser correspondent), 134–35
Beardsley, Aubrey, 92

Benedict, Harriet, 126–27
Bhagavad-Gita, 183, 184
Bible, 162, 172. *See also* Dreiser, Theodore: and the Bible
Book About Myself, A (Dreiser), 10, 14, 70
Bookman, 147
Book of Discipline (Quaker), 155, 160
Booth, Beatrice, 146
Booth, Franklin, 146
Bourguereau, Guillaume-Adolphe, 92, 101
Bourne, Randolph, 12
Bowers, Claude, 65–66
"Brahma" (Ralph Waldo Emerson), 149, 184
Bridges, Calvin, 150
Brothers Karamazov, The (Fyodor Dostoevsky), 172
Browder, Earl, 192
Brown, Grace, 126
Bryant, William Cullen, 8
Buddhism, 111
Bulwark, The (Dreiser): author's evaluation of, 153, 170–75 passim, 177–79, 195; compared to *An American Tragedy*, 131, 134, 135, 140, 158, 159, 174, 175, 177–78; compared to *The Financier*, 80, 161–62, 174; compared to *The "Genius,"* 82, 109, 156, 158, 175; compared to *Jennie Gerhardt*, 165, 173, 174, 175; compared to *Sister Carrie*, 61, 158, 162, 164, 167, 168–69, 179; compared to *The Stoic*, 180, 184, 185, 188, 189, 191; compared to *The Titan*, 82; composi-

tion of, 154, 156, 165; critics' responses to, ix, 162, 165, 168–75 passim; love-service ethic in, ix, 163–65, 169, 177, 185, 189; manuscript controversy over, 165–66; mentioned, ix, x, 8, 11, 14, 16, 52–53, 61, 80, 82, 106, 120, 124, 141, 146, 152, 180; nature in, 9, 160–62, 170; plot of, 156–65 passim; 167; reception of, 153, 154, 166–67; Rufus Jones's influence on, 154–55, 156, 204n6
Bunyan, John, 19
Burke, Thomas, 148–49
Butterick Publications, 48
B. W. Dodge and Company, 48

Campbell, Louise, 165–66, 206n1
Canterbury Tales (Chaucer), 113
Cargill, Oscar, 64–65
Carlyle, Thomas, 94
Cash McCall (Cameron Hawley), 89
Catholicism, Roman. See Dreiser, Theodore: and Catholicism
Catholic World, 111
Century, 119
"Chains" (Dreiser), 120–21
Chaplin, Charlie, 206n1
Chaucer, Geoffrey, 113
Chicago, University of, 7
Chicago Globe, 9
Christian Science. See Dreiser, Theodore: and Christian Science
Churchman, John, 147
Cold Spring Harbor Biological Laboratory, 150, 151, 160, 169
Collecting Net, The (Woods Hole Publication), 146
Color of a Great City, The, 112, 170
Committee for the Defense of Political Prisoners, 142
communism. See Dreiser, Theodore: and communism
Cooper, James Fenimore, 8
Cornell Medical Laboratory, 147
Corot, Jean Baptiste Camille, 92
Cosmopolitan, 16, 113, 115
"Crack Up, The" (F. Scott Fitzgerald), 194
Crashaw, Richard, 99
Creative Force. See Dreiser, Theodore:

and the Creative Force
Crile, George W., 150
Crime and Punishment (Fyodor Dostoevsky), 195
Cudlipp, Mrs. Annie Ericsson, 48, 105
Cudlipp, Thelma, 48, 49, 73, 84, 93, 100, 103, 108

Darrow, Clarence, 139
Darwin, Charles, 88, 100, 132, 187. See also Darwinism, Social
Darwinism, Social, ix, 71, 77, 79, 142, 182, 191
Daubigny, Charles, 92
Dawn (Dreiser), 3, 7–8, 19, 20, 63, 100
Degas, Edgar, 92
Delineator, The, 48
determinism. See Dreiser, Theodore: naturalism of
Detroit Free Library, 30
Dickinson, Emily, 63
Dinamov, Sergei, 139
Direction, 165
"Doer of the Word, A" (Dreiser), 45–46, 51, 66, 137, 143–44, 173
Doré, Gustave, 92
Dostoevsky, Fyodor, 132, 140
Doubleday, Frank N., 45
Doubleday, Mrs. Frank N., 45
Doubleday, Page and Company, 45, 48, 49
Doubleday and Company, 165
Dream of Success, The (Kenneth S. Lynn), 144
Dreiser, Emma Wilhelmina (Theodore's sister), 18
Dreiser, Helen Richardson (Theodore's second wife), 53, 141, 165, 168, 176–77, 182, 183, 189, 191, 202n2, 204n10, 206n1, 207n15
Dreiser, John Paul (Theodore's father), 3, 6, 52, 174, 177
Dreiser, John Paul, Jr. (Paul Dresser, Theodore's brother), 8–9, 30, 48, 65
Dreiser, Marcus Romanus (Theodore's brother Rome), 6, 62
Dreiser, Mary Frances (Theodore's sister Mame), 50, 65, 66, 192, 202n5
Dreiser, Sarah Schänäb (Theodore's mother), 4–6, 9, 30, 50, 65, 145, 174
Dreiser, Sara Osborne White (Theo-

dore's first wife), 15–16, 48, 73, 93,
94, 95, 98, 101, 105, 112–13,
198n3, 199nn9, 11, 12
Dreiser, Theodore: and the Bible, 4, 7,
46, 60–61, 62, 79, 104, 191, 193;
and capitalism, ix, 130, 142, 143,
144, 178; and Catholicism, 3–4, 5, 7,
17, 47, 52, 60, 63, 99, 105, 108, 111,
145, 170–71, 172, 174, 175–76,
204n10; and Chicago, 3, 7, 9, 12,
17, 18–19, 43, 91; and Christian
Science, 104–5, 106, 108–9, 110,
111, 170, 183, 188, 191, 202n5; and
communism, 141–42, 167, 192–93,
206–7n15; and the Creative Force,
ix, 47, 104, 111, 149, 151–52, 153,
160–62, 163, 164, 170, 176, 177,
192, 193; and desire, 9, 11–14, 16,
19, 20, 21; Edison's influence on, 11–
12, 30–32; education of, 3–4, 7–8,
17; "equation" theory of, 8, 68, 88,
112, 130, 174, 183, 190; existen-
tialism in, 15, 21, 53, 54, 88; family
influence on, 3, 4–7, 8–9, 16–17, 21,
50; and Hinduism, 7, 173, 183–92
passim, 204n10; humanitarianism of,
42, 141–46, 156, 171; literary
influences on, 7–8, 106, 132; marriage, attitude toward, 15–16, 17, 54–
55, 91, 96, 103, 104, 105, 113;
mental breakdown of, 46–48, 91;
naturalism of, ix, 3, 5, 7, 9, 10–11,
12, 14–15, 17, 22, 23–24, 42, 56, 61,
62, 63, 79–80, 88, 91, 104, 105, 106,
130, 131, 132, 133, 139, 140, 142,
143, 153, 169, 173, 174, 179, 194;
and nature, 8–9, 14, 59, 109, 142,
149, 160–62, 163, 179, 195; newspaper and magazine experience of, 9–
10, 48, 91, 138, 166; and Quakerism,
7, 153, 154–77 passim; romanticism
of, 7–8, 9–10, 140; and science, 4, 6,
7, 13, 107, 112, 146–52, 160, 195;
selfishness, attitude toward, 14–15,
42, 46, 156, 177, 188, 194, 195;
selflessness, attitude toward, 4–6, 14–
15, 42, 46, 143, 188, 194, 195;
sexual varietism of, 5, 15, 16, 17, 91,
98, 102–3, 109; and socialism, 139,
143, 192; supernaturalism in, 6–7;
and the twentieth century, 11, 13,

17, 19, 194–95
Dreiser, Theodore, Mrs. See Dreiser,
Sara White; Dreiser, Helen
Richardson
Dreiser, Vera (Theodore's niece), 5
Dresser, Paul. See Dreiser, John Paul, Jr.
Drummond, Edward, 173

Eddy, Mary Baker, 104, 108, 183,
202n5
Edison, Thomas Alva. See Dreiser,
Theodore: Edison's influence on
Elder, Donald, 165–66, 204n10
Elias, Robert H., 108, 143, 167, 168,
175, 176, 192
Emerson, Ralph Waldo, 94, 104, 149,
173, 184
Epictetus, 100
Esther Waters (George Moore), 64
Ethan Frome (Edith Wharton), 120

Fabri, Ralph, 149
Farrell, James T., 165–66, 189, 190
Faulkner, William, 17
Ficke, Arthur Davidson, 176
Fiedler, Leslie, 33
Financier, The (Dreiser): art in, 75, 77;
author's evaluation of, 89–90; compared to An American Tragedy, 76, 89;
compared to The Bulwark, 80, 161–62,
174; compared to The "Genius," 76;
compared to Jennie Gerhardt, 54, 79,
80; compared to Sister Carrie, 72, 74,
89; compared to The Stoic, 80, 81, 89,
182; compared to The Titan, 78, 89;
critics' responses to, 88–90; epilogue
of, 79–80; mentioned, 68, 69, 91,
155, 182; plot of, 71–80 passim;
sources for, 70–71, 72–73; sympathy
in, 76–79, 201n3; women in, 71–79
passim. See also Trilogy of Desire, A
Finding the Trail of Life (Rufus Jones), 156
First Principles (Herbert Spencer), 10
Fitzgerald, F. Scott, 40, 84, 194
Fort, Charles, 107
Foster, William Z., 192
Fox, George, 162
Francis of Assisi, 69, 162, 173
Free and Other Stories (Dreiser), 175–76
"Free" (Dreiser), 16, 116–19, 195

Gallery of Women, A (Dreiser), 101, 124, 148, 165
Gates, Elmer, 23
"Genius," The (Dreiser): art in, 13, 76, 91–92, 95, 97, 105; author's evaluation of, 91, 109; compared to *An American Tragedy*, 76, 135, 140; compared to *The Bulwark*, 82, 109, 156, 158, 175; compared to *The Financier*, 76; compared to *Jennie Gerhardt*, 94, 106, 108; compared to *Sister Carrie*, 50, 51, 54, 94, 105–6; compared to *The Stoic*, 82, 183, 188; compared to *The Titan*, 82, 99–100, 101, 183; holograph "happy ending" of, 107–8; mentioned, 12, 13, 16, 69, 81, 82, 90, 113, 119, 145, 170; plot of, 91–100 passim; womanly ideal in, 13, 92–103
Gerber, Phillip, 40, 41, 56, 59, 85, 93, 99
Gerôme, Jean Léon, 83
"Giff" (Dreiser), 148
Gillette, Chester, 126, 127
Glackens, William, 92
Goldsmith, Oliver, 8
Gould, George M., 106
Grapes of Wrath, The (John Steinbeck), 140
Great Gatsby, The (F. Scott Fitzgerald), 40
Great Man from the Provinces, The (Honoré de Balzac), 26
Grigsby, Emilie, 84, 85, 184

Hals, Franz, 75
Hardy, Thomas, 26, 198n3
"Harness, The" (John Steinbeck), 119
Harper and Brothers, 56–57
Harper's Bazaar, 122
Harris, Marguerite Tjader, 151, 154, 165–66, 168, 178, 182, 191, 202n2, 204n10, 206n1
Hawthorne, Nathaniel, 8
Heinemann, William, 48
Helleu, Paul Cesare, 92
Hemingway, Ernest, 13
Henry, Arthur, 16, 198n3, 199nn9, 11, 14
Hey Rub-a-Dub-Dub (Dreiser), 102, 111, 134, 155
Hicks, Granville, 145, 170
Hinduism. *See* Dreiser, Theodore: and

Hinduism
Hirsch, Emil Gustav, 7, 103
History of the Great American Fortunes (Gustavus Myers), 70
Hitler, Adolph, 145
Hoosier Holiday, A (Dreiser), 4, 14, 110, 111
Hovey, Ralph B., 101
Howells, William Dean, 20
Huckleberry Finn (Samuel L. Clemens), 66
Hunter, Rev. Allan, 206n1
Huxley, Thomas Henry, 10, 12, 17, 100

Ingres, Jean Auguste Dominique, 75
Inner Light, the, 7, 158, 159, 160, 163, 165, 168, 169, 175, 177. *See also* Dreiser, Theodore: and Quakerism
Irving, Washington, 8

"Jealousy" (Dreiser). *See* "Shadow, The"
Jennie Gerhardt (Dreiser): author's evaluation of, 63–68 passim; Christianity in, 52–53, 59–61; compared to *The Bulwark*, 165, 173, 174, 175; compared to *The Financier*, 54, 78–79, 80; compared to *The "Genius,"* 94, 106, 108; compared to *Sister Carrie*, 50–51, 54, 56, 57–58, 59, 61–68 passim; compared to *The Stoic*, 190; compared to *The Titan*, 88, 89; critics' responses to, 56–57, 61–62, 64, 66, 144; Dreiser's attitude toward, 65–66; epilogue to first edition of, 57–58; "goodness of heart" in, 57–59, 61, 62, 173; mentioned, 4–5, 15, 49, 132, 137, 144; mysticism in, 62–63; plot of, 50–56 passim
J. F. Taylor & Co., 45, 48
John Lane Company, 154
Jones, Jenkin Lloyd, 7, 103
Jones, Rufus. See *Bulwark, The*: Rufus Jones's influence on
Journal (Henry David Thoreau), 161
Journal (John Woolman), 155, 164, 167, 168, 175
Joyce, James, 4, 13

Kazin, Alfred, 3
Kennell, Ruth Epperson, 147

Lacosky, Rev. Paul, 175–76, 206n36

Lanier, Henry, 199n14
Larkin, Edgar Lucien, 106
Laughing Gas (Dreiser), 110
Lawrence, D. H., 13
League for the Abolition of Capital
  Punishment, 134
League of American Writers, 142
Lehan, Richard, ix, 41, 56, 60, 173
Lenin, Nikolai, 192–93
Lewis, Clive Staples, 19, 171, 186
Libby, Laura Jean, 8
Library Associates of Haverford Col-
  lege, 174
"Lions, Harts, Leaping Does" (J. F.
  Powers), 66
Living Thoughts of Thoreau, The (Dreiser),
  145
Loeb, Jacques, 111
Longfellow, Henry Wadsworth, 8
"Lost Phoebe, The" (Dreiser), 119–20
Lubbock, Sir John, 100
Lucretius, 13
Luks, George, 92
Lundquist, James, 191
Lyndenberg, John, 167–70
Lynn, Kenneth S., 41, 144, 170

McAleer, John, 56, 89, 190
Madame Bovary (Gustave Flaubert), 195
Mahler, Gustav, 195
Mailer, Norman, 64
Manet, Edouard, 92
"Man with the Blue Guitar, The" (Wal-
  lace Stevens), 13
Marcus Aurelius, 100
Markham, Kirah, 73, 201n7
Marriage, 121
"Marriage—For One" (Dreiser), 121–22
"Married" (Dreiser), 16, 113–15
Matthiessen, F. O., ix, 41, 52, 55, 73,
  88, 108, 109, 133, 167, 188–89
Mencken, Henry Lewis, 66, 70, 89
Metropolitan, 16
Millais, John Everett, 92
Millikan, Robert Andrews, 150
Mirage (Dreiser), 127. See also *American
  Tragedy, An*
Moers, Ellen, ix, 23, 29
Mohammedanism, 111
Molineux, Roland, 126
Monet, Claude, 92

Monticelli, Adolphe, 92
Mookerjee, R. M., 185
Mooney, Tom, 142
Moore, George, 64
Morris, Emmanuel, 147
Mt. Wilson Observatory, 150, 151
Munsey's, 48
Mussolini, Benito, 145
"My Creator" (Dreiser), 151
Myers, Gustavus, 70, 201n4
"Myth of Individuality, The" (Dreiser),
  149

Nation, 171
naturalism. *See* Dreiser, Theodore:
  naturalism in
New Criticism, the, ix, 44
New York Society for the Suppression of
  Vice, the, 110
New York Times, 120
New York World, 127
Nietzsche, Friedrich, 70, 88
Norris, Frank, 45, 106, 191
North American Review, 189
Notes on Life (Dreiser), 151

Octopus, The (Frank Norris), 106
O'Neill, Eugene, 148, 149
O'Neill, John, 89
Ouida. *See* Ramée, Marie Louise de la

Père Goriot (Honoré de Balzac), 32, 195
Phenomena of Life, The (George Crile), 150
Pilgrim's Regress (C. S. Lewis), 19
Pit, The (Frank Norris), 106, 191
Pittsburgh *Dispatch*, 10
Pizer, Donald, ix, 39, 56, 62, 65, 80,
  85, 89, 132, 162–63, 173
Plato, 12, 104
Plays of the Natural and Supernatural (Drei-
  ser), 110
"Portrait of a Rabbi" (Rembrandt), 75
Powers, J. F., 66

Quakerism. *See* Dreiser, Theodore: and
  Quakerism

Rake, The (Dreiser), 126. See also
  American Tragedy, An
Ralph, Ruth S., 101
Ramée, Marie Louise de la (Ouida), 8

214 · INDEX

Rand, Ayn, 79
Rascoe, Burton, 108
"Rebellious Women and Marriage"
(Dreiser), 123–24
"Reina" (Dreiser), 124
Relations and Development of the Mind and
Brain, The (Elmer Gates), 23
Rembrandt van Rijn, 75
Ribera, José de, 92
Richards, Grant, 68, 202n5
Richardson, Helen. See Dreiser, Helen
Richardson
Rockefeller, John D., 71
Rodin, Auguste, 92
Roe, E. P., 25
Ross, Woodburn O., 172
Rousseau, Henri, 75, 92
Rousseau and Romanticism (Irving Babbitt),
8
Rossetti, Dante Gabriel, 92
Rubinstein, Annette, 167
Russia. See Union of Soviet Socialist
Republics

St. Louis Republic, 15
Salzman, Jack O., 204n10
Santayana, George, 14
Saturday Evening Post, 116
Schopenhauer, Arthur, 70, 71, 100, 186
Science and Christian Tradition (Thomas
Henry Huxley), 10
Science and Health (Mary Baker Eddy), 104
Science and the Hebrew Tradition (Thomas
Henry Huxley), 10
Scottsboro Boys, The, 142
"Second Choice, The" (Dreiser), 16,
115–16
"Shadow, The" (Dreiser), 122–23
Shapiro, Charles, 89, 168, 191
Sherman, Stuart Pratt, 81, 131
Shinn, Everett, 92
Shintoism, 111
Sinai Congregation (Chicago), 7
Sing Sing prison, 139
Sister Carrie (Dreiser): Ames in, 24–34,
39, 42, 67, 198n3, 199n8, 199n11;
author's evaluation of, 42–45, 195;
compared to An American Tragedy, 129;
compared to The Bulwark, 61, 158,
162, 164, 167, 168–69, 179; com-
pared to The Financier, 72, 74, 89;

compared to The "Genius," 50, 51, 54,
94, 105–6; compared to Jennie Gerhardt, 50–51, 54, 56, 57–58, 59,
61–68 passim; compared to The Stoic,
61, 189; compared to The Titan, 87,
88, 89; composition of, 16, 21;
critics' responses to, 40–42; desire in,
18–21, 23–28 passim, 33, 35–40
passim, 44–45; Doubleday, Page first
edition of, 28, 32, 33–34, 40, 42,
57–58, 87, 198n3, 199n9, 199n12;
holograph of, 198n3, 199n9, 199n11,
199n14; mentioned, 7, 9, 11, 13, 15,
16, 61, 78, 94, 113, 132, 155, 168,
195; plot of, 18–28, 32; publication
history of, 45, 48; selflessness vs.
selfishness in, 27–32 passim, 33–40;
sources for, 18, 30–32
Small Town Boy, A (Rufus Jones), 156
Smith, Edward H., 110, 112, 127
Smith, Huston, 6
Snell, George, 167
Snow, Charles Percy, 43
Social Gospel, The, 7
Society of Friends. See Dreiser, Theo-
dore: and Quakerism
Sonntag, W. L., 92
Soul of the Universe, The (Gustav Strom-
berg), 151
Spanish Civil War, 142, 154, 156
Spectator, The, 145
Spencer, Herbert, 10, 12, 17, 20, 68,
100, 105–6, 107, 173, 187
Spiller, Robert, ix, 166, 175
Spinoza, 100
Stalin, Joseph, 192
Stebbins, Joel, 150
Steinbeck, John, 13, 119, 140
Stevens, Wallace, 13
Stoic, The (Dreiser): author's evaluation
of, 190–91; compared to The Bulwark,
180, 184, 185, 188, 189, 191;
compared to The Financier, 80, 81, 89,
182; compared to The "Genius," 82,
183, 188; compared to Jennie Gerhardt,
190; compared to Sister Carrie, 61,
189; compared to The Titan, 81, 82,
89, 182, 183, 187; composition of,
180; critics' responses to, ix, 190–91;
epilogue expunged from, 189–90;
mentioned, ix, x, 8, 11, 61, 80, 81,

82, 106, 146, 152, 154, 166, 168,
179, 204n10; plot of, 180–91 passim
Strange Interlude (Eugene O'Neill), 148,
149
Stromberg, Gustav, 151
Success, 11, 30
Swanberg, W. A., 207n15
Synthetic Philosophy (Herbert Spencer).
See *First Principles*

TASS (Soviet News Agency), 192
Tatum, Anna, 154, 178
Teilhard de Chardin, Pierre, 186–87
Thaulows, Fritz, 92
Thoreau, Henry David, 145, 161, 173,
193
Titan, The (Dreiser): author's evaluation
of, 88–90; compared to *An American
Tragedy*, 129, 140; compared to *The
Bulwark*, 82; compared to *The Financier*,
78, 89; compared to *The "Genius,"* 82,
99–100, 101, 183; compared to *Jennie
Gerhardt*, 88, 89; compared to *Sister
Carrie*, 87, 88, 89; compared to *The
Stoic*, 81, 82, 89, 182, 183, 187;
critics' responses to, 88–90; epilogue
of, 87, 88; and Emilie Grigsby,
84–86; mentioned, 91, 95, 180, 181,
182, 183; plot of, 80–87 passim;
womanly ideal in, 81–86, 99. See also
Trilogy of Desire, A
Tjader, Marguerite. See Harris, Marguer-
ite Tjader
Tolles, Frederick B., 155
Tolstoy, Leo, 43
Tragic America (Dreiser), 145, 170–71
Trail of Life in the Middle Years, The (Rufus
Jones), 168
Transgressor, The (Dreiser), 45, 49. See
also *Jennie Gerhardt*
Traveler at Forty, A (Dreiser), 68–69, 70
Trilling, Lionel, 134, 144, 166, 171–72
Trilogy of Desire, A (Dreiser): Berenice
Fleming in, 202n6; compared to *An
American Tragedy*, 127, 140; Cowper-
wood in, 13, 15, 54, 87; critics'
responses to, 88, 90; mentioned,
180, 191; sources for, 70–71,
202n10. See also *Financier, The; Stoic,
The; Titan, The*
Trilogy of Wheat, The (Frank Norris), 191

"True Patriarch, A" (Dreiser), 45
Turner, J. M. W., 92
Twelve Men (Dreiser), 45–46, 65, 173
Tyndall, John, 10, 12, 17, 100

Union of Soviet Socialist Republics,
139, 141, 142, 143, 144, 147, 192
Unitarianism, 7
Unity Clubs, 7
Upanishads, 183

Vaughan, George, 183
Verestchagin, V. V., 92

Wagenknecht, Edward, 173
Walcutt, Charles Child, 59, 61, 132,
139, 167
Wallace, Alfred Russell, 106
Warren, Robert Penn, 90, 108, 109
Watts, George Frederick, 92
Wharton, Edith, 120
White, Rev. Eliot, 149
White, Sara. See Dreiser, Sara White
Whitman, Walt, 94
Whittier, John Greenleaf, 8, 155
Who's Who in America, 16
Willkie, Wendell, 192
"Winter Dreams" (F. Scott Fitzgerald),
84
Wolfe, Thomas, 109
Woods Hole Marine Biological Labora-
tory, 146–47, 150
Woolf, Virginia, 13
Woolman, John, 155, 164, 167–68, 175
World Parliament of Religions, 7
World's Columbian Exposition, 7
World War II, 142, 155, 195

X (Charles Fort), 107

Yerkes, Charles Tyson, 69, 71, 72, 73,
81, 84, 85, 86, 87, 184, 202n10